SEX EDUCATION 101

APPROACHABLE ESSAYS ON FOLKLORE, CULTURE, & HISTORY

DR. JEANA JORGENSEN

CONTENTS

THE HISTORY OF SEX EDUCATION

TABOO TOPICS

THE CASE FOR SEX ED

RESOURCES

I dedicated my first book, Folklore 101, to my family, but I'm going to dedicate this book to them as well: thank you for not messing me up about sex. Thank you for explaining concepts and anatomy to me in plain language, for not shaming me for any of my undoubtedly weird behaviors, for being chill during my gender-expansive youth (I damn near gave myself whiplash going from being a tomboy to high femme), and for being generally sex-positive, tolerant, and awesome.

I wish everyone could experience life with as wonderful and supportive a family as I did (and do!) with my parents, my sister, my grandparents, and the rest of the crew.

I also owe gratitude to my folklore mentor, Alan Dundes, for asserting that studying the intersections of folklore and sexuality is a worthy endeavor, and to my first sex ed mentor, Debby Herbenick, for believing in me.

INTRODUCTION

What's a folklorist doing writing about sex? It's not as weird of a fit as you might think!

This book offers an original analysis of the history and culture surrounding sex education from the lens of a folklorist. I look at how folklore topics like urban legends, moral panics, and conspiracy theories have actually shaped U.S. sex education history and policy. And I examine some ways that folklore can stand in for formal sex ed, for better or for worse, as when we learn slang words to refer to genitals instead of medically accurate terms.

Also, let's address the title ASAP: this is not a how-to book of sex education (there are already some excellent resources out there, and I'll talk about them later on), but it's more of a *why* of sex education. I address questions like why sex ed looks the way it does today, why we need to understand the role of folklore in shaping human sexuality, why knowing about folklore helps us to understand the whole picture, and more.

Why this book, why now? This is a paraphrase of a question I often ask my college students, when I want them to think about why we're reading something in the context of a given course. In case you hadn't connected the dots, the state of sex education in the U.S. is pretty dismal and has been for some time; according to a 2019 article in the *American Journal of Public Health*, the U.S. federal government has spent over $2 billion on abstinence-only sex education...and there's no evidence that it actually does what it says it does (Fox et al.).

Why would we waste money on useless—and indeed harmful—interventions? That's what I want to know, and that's what started me on a path of researching the history of sex education around a decade ago, having already earned my PhD in folklore with a minor in gender studies. Now, I teach college classes on culture, folklore, and sex education, and I've also grown a network of sex educator and researcher friends all over the U.S. with whom I can chat about the whys and hows of the field. I have amassed enough knowledge to step in with sex ed info when someone needs it, and I teach workshops for a variety of adult audiences. But I believe that being more socially aware of all the historical and cultural things about sex that led us to this present moment is super important for informed citizens, hence this book.

Further, a lot of this history isn't made easily available to the general public. John Knowles wrote his two-volume history of sexuality because he wanted "to make the whole story available to the general reader" (xi). Unlike him, I didn't spend twenty-plus years churning out a two-volume set of books that spans thousands of pages, because I really do want this to be something anyone can pick up and read and learn the basics of in a shorter, more accessible format. But kudos to him!

I also relish any opportunity to step on the "Folklore is amazeballs!" soapbox and talk about how folklore is one of the best tools for understanding damn near everything, including the past and present state of sexuality education. So you're gonna learn about what folklore is and how it relates to sex in this book too.

You can read the chapters in any order that you like, though I'll lead with a brief content note (and there's a more detailed one right after this chapter if you find it helpful): I sometimes discuss things like trauma and sexual assault, though rarely with any great amount of graphic detail. The same goes for racism, ableism, and eugenics, plus homophobia and transphobia and whorephobia and misogyny, which are unfortunately a huge part of the backstory of sex ed in the U.S. I try to describe these phenomena so that we can better understand them and hopefully not be doomed to repeat the past, not because I endorse these things…which sounds pretty dang obvious, but the entire field of sex ed is plagued by the assumption that talking about sex is the same as encouraging people to have it, which is, err, not true. Unless, in some twisted form of logic, you live in a highly sex-negative society like this one, I guess. We'll get more into that soon!

Another note: I can't cover every single sex topic in this book, because if I tried, I'd still be writing it and you would never get a chance to read it. Plus, even though the process of earning a PhD trained me with mad research skills, I know my limits; I'm not a neuroscientist, for example, so I rely on approachable explanations of brain science to get across points about trauma and memory in the chapter on trauma. But I always provide citations and references so you can follow the research on your own if you choose.

Mostly, I maintain a tight focus on folklore, culture, and

history as these subjects relate to sexuality and to sex education in particular, with occasional romps into related topics that make my nerdy little heart sing. Out of necessity, I also touch on topics like physiology and psychology, but if those are your specialties and you're like, "Dang, I wish there was more on this stuff", then maybe you should add your knowledge to the conversation by writing your own book!

Also, I'm assuming some basic familiarity with gender and sexuality terms, but in case you need a brush-up before we dive in, I've got you:

- We usually use "sex" to mean an array of anatomical/biological traits (chromosomes, anatomy, hormones, etc.) that tend to get sorted as male or female, but sex is often more complicated than this simple binary makes it out to be.
- However, "sex" can also refer to acts thought of as sexual acts, not just penetrative or genital-focused sexual acts but an array of things that convey intimacy, romance, passion, eroticism, or really anything humans can imagine, since we are a very creative species.
- Anatomical sex is distinct from "gender," or the variety of ways people experience and present their identities, often thought of as a range from masculine to feminine, but again, it tends to be more complex than those two or even those two on a spectrum.
- Finally, "sexuality" encompasses sexual orientation (heterosexual, homosexual, bisexual, pansexual, asexual, demisexual, etc.), but also one's entire set of

erotic/relational experiences, fantasies, ideas, ideals, and so on.

So, um, there's a lot of "it's complicated" nuances around these terms and how they interact, but I do think it's important before we proceed to emphasize that these concepts don't exist in a direct or one-to-one correlation with each other. Assuming that male-bodied people *should* have masculine gender identities and presentations and *should* be attracted to female-bodied people with feminine gender identities and presentations is one example of being a tad too narrow-minded about this stuff, given the amazing diversity of human experience. There's nothing wrong if that's your experience, just don't assume it's what everyone else can, does, or should experience.

Oh, and while I try to use inclusive language throughout this book, in order to acknowledge this complexity of lived experience, I do use the original language of authors when I directly quote them. For example, in the chapter about folklore and sex education, I quote from one of my favorite (older) books on the topic, which describes the beliefs around how a woman may or may not get pregnant (among which, ew, please do not douche with Coca-Cola or 7-Up or anything, really). But it would be a little misleading to only use the language of womanhood in connection with pregnancy, since some women don't have a uterus anymore or at all, and some non-binary people and transgender men are capable of getting pregnant. Using inclusive language doesn't take anything away from the people having the bulk of these experiences, as we'll see when I talk about some of the moral panics around gender and sexuality later on.

Yes, I probably come across as very social-justice-y in this book, and...I don't think that's a bad thing? We don't need to agree on all the particulars beyond the baseline of "please don't commit or advocate for human rights violations" in order for you to get something out of this book, but if you're interested in understanding sex education, then presumably, you're also interested in things like bodily autonomy and how we can try to have more of in it all of our lives.

As you'll see, the history of sex education has not always been egalitarian. Lots of people have been excluded, sometimes deliberately, sometimes not. I'm beginning from the premise that we all deserve access to medically accurate information about our bodies, as well as the kinds of cultural information that help people make sense of their relationship options, their life path, and so on. Hopefully that's something we can all agree on, at a bare minimum!

A bit more about me and this book: you'll notice that my writing style is heavily irreverent (yes, there will be both slang and swear words) but also densely cited. If I don't have a good citation for something, I will try to tell you why, because I believe thinking about where knowledge comes from and how it comes to be is a super important part of the education process. I also think it's important to be up front about this stuff because a lot of info about sex remains shrouded in mystery due to shame, taboo, and so on. Plus, it can be difficult to ethically study stuff related to sex, which then impacts our lack of knowledge around it.

I've done my time learning about sex ed with and from experts; my first paid blogging gig was with Dr. Debby Herbenick at Indiana University, a Kinsey-affiliated researcher whose work I'll discuss at length in this book because it's just so good. My gender studies coursework at Indiana University armed me with a ton of feminist and queer theory to make sense of the world, and my folklore and anthropology back-ground taught me to listen to the people most impacted by the issues at hand. I attended the inaugural Sex Geek Summer Camp with famed sex educator Reid Mihalko in 2014, have been an on-and-off member of AASECT (the American Associ-ation of Sexuality Educators, Counselors, and Therapists— on-and-off because academic society memberships are expensive, yo) and presented at their annual conference. While at one AASECT conference I also did a SAR training, which stands for Sexual Attitude Reassessment, so I'd be better suited to understand my own biases when doing this work. I helped wrangle a Sex Geekdom community in Indianapolis for a while that provided a venue for sex-positive discussions on a variety of topics. I've attended not only the annual AASECT conference a number of times, but also CatalystCon and Woodhull's Sexual Freedom Summit and other educational events.

Plus—and I'm sure many sex-positive people can relate— I've just always accrued a lot of knowledge around sex, to the point where a lot of friends and acquaintances will ask me about stuff they've experienced, like if it's normal or not (and often, the answer is: "yes, perfectly normal, just put down a towel beforehand"). As sex educator Al Vernacchio quips in the introduction to his book *For Goodness Sex*, he's gifted with being able to talk openly and easily about sex, and hey, me too! Might as well put that skill to use.

Oh, and me personally? I actually grew up without much shame or mystery around sex. My parents are hippies and were fairly chill about all these topics, and when I was 5 with a newborn baby sister, I found the "where babies come from" book and taught myself the facts. I didn't go on to become sexually active until much later, but my reading outpaced what my parents could keep up with (sorry, Mom and Dad, I know you tried!) so that's part of why I became extremely knowledgeable about sex early on. We were a pretty secular household, too, so I didn't have much religious socialization, which can skew sexuality for many people. Please note: I'm not necessarily anti-religious, though I lean atheist/agnostic and think our laws and our (sex) education should do the same...but I have noticed that a lot of people in the U.S. with religious convictions pass on a lot of sex-negative as well as inaccurate facts and beliefs, which in my view shouldn't be part of the discourse tied to curricula that get federal funding, at the very least. But here we are.

And the sex ed that is often taught is more about what adults believe is appropriate than what is beneficial for young people. This will be a running theme in the book, and it goes back at least one hundred years in the U.S.

The other weird thing I want to note is that medically-accurate, scientifically-based sex ed isn't necessarily inherently better than the alternatives; as Nancy Kendall writes in her amazing anthropological study *The Sex Education Debates*, even the pro-science lesson plans can be exclusionary when it comes to LGBTQ+ folks, for example. So when we start to dig in and study sex education, we might actually find some things that are counter-intuitive at first.

...or are they? One of my arguments in this book is that culture (often expressed through folklore) remains constant until it's given a reason not to, and we can make all kinds of curricular interventions and change all kinds of laws, but if the underlying cultural values stay the same? Not much is actually going to change. I've got a few alarmingly enthusiastic rants on this that many unfortunate college students have suffered through when it comes to the history of sex ed, and which I try to capture here for your reading enjoyment, in the history section.

To give you a bit more of a tour, the book opens with concepts, definitions, and examples from folklore and culture. We'll talk about sexual folklore such as slang and moral panics, as well as why folklore and sex ed go hand-in-hand in so many ways.

Next is a section on how sex actually works; again, it's not the main focus of the book, but dang, I can't resist the opportunity to clear up some misunderstandings that are actively hurting people. From the mistaken belief in a thing called the sex drive to some fun facts about orgasms, I share some of the interesting scientific findings many people aren't aware of yet.

After that is my massive section on the history of sex ed and sex-related phenomena. Buckle up since there's a lot, and reading the section (as well as researching it) made me feel like I was living in some bizarre time machine because—another theme of this book—we keep repeating history! It's wild!

Next comes a series of short essays on taboo topics, like gasp, porn addiction isn't a thing (the neuroscience says so). Again, not the main point of this book, but it's stuff I've researched and I really want people to be better informed about it, in part because these issues are tangled up with the persistent sex-negativity in America that keeps people feeling isolated and ashamed.

Finally, I've got a section building a case for sex ed, explaining the importance of sex ed through a variety of inter-connected lenses. Then, I've got a concluding essay, followed by a bunch of resources and recommendations for books, podcasts, and the like.

Ready to dive in? Let's do this!

References:

Fox, Ashley M., et al. "Funding for Abstinence-Only Education and Adolescent Pregnancy Prevention: Does State Ideology Affect Outcomes?" *American Journal of Public Health*, vol. 109, no. 3, 2019, pp. 497–504.

Knowles, Jon. *How Sex Got Screwed Up: The Ghosts That Haunt Our Sexual Pleasure. Book Two, from Victoria to Our Own Time.* Vernon Press, 2019.

CONTENT NOTES

Welcome to the "this is why we can't have nice things" section of the book. Well, one of them, anyway.

Trauma is one of those shared human experiences that also can be strangely specific to an individual, so please trust that I'm trying to note all the potential triggers for folks in this section, but I still might fail. I will describe how trauma works more fully in the chapter titled "Body, Brain, and Trauma," but for now, here is a list of potential triggers and which chapters they appear in:

- Sexual assault and rape are discussed in "Folklore and Sex Education," "Sexuality Moral Panics in Folklore and Pop Culture," and "The Case for Sex Ed Part 5."
- Anti-sex worker sentiment and actions appear in most chapters in the History section of the book.

- Forced medical and gynecological exams are touched on in "World War I and the American Plan."
- Racist violence and medical neglect appear in "World War I and the American Plan."

THE FOLKLORE OF SEX

FOLKLORE AND SEX

IN GENERAL

WHAT IS folklore and why is there a whole section on it in this book about sex education? Why, I'm so glad you asked! This chapter defines folklore and describes the myriad ways in which folklore touches on a variety of aspects of sex, ranging from sexual acts to interrelated things like gender expression, sexual orientation, and relationship structures.

At its most basic, folklore is, as defined by my colleague Lynne McNeill, "informally transmitted traditional culture." Folklore refers to those parts of culture (a.k.a. shared/transmitted group knowledge) that are passed along informally rather than formally and that are considered traditional since they have some kind of history to them. Being traditional doesn't have to mean being super old, and being informal doesn't have to mean there are no rules, just that there's less official infrastructure keeping the folklore alive.

One aspect of folklore that's super important for our purposes is something I discuss in *Folklore 101*:

Folklore has a neutral orientation towards truth value. Calling something "folklore" in the slang sense of the word might mean you're saying "oh, that's just folklore" or "oh, that's just a myth" or "oh, that's just a fairy tale" or "oh, that's just an urban legend" – all of which are used to mean "oh, that's fake." We don't use any of those terms in folklore studies to mean fake...When we're categorizing something as folklore, we generally want to know more about the how of its transmission than the what of its contents, though that turns out to be important on the level of genre classifications later on, too. (7-8)

THIS GETS ITS OWN BLOCK QUOTE BECAUSE THERE IS A *LOT* OF folklore circulating about sex that is totally untrue...but that doesn't make it either more or less accurately called folklore. Because folklore lacks the same gatekeeping mechanisms as other types of culture (think medicine, education, the law), it proliferates in tons of variations that again, may or may not technically be real or true. This is fine, when we know we're dealing with something that is folklore. But it's less fine when a folklore text is being transmitted as though it's objectively true, like with some of the "how to prevent pregnancy" beliefs we'll talk about shortly.

And normally we folklorists don't get excited to play MythBusters and go out there and debunk a bunch of stuff because that is not the point of studying folklore (we're more about understanding why something resonates with people enough to keep transmitting it)...but when a false belief is impacting people's lives? Yeah, we might speak up.

The point of studying folklore, since it's not to be the truth police, is actually to better understand culture (and this is extra true around sexuality topics in my opinion). Since folklore is not preserved by laws or other institutions, it only sticks around in oral or digital tradition when it's relevant to people's needs. The connections may not be obvious, and they may not be something the people transmitting the folklore can easily articulate, but there is always *some* kind of connection between the folklore people transmit and the need it fulfills in their lives. So when we study folklore, we are tuning into the kinds of beliefs and stories and so on that people share because they want to, not because they have to, which is a great way of taking the temperature of social relevance and concerns.

When it comes to sex and folklore, we see the pretty typical breakdown in genres (categories or types of folklore) that we see with non-sexual things. Most kinds of folklore are transmitted either as things people say, things people do, or things people make (which we call verbal folklore, customary folklore, and material culture, respectively). I'll give a rundown of some examples of each of these, along with some explanations of why this all matters and how it connects back to the larger topic of sex education.

Verbal folklore, or things people say, encompasses all the folklore genres transmitted vocally and/or in language: proverbs and sayings, chants and charms, slang, jokes, myths, legends, folktales/fairy tales, jump-rope rhymes, and more. And all of these can be *quite* sexual in nature.

Let's take slang, for example. Also called folkspeech (and sometimes dialect) by folklorists, it refers to any non-official use of language that circulates among a group of people (what we also call "the folk," and this group can be practically any size and united by any common characteristic). Slang is more likely to show up in Urban Dictionary than the actual dictionary, though of course language shifts over time, and something that begins as slang may eventually become a part of official/accepted language use.

Sooo much of slang is sexual in nature. So much! What do we call body parts when we're not calling them their anatomically correct names? Yep, slang. Depending on which folk groups you're a member of, you might use words like cock or pussy for penis or vagina (more on this in a few chapters), and you might call the act of coupled sex bangin' while masturbation might be banging one out (or pounding one out).

Some of the results of sex get their own folkspeech names, too: when someone is pregnant you might say they're with child or knocked up. These examples are from my own knowledge of generic American folkspeech; there are more to be found on the internet if you want to go there. There are lots of names for sexually transmitted illnesses (STIs, also called STDs), too: I've heard chlamydia called "the clap," for instance. The both amusing and disturbing thing, as my mentor Alan Dundes points out, is that "it is common xenophobic practice to attribute sexual perversity or illness to another nation of people" leading to the English calling syphilis "the French disease" while "the French, however, call syphilis 'the disease of Naples'" ("Sweet Bugger All" 221).

These examples lead me to one of my first interpretive points about folklore and sex: folklore can be used to convey and deal with social anxieties around a topic. America is a pretty sex-negative society, so we don't like to speak directly about sex very often, hence all the indirect ways of referring to sex acts. All the various slang insults to people of non-normative genders and sexualities? Yeah, also a way of coping with cultural anxieties as well as asserting and enforcing hierarchy.

And these differences are cultural, too. As Dundes points out in an article about the origins of the British slang term bugger, there are distinct differences between American and British uses of the word: an American might tell someone to "bug off," meaning to go away, while the British version, "bugger off," is a bit more intense, with connotations of "piss off" or "sod off," which Dundes notes "is another expression totally absent from American folk speech" ("Sweet Bugger All" 218). Dundes suggests that all the British slang around the act of buggery, which has male homosexual connotations, developed as "a verbal attempt to resist any attempt to be put in the humiliating position of serving as a 'female' homosexual victim of a predatory male" (224). In other words, the stigma of being called gay is lessened in some European contexts when one is the active participant rather than the recipient of the act...which can be debated, yes, but at least Dundes made an attempt to look at the slang's connotations in its cultural context.

Even something as innocuous as jump-rope rhymes and playground chants can convey sexual information. When I was a kid on the playground in the 1980s in California, I remember a bunch of them being about kissing, and looking back this seems a bit premature at first. Other folklorists have documented a bunch of these, so while I remember the hand-clapping rhyme being about Miss Suzy and her steamboat, Simon Bronner in his book on American children's folklore documented a version about Lulu and her steamboat (61). Thankfully it's still Cinderella dressed in yellow who goes upstairs to kiss a fellow (70-71).

Now, as a folklore scholar, I know that children's folklore is often more violent and sexual than most adults expect, because kids live their lives according to hierarchy imposed by adults, so much of their folklore revolves around examining these power structures (think of permission-asking games like "Mother, May I?") and pushing the boundaries of what is deemed appropriate. If kids' games showcase folklore about kissing (and sometimes more), it's not necessarily because they're literally interested in kissing, but rather, they are playing the verbal equivalent of dress-up with adult ideas: trying them on and trying them out without actually engaging in them, as part of learning about society.

When it comes to the narrative or storytelling genres—myth, legend, and folktale/fairy tale are the major ones found in every culture—then yeah, there is also a ton of sex. Origin myths (sacred narratives about the creation of the world) detail the first gods and humans and how they procreated; tons of urban legends (told as realistic even though they probably didn't actually happen) talk about sexual adventures gone wrong; and folktales and fairy tales (explicitly positioned as fictional) also convey sexual adventures, from the characters in medieval folktales like *The Arabian Nights*, or *The Canterbury Tales* who cheat on spouses, to the characters in lesser-known fairy tales who have affairs or virginity tests. In fact, I discuss all sorts of unexpected sexy-times in fairy tales such as the aforementioned virginity tests in my e-book *How to Get Laid in Fairy Tales* (join my newsletter at folklore101.com to get a free copy!) along with sexual assault and serial monogamy, not what most people expect to see in fairy tales.

Storytelling traditions about sex are far from new, as should be clear from the mention of mythology above. To take just one example of those, Polynesian mythology depicts

8

demi-god Maui going on vaginal adventures with the death goddess Hine-nui-te-po, who it turns out has a vagina dentata (toothed vagina; discussed in Woods 32-33). And even during as dark a time as the witch trials in medieval Europe, we see a joke about a penis-stealing witch in the *Malleus Maleficarum*. Folklorist Moira Smith insightfully analyzes this "bawdy joke" as being in connected to jokes still in circulation today, about "a man recognized by his penis alone" (102). And there are reports of supernatural penis theft circulating throughout the world today, so again, folklore about sex is simultaneously old and new.

A lot of urban legends (also called contemporary legends) explicitly tackle sex topics, so I'll mention a few here. Mari-amne Whatley and Elissa Henken document a ton of them in their excellent book *Did You Hear About the Girl Who...?: Contemporary Legends, Folklore, and Human Sexuality*, such as the story where a girl masturbates with a hot dog (and gets it stuck and must be surgically removed) or the story where a college girl goes to an exotic location on spring break, is seduced by a new lover, and comes back with a tiny box that turns out not to contain an engagement ring as she'd assumed, but rather a tiny coffin reading "Welcome to the World of AIDS."

Pro tip: a lot of these legends talk up the danger women pose to themselves, or that strange/foreign men pose to women, rather than acknowledging the reality that most women are victimized by men they know. So, folklore some-times has a convoluted relationship with reality.

Dirty jokes should really get their own chapter on verbal folklore that is also highly sexual, but alas, I am trying to keep this chapter manageable, so I'll just list a few examples. In addition to all the jokes about screwing in lightbulbs which focus on the screwing part, there are jokes about Cinderella going to the ball wearing a pumpkin tampon and meeting Peter Peter Pumpkin Eater (analyzed as transgressive humor in a great article by Cathy Lynn Preston) and jokes that play on antisemitic stereotypes about the Jewish American Princess and her stinginess when it comes to sex (analyzed in yet another piece by Dundes).

Finally, personal narrative is a verbal genre of folklore that is a bit wonky because it's more individualistic than most folklore genres. Personal narratives are unique to the individual, since they're about you and your life experiences, but they're still of interest to folklorists since we know that storytelling is culturally patterned. And once you tell one (or more) of your stories often enough, it becomes traditional to you, so it's kinda like a microcosm of tradition.

I would wager that most people have personal narratives that pertain to sex or sexuality-based topics, such as notable early experiences with menstruation, partnered sex, and so on. In fact, Dixie de la Tour runs Bawdy Storytelling, which has a podcast and a live show as components in which people can share their personal narratives with audiences, leading to hilarity, empathy, and more (I'll link her stuff in the resources section). Like many people, I have some personal narratives around sex, but blah blah blah professionalism and sex-negative American society, so it's mostly just my close friends who get to hear them.

In terms of customary folklore, or things people do in a traditional vein, there is, you guessed it, tons of sex. I'll discuss this stuff more in the next chapter, since traditional beliefs and behaviors around sex can actually be a stand-in for formal sex education, but in brief, you'll find superstitions and folk beliefs around everything from menstruation to pregnancy (both causing and avoiding it). Beliefs around masturbation are also prevalent, though I think the whole "masturbating will make the backs of your hands hairy" belief is thankfully falling out of circulation. Again, folklorists aren't necessarily in it to prove or disprove superstitions and folk beliefs, more to document and study them...but it can be quite telling to realize just how many mistaken beliefs there are around sex.

Rituals and rites of passage, another mode of customary folklore, also have tons of connections to sex and sexuality. A ritual is a "a type of traditional repeated behavior with symbolic weight" (Jorgensen 196) and a rite of passage is "a transitional time in life when you attain a new identity, whether social, religious, sexual, occupational... [it is] the collection of ceremonies and rituals that moves you from your old identity to your new identity" (Jorgensen 200). Most cultures have rites of passage to move young adults from childhood to adulthood, and many of these center around sexuality-related things like menstruation and circumcision. And nearly all cultures also have rites of passage along the lines of marriage, which again, goes back to the relational aspect of sexuality and the emphasis on procreation found in many people's attitudes. The idea that there is anything one "should" do or not do when losing one's virginity—an ill-defined concept if ever there was one—also connects ritual to sex.

Games are yet another genre of customary folklore that relate pretty heavily to sex. From teenage games like "spin the bottle" (where a group of teens sit in a circle and one person spins a bottle around on the floor, and is in theory supposed to kiss the person the bottle points to) to "truth or dare", games can be a way of dipping a toe in the taboo. And plenty of cultures have divination rituals that resemble games, in which you're supposed to do something that will reveal the face or name of your future lover or spouse. I remember twisting the stem of an apple while reciting the alphabet, and the letter I was saying when the stem came off would supposedly be the letter starting the first name of my future love.

And finally, in terms of material culture, or things people make or adapt, we see yet more sex. Folk medicine is a natural fit here, with people worldwide brewing teas and tinctures to help with menstrual cramps or induce abortion. Folk remedies for impotence, along with aphrodisiacs, are also a fascinating area to study (and perhaps sample; I am an adventurous eater, but I'm not sure how I feel about Rocky Mountain oysters, a folk name for bull testicles). And what did people do before tampons and pads were commercially available? They used some DIY version influenced by the materials at hand in their environments.

Body art—intentional supplementations or modifications to the body—also relates to sex in a number of ways. Many clothing items are quite gendered, and there are derogatory slang terms for those who transgress what they "should" wear according to their presumed gender. People advertise whether or not they're sexually available by "putting a ring on it," and the hanky code has provided a way for the LGBTQ+ community to subtly indicate their availability and interests without alerting a potentially hostile mainstream culture to the fact that they're even queer in the first place.

Other forms of folk art connect directly back to sex, as with latrinalia (the scholarly term for public bathroom wall graffiti, and there's evidence that it dates back to ancient Roman latrines). Dundes studied precisely this oft-obscene genre of material culture, providing a number of amusing examples. Some of it advertises who to call for a good time or makes jokes about genital size. Much of it gives advice: "Stand close, the next person might be barefoot" or, in taking a jab at a certain state: "Shake well. Texas needs the water" ("Here I Sit" 364). This is a great example of how folklore about sex isn't always just about sex; it can touch on other aspects of identity, too.

One type of folklore that doesn't sort so easily into a large category (verbal, customary, or material) is folk ideas. This is a bit of a murky category, for reasons I explain in *Folklore 101*: "what happens when you've got folklore that crosses genres, or could fit in multiple genres depending on context, meaning, or intention? What then? (other than the anguished cries of thwarted archivists)...[Those] notions that are expression in folklore, but which are a poor fit for established genres, might be classified instead as folk ideas" (189).

Do you know any folk ideas? I bet you do. These tend to bump up against stereotypes, so what if I asked you to think about which type of person is a good or bad driver, or who is more or less likely to be faithful...yeah, I bet some images are coming to mind (e.g. that women are bad drivers, or that bisexual people are flighty, neither of which I endorse by the way since I belong to each category and I think I am a very good driver). My point is, folk ideas are yet another kind of folklore that pretty directly relate to sex, gender, and sexuality, for better or for worse.

In addition to folklore that's explicitly about sex or a linked topic, there is plenty of folklore that perhaps can and should be interpreted in a sexual light. Debates about how to interpret folklore can get pretty heated, but here are a few examples that you may find interesting to chew on. Alan Dundes was famously Freudian, and he, to take just one example, advocated for viewing American football as "analogous to male verbal dueling" ("Into the End Zone" 79), which is itself about sexual domination under patriarchy. After reviewing a variety of folk speech items that reinforce this sexual interpretation, Dundes concludes that

[A] good many football players and fans will be sceptical [sic] to say the least of the analysis proposed here. [...] Yet I think it is highly likely that the ritual aspect of football, providing as it does a socially sanctioned framework for male body contact—football, after all, is a so-called "body contact sport"—is a form of homosexual behavior. The unequivocal sexual symbolism of the game, as plainly evidenced in folk speech coupled with the fact that all of the participants are male, make it difficult to draw any other conclusion. Sexual acts carried out in thinly disguised symbolic form by, and directed towards, males and males only, would seem to constitute rival homosexuality" (86-87).

Love it or hate it, this is one example of a sexual interpretation of folklore (folkspeech and ritual surrounding a game, even if that game has become highly commercialized and thus less inherently folkloric) that may not seem immediately sexual to a different observer. Another, perhaps less controversial, example of this kind of interpretation is when fairy-tale scholars look at earlier versions of fairy tales like "Little Red Riding Hood" that don't have sexual acts described in the text, but do have symbols that seem to resonate with sexual topics. French folklorist Yvonne Verdier not only connected Little Red's hood with menarche but also the "language of the pin and needle" seen in French versions of the text with puberty and maidenhood (106). These versions of the tale also often involve cannibalism and a striptease for the wolf, so, fun times, but this remains one of my favorite examples of how folklore needn't be explicitly about sex to perhaps convey sexual messages.

Not all folklore revolves around sex, but as I hope I've shown here, a fair bit of it does. Similarly, a lot of folklore relates to national identity, or religious identity, or career, or hobby, or...take your pick. Human experience is pretty darn vast, and folklore reflects that. So I don't want anyone to come away with the idea that folklore is inherently sexual, which it's not...but when folklore revolves around sex, that's only because the people creating and transmitting it are *super* into the topic for whatever reason.

The downer part of this topic is that folklore about sex hasn't always been studied with the seriousness it deserves. This is in part due to straight-up sex-negative bias and Puritan attitudes in academic and publishing arenas, and in part due to the trivialization of sexuality topics as not worthy of study, even if they weren't seen as too taboo/dirty in the first place. But it's like...sex and sexuality weave in and out of every aspect of human life, and when we talk about past and present public health crises, such as the AIDS epidemic or the maternal mortality episode that is particularly affecting Black American women...it's like, my peeps, how do we talk about these things and not also talk about sex?! And both of these crises are/were, unfortunately, informed by stereotypes and attitudes around certain groups of people, which stem from and can be documented in...drumroll, please...folklore and culture.

The censorship aspect is real, unfortunately. Sometimes censorship is self-imposed, as when American folklorist Stith Thompson was writing the *Motif-Index of Folk Literature* (first in the 1920s–1930s, then the revised edition came out in the 1950s, and yeah, this staggered time span was because it was a monumental reference work completed before the age of computers). As Dundes notes in his essay critiquing this index work, Thompson explicitly left "obscene motifs" out of the motif index, leaving some classification spots for them to be filled in perhaps later under the heading of "X," and gave descriptions that were so vague as to be unhelpful: "The lover retains his gift by a ruse (obscene)" (qtd. in Dundes, "The Motif-Index" 103). Gershon Legman was one of the rare scholars who went all-in on studying obscene and taboo folklore, but unless you're in the know, he's not necessarily taught as part of our discipline's history.

Subtler forms of bias exist, too, as when Torborg Lundell analyzed gendered terminology in Thompson's *Motif-Index* as well as in his revision of the tale type index, noticing discrepancies around sexual roles: "Thompson simply tends to give men who commit adultery a less shameful label" than their female counterparts, among other odd takes (157). Because there's definitely a lot of infidelity in folktales, and it definitely gets committed by people of both genders, so why the reluctance to name it?

As Dundes writes in one of his section introductions in *International Folkloristics*, there were two main journals dedicated to documenting and analyzing "obscene" folklore in the last century: *Anthropophyteia* (which ran 1904–1913) and *Kryptadia* (which ran 1883–1911). These journals were sometimes accused of publishing pornographic materials, to the point where Sigmund Freud wrote a letter of support that was published in *Anthropophyteia* in 1912 (*International Folkloristics* 178). Yes, Freud sometimes dipped into folklore research, which is a fascinating topic for another time. But the point stands: early attempts to study and catalogue folklore about sex were sometimes thwarted by social norms and censorship, even to the point where printing certain things in the early twentieth century would run people afoul of censorship laws (more on this, especially the Comstock Laws, in the history section of this book).

I was lucky enough to come of age in a time when scholars are a bit freer to pursue sexual topics in our research (in fact, one of my early peer-reviewed publications was on contemporary erotic retellings of fairy tales), though we do generally have to think twice about whether anything could be misconstrued and whether our reputations might take a hit.

To wrap up, the point of this chapter was both to define folklore and to demonstrate the myriad ways in which folklore has always been about sex. Sure, there is plenty of folklore that revolves around non-sexual topics, too, but I think it's a gamechanger to realize that people have *always* had ways of discussing sex and related topics within their traditional communities. Sometimes this is because sex can be an uncomfortable topic, so people are like "yeah let's encode this metaphorically so it's easier to talk about," and other times it's because folklore can also be weaponized to put down certain groups and uplift others.

Folklore is not, as many people assume, always uplifting magical fairy tales and unicorns and stuff like that. It can be, but folklore is also dirty jokes and ethnic stereotypes and urban legends about how we should fear immigrants and people with mental illnesses.

Folklore is a mirror held up to society: it shows us the good, the bad, and the ugly. Because folklore is opt-in culture rather than mandated culture, it reveals the things we *choose* to do: telling jokes, celebrating holidays, making and sharing memes, and making crafts. With sex and any other facet of human experience, folklore gives an uncensored (at least by the folk; censorship on other levels is a whole different thing) glimpse into people's *real* attitudes and values. It ain't always pretty, but it sure as hell is valuable if you want to understand people better. And culture. And cultural views around sex. And so on.

References:

Bronner, Simon J. *American Children's Folklore*. 1st ed., August House, 1988.

Dundes, Alan. "The Motif-Index and the Tale Type Index: A Critique." *The Meaning of Folklore: The Analytical Essays of Alan Dundes*, edited by Simon J. Bronner, Utah State University Press, 2007, pp. 101-06.

---. "Here I Sit: A Study of American Lartrinalia." *The Meaning of Folklore: The Analytical Essays of Alan Dundes*, edited by Simon J. Bronner, Utah State University Press, 2007, pp. 360-74.

---, ed. *International Folkloristics: Classic Contributions by the Founders of Folklore*. Rowman & Littlefield, 1999.
---. "Into the Endzone for a Touchdown: A Psychoanalytic

Consideration of American Football." *Western Folklore* vol. 37, no. 2, 1978, pp. 75-88.

---. "The J.A.P. and the J.A.M. in American Jokelore." *The Journal of American Folklore*, vol. 98, no. 390, 1985, pp. 456–75.

---. "Much Ado About 'Sweet Bugger All': Getting to the Bottom of a Puzzle in British Folk Speech." *The Meaning of Folklore: The Analytical Essays of Alan Dundes*, edited by Simon J. Bronner, Utah State University Press, 2007, pp. 215-28.

Jorgensen, Jeana. *Folklore 101: An Accessible Introduction to Folklore Studies.* Fox Folk Press, 2021.

Lundell, Torborg. "Gender-Related Biases in the Type and Motif Indexes of Aarne and Thompson." *Fairy Tales and Society: Illusion, Allusion and Paradigm*, edited by Ruth Bottigheimer, University of Pennsylvania Press, 1986, pp. 121-39.

McNeill, Lynne S. *Folklore Rules: A Fun, Quick, and Useful Introduction to the Field of Academic Folklore Studies.* Utah State University Press, 2013.

Preston, Cathy Lynn. "'Cinderella' as a Dirty Joke: Gender, Multivocality, and the Polysemic Text." *Western Folklore* vol. 53, no. 1, 1994, pp. 27-49.

Smith, Moira. "The Flying Phallus and the Laughing Inquisitor: Penis Theft in the *Malleus Maleficarum*." *Journal of Folklore Research* vol. 39, no. 1, 2002, pp. 85-117.

Verdier, Yvonne. "Little Red Riding Hood in Oral Tradition." *Marvels & Tales*, vol. 11, no. 1/2, 1997, pp. 101–23.

Whatley, Marianne H, and Elissa R Henken. *Did You Hear About the Girl Who...?: Contemporary Legends, Folklore, and Human Sexuality.* NYU Press, 2001.

Woods, Emma. *Bite Me: The Myth of Vagina Dentata.* Independently published, 2022.

FOLKLORE AND SEX EDUCATION

Now that we've established in the previous chapter the many ways in which folklore and sex intertwine, it's time for the good stuff: the intersections of folklore and sex education, both formal and informal.

Whenever I get to teach a semester-long college course on the history and cultural context of sex education (yep, I'm livin' the dream), I start with a unit on folklore. Which might not be the most obvious starting point in most people's brains, but as I establish (both in the class and in this chapter), folklore *is* where most people's sex education begins.

In this chapter, I make three interrelated claims:

- Folklore serves as informal sex education for many people before they ever receive school sex ed.
- Folklore influences how school sex ed is perceived and executed, in the form of urban legends about school sex ed gone wrong and moral panics that impact school sex ed, for example.

- School sex ed is more effective if it takes folklore into account, just not as something to (occasionally, where appropriate) debunk but also as one of the major ways we all participate in and contribute to culture.

When it comes to my first point—that folklore *is* a form of sex education, like it or not—I have to start out by mentioning one of the best books written on this topic: *Did You Hear about the Girl Who…? Contemporary Legends, Folklore, & Human Sexuality* by Mariamne H. Whatley and Elissa Henken. I know Elissa Henken, she's a folklorist like me, and to write this book she teamed up with health educator Mariamne Whatley to collect and analyze all the folklore that revolves around sex ed topics: contraception and pregnancy, menstruation, STIs, and more. It's an amazing book and if my book is at all your vibe, you should definitely read theirs as well.

To briefly summarize the main point of the book, the authors "use folklore in this book as a way of understanding groups' and individuals' current concerns around sexuality" (15), providing numerous examples and case studies of how students may arrive at the sex ed classroom with sexuality information derived from folklore that is ultimately not true, but may escape the educator's notice if it is not explicitly discussed.

Again, the point of studying folklore is *not* necessarily to play MythBusters and hold up every item of folklore against the truth to see where it falls short. Because we define folklore as informally transmitted traditional culture, we know that folklore circulates among peer groups, when people have shared identities, values, and hence stories, customs, and so on. By tuning into a group's folklore, we can get a better sense of what people actually believe about themselves, the world, other groups, and so on...which is quite valuable when we're looking at a topic as broadly human as sexuality.

For instance, one of the major folklore genres analyzed in their book is folk belief (also called superstition). While some of these beliefs may sound outlandish, Whatley and Henken make the important point that "Even folk beliefs that are not fully believed may be acted upon, as anyone will recognize who has searched for a piece of wood on which to knock, picked up a penny for luck, avoided walking under a ladder, or avoided stepping on a crack in the sidewalk" (9). We all have beliefs about causation and correlation that may or may not be grounded in scientific fact, that we learned from friends or family, and that we consciously or unconsciously perform. Labeling these kinds of folklore folk belief or superstition isn't a dig at anyone who believes in or transmits them, but rather a way of acknowledging that these things are passed along in folkloric ways.

Whatley and Henken document a large number of folk beliefs that revolve around pregnancy and fertility, for example. Some of my favorites include that it's impossible for a woman to get pregnant if or when:

- she has intercourse standing up
- she only has sex a few times
- she holds her breath when the man comes
- she sneezes after sex
- the man drinks alcohol before intercourse
- she is raped. (Whatley and Henken 25)

Obviously none of these are true, but as Whatley and Henken point out, students of all ages might walk into the sex ed classroom (or even worse, miss out on having any sex education at all) with these beliefs: "These beliefs may be held by middle school, high school, and college students, and even by adults beyond college age" (25). They encourage sexuality educators to solicit these kinds of beliefs from students as a starting point to lead a discussion about fertility, and the educators can then add related facts to help students reach a more accurate understanding of human reproduction.

People are exposed to folklore about sex long before they set foot in the sex ed classroom: playground rhymes and games about kissing, stories about where babies come from (ranging from storks to more inventive explanations, rarely anything like the truth), and even the segregation of certain activities and toys by gender. These things all send messages, trivial as they may seem and subtle as they may be.

These folk beliefs aren't just quaint and interesting relics, either (as is often the mistaken assumption about folklore in general, sigh). As Whatley and Henken point out, "It is imperative to examine these beliefs for their possible influence on behavior and to note how folklore is used to justify behavior, such as a woman not using contraception because she only has infrequent intercourse" (30). Folklore can actually guide our behavior in a ton of ways; just look at the whole Disney and fairy-tale wedding industry, which is (I believe) based on the premise that having a fairy-tale-esque wedding guarantees a fairy-tale happily-ever-after. Which, er, go read some of the older versions of fairy tales before making that assumption, but the point stands: people look to folklore as models for our values, ideals, dreams, and choices. And when the folklore gives misguided sex advice, what are we supposed to do with that?! (Hopefully, listen nonjudgmentally and then offer correct information.)

As sort of a sub-point to my first point about how folklore is often the first—and sometimes the only—contact a young person has with sex education, I would also like to mention that since teaching styles vary, and sex ed teachers are especially constrained in what they can or cannot say in the classroom, there may be a lot of gaps in terms of the material that a sex ed teacher can feasibly cover. Or a student may have transferred schools at a critical juncture, causing them to miss "Health" class in one grade, and that particularly relevant unit of "Biology" in another grade. Guess what steps in? Yep, folklore.

Sometimes I see the argument that school sex ed shouldn't exist because parents can and should educate their kids themselves. Which sounds fine in principle to a degree (later in this book, I argue why comprehensive sex ed for all is a public good) but will still probably leave a lot of gaps. I've heard many personal narratives about how a young person experienced the onset of menstruation and had to piece together from bits and pieces they've overheard (a.k.a. folklore) what was happening to them and how to handle it.

If not for the simple goal of preventing a first-time menstruant from freaking the fuck out when they bleed from their genitals, there are other good reasons to have sex ed around menstruation universally taught. As Whatley and Henken point out, "Whether or not they have formal education, young women often depend on beliefs about menstruation for advice and warnings" and go on to deliver gems of folk beliefs such as this one: "If you have sex during your period, it will damage you internally and you will never be able to have children" (45).

From a human sexuality standpoint, this is untrue: there's nothing wrong with having sexual contact during one's

25

period, though one should be aware that menstrual blood can carry STIs. But since people lacking a formal education in a topic often don't know what they don't know, they may rely on folklore and overheard wisdom from their peers to navigate these biological changes.

And this is nothing against school sex ed, but the classroom delivery of material will always have some gaps. Whatley and Henken observe:

> In matters of sexuality, folklore goes beyond classroom learning of mechanics to fill in, satisfy, and answer—in piecemeal fashion—all those questions about what people actually do and how they do it. A joke laughed at by a young teenager without understanding, lest the puzzled listener disclose naivete, can be mulled over in private, pieced together, and collated with other bits of information until an explanation arrives. (8)

School sex ed might deliver a lot of the "hows" of sexual behavior, but folklore can deliver many more of the "whys" of it, with urban legends of desire and infidelity, fairy tales driving the heterosexual monogamous happily-ever-after as the only happily-ever-after, folkspeech detailing a variety of names for taboo body parts and sex acts, and so on. Diagrams and quizzes can be great learning tools, but so are stories, after all.

Now, on to my second organizing point, about how folklore actually impacts school sex education: folklore doesn't live in a little compartmentalized box away from all the other parts of culture, those parts of culture that are highly institutional hence not super folkloric in nature; rather, folklore weaves in and out of human experience, even those experiences that are quite regulated and by-the-book.

I'll be mentioning folklore as it darts in and out of the chapters in the history of sex education section of this book, so please keep an eye out for that, but in brief, lots of different types of folklore have shaped the way school sex ed looks today. Moral panics and conspiracy theories from a century ago over "white slavery" and "race suicide" had white Americans freaked out over the supposed victimization of white people at the hands of other races, when—guess what?!—it was usually the reverse, which then guided early sex ed efforts to keep white middle-class and upper-class women popping out babies by withholding contraceptive info from them.

This happened to the point of making disseminating information about contraception illegal (see the chapter on Comstock), which of course influenced what could be taught in schools.

Furthermore, the beliefs about what kinds of people contracted and transmitted STIs—again, shocker, it was never the nice heterosexual white people at fault—went on to inform early sex ed messages conveyed by the U.S. military to soldiers in World War I, for example. I cover this later on in its own chapter in the history section, but basically, sex workers and non-white people (almost always women) were blamed for the spread of STIs, and sometimes even violently corralled to stop their oh-so-immoral activities.

The wartime discovery that a lot of men were enlisting who'd contracted STIs on the home front also spurred U.S. government efforts to support sex ed among civilians after WWI. So, weirdly, folk beliefs around who wasn't likely to be infected with STIs butted up against the reality that a lot of white dudes *were* infected with STIs, which influenced sex ed efforts in the early- to mid-twentieth century.

More recently (like in the 1960s and 1970s), a series of urban legends have circulated, going into vicious amounts of detail about sex ed encounters gone wrong in the classroom. Some of them allege that a sex ed teacher stripped in front of her students to deliver a very, er, hands-on anatomy lesson. Others told that "male students had raped a sex education teacher after watching a film in class" (Irvine 55). As with many urban legends that gain credibility from their attention to detail, a 1979 version specified that it was twenty male students who did the deed, one of whom said, "Didn't she spend the whole year telling us how to do it, when to do it, and how much fun it would be?" (Irvine 55)

Finally, I assert in this chapter that school sex ed is even more useful when it takes into account folklore as a major mode of human interaction and learning.

Like, yes, not gonna lie, in my ideal world we're organizing folklore workshops for every sexuality educator on the planet so they are better equipped to handle folklore when it inevitably arrives in the sex ed classroom, or in the school board meetings where the next folklore-driven moral panic or conspiracy theory crops up. But, earth to Dr. Jeana, that is probably not happening, so the best I can hope for is to help spread the good folklore word and hope that this book (or one like it, such as *Did You Hear about the Girl Who...?*) gets picked up by more sex educators.

Why? Because school sex ed is incomplete when it's just biology and facts. Human sexuality is simultaneously biological and cultural, so if we leave out the cultural side of things (which folklore taps into and expresses), we're leaving out a big chunk of the puzzle. That doesn't serve our students or our citizens. Like, at risk of coming across as kinda snarky, we live in a democracy, so it'd be cool if more people were on the same page about how human biology actually works, for starters, so we could elect officials to make laws that are grounded in scientifically accurate and culturally nuanced understandings of these things.

For example, when teaching about the relevance of feminism in my college courses, I often assign an essay called "The Blame (and Shame) Game" by notable American feminist Jessica Valenti. In it, Valenti gives statistics to reveal just how prevalent rape and sexual assault are in the U.S., and also talks about how "rape illiterate" our country is (63). To demonstrate this, she quotes notable politicians such as Todd Akin, who told a journalist that a woman who is raped can't get pregnant if it's a "legitimate rape" because "the female body has ways to shut that whole thing down" (64). This is a restatement of the folk belief mentioned above that women can't get pregnant when raped...so an elected U.S. official basically believes in a folk belief about conception, which, on the one hand, no big deal because we *all* believe in some folk beliefs, but if the people responsible for making laws believe egregiously erroneous folk beliefs and are modeling the laws on those beliefs? That's kinda problematic.

Similarly, if the people voting and the people making laws have uncritically opted into folk beliefs about, for instance, all queer people being predators, that's super problematic. Or about how only gay men can get or transmit HIV/AIDS. And so on. We all need to be more aware of our folklore and its implications, especially when marginalized groups are further blamed or oppressed as a result of beliefs about them.

Some sex educators are even using folklore in their lesson plans already! Al Vernacchio has a TED talk on the "baseball metaphor" for sex, which he expands on in his book *For Good-ness Sex*. This metaphor is a folk idea, or an underlying belief about something that circulates and is apparent in a variety of folklore items. And it uses folkspeech or slang to express the folk idea that sex is just like baseball, for the following reasons.

Vernacchio documents a lesson plan, starting with telling his students they'll be playing baseball that day, which begins to elicit slang about "rounding the bases" and "scoring runs" (49). From there, he talks about how baseball has wound up providing "a conceptual model in our country...a basic frame-work for the way most young people learn about sex from our peers" (51). Again, this is basically a folk idea, or a notion that circulates among a group of people about how/why some-thing is the way it is, and that may be expressed through a variety of folklore genres.

The how/why of the baseball model of sex is pretty sexist, heterosexist, and overall flawed; it's competitive, pitting men and women against each other, and further assuming that the players are one of two binary genders and are heterosexually interested in one another. It makes sex, like baseball, into a scheduled and routinized act, ruled by external factors (it's baseball season! Do what your coach tells you to do!) rather than internal factors (how do I feel? What do I enjoy?).

How do we reach this conclusion? By utilizing folklore, in addition to our critical thinking skills. The "bases" refer to sexual activities that should happen in a specific order, "striking out" means no sex for you, "playing for the other team" means being gay or lesbian, and so on (Vernacchio 51-52). The best part is that since these are folkspeech terms, they come from the folk, and it's not just the teacher lecturing their students and providing terms. It's more participatory this way, and allows educators to meet students where they're at.

Rather than stick with the baseball model, Vernacchio has a delightful alternative to suggest; I'll let you discover it for yourself via his TED talk or book. But it's much more pleasure-centered and inclusive, so yay for that!

Following where folklore leads can help educators pinpoint concerns that students may have but may not think to vocalize (or may not be given the opportunity to voice; not every classroom is set up in a fashion that gives students a lot of agency). Whatley and Henken once again share a very incisive statement: "While some folklore may appear frivolous and merely entertaining, much of it reflects very real concerns and anxieties. Legends about AIDS contracted from romantic strangers and gang-rape at a fraternity speak to shared fears about STD and HIV transmission and the prevalence of sexual violence" (187). If you imagined folklore as being a giant neon sign pointing at people's social insecurities, why *wouldn't* you want to study it further to understand what freaks people out about a given topic?

Furthermore, folklore lets us bring up tough topics in a potentially less-scary way. To quote Whatley and Henken again, "Folklore provides an opening to a difficult conversation. Rather than beginning with a discussion-stopper such as 'Let's talk about gang rape,' the legend of the frat boy's sister, while an uncomfortable story to tell or hear, will create a better starting point" (87). And yes, as someone who has to teach uncomfortable and difficult topics all the time—All right, students, today we're talking about femicide!—I can assure you that folklore often provides a better path in to a tough topic than simply asking students to weigh in on the topic right away.

Including folklore and sex education in the same conversations is important if you want to reach people where they're at, and values of accessibility are central to both disciplines. So let's get to it!

References:

Irvine, Janice M. *Talk About Sex: The Battles Over Sex Education in the United States.* University of California Press, 2004.

Valenti, Jessica. "The Blame (and Shame) Game." *Full Frontal Feminism.* Seal Press, 2006, pp. 63-83.

Vernacchio, Al, with Brooke Lea Foster. *For Goodness Sex: Changing the Way We Talks to Teens about Sexuality, Values, and Health.* Harper Wave, 2014.

Whatley, Marianne H, and Elissa R Henken. *Did You Hear About the Girl Who...?: Contemporary Legends, Folklore, and Human Sexuality.* NYU Press, 2001.

CULTURE THAT IS NOT FOLKLORE
AROUND SEX

OKAY, some of you may be thinking, folklore sounds like it encompasses a lot of culture, so what *isn't* folklore? And for those of you who picked up this book specifically wanting to learn about sexual stuff, what are the parts of non-folklore culture that still mostly revolve around sex?

Let's remember, folklore is informally transmitted traditional culture. It's all the parts of culture that we share peer-to-peer and face-to-face that aren't upheld by official or institutional parts of culture. Folklore is an opt-in culture, ranging from serious stuff like rituals to funny stuff like jokes; there's usually not one "right" way to go about it, unlike parts of official culture that are governed by laws.

What are some institutions, then, that are distinct from folk culture? The law and the government. Medicine and science. Religion (in many if not all aspects; folk religion is also a thing). Popular culture and the mass media. The educational system, K-12 plus higher ed. If it's got an HR (Human Resources) office and a handbook, or someone with money/power acting as a gatekeeper or barrier to entry, or if you could go to jail for doing it wrong, we're probably talking about some facet of institutional culture rather than folk culture.

Institutions govern much of our daily lives in the Western world, and this can be traced back to the Enlightenment and Industrial Revolution and stuff like that. As people in many societies migrated from villages to cities, and as governments solidified their hold on, well, governing, that meant increased regulations. And not just regulations in the sense of norms, or "this is how people should behave, and socially we all agree on this," but regulations in the sense of rules that could be enforced with consequences like the criminal justice system and credit scores.

Rules and regulations about sex go way beyond "it's illegal to have sex in public" in pretty much every society. Once you start looking for all the ways in which official culture can order sex, it's everywhere.

To take a pretty basic example, let's look at identifying documents and cards. When someone is born in the U.S., they're usually issued a birth certificate, and that document, along with the ensuing ID documents like driver's licenses, passports, and so on generally note the person's sex. Having a divergent gender identity is thus one point of friction governed by official culture, since some states make it harder or easier to officially change one's gender on these kinds of documents.

Why do we need someone's assigned-at-birth sex on these ID cards? This is something that's puzzled me for a while, and at my most cynical, I think of it as an attempt to uphold binary gender as an identity system that is supposed to shape us to our core. In reality, I don't really see why it matters to have an

M or F on our identifying documents...I can't imagine that a person's gender is as important in, like, a police chase as how tall they are. And I say this while trying to be as gender-affirming as possible, since I know for a lot of people their gender identity *matters* and they have to fight for validation and recognition. But, like, why do we need to check one box of two on identifying documents? I'm still confused.

One apparent reason to encode sex and gender into legal documents might be to keep hierarchies where they are. Let's recall, (most) women couldn't vote in the U.S. until 1920, nor could they get a credit card in their own name without approval of a male relative until 1974. The need to reinforce these kinds of rules might have been considered a justification for deciding that gender needs to be on all these documents (and I thank my friend Tammy Coxen, mixologist extraordinaire, for this insight).

Another example is name changes when people get married. I have some rather feminist opinions about the practice, but love it or hate it, what we essentially have here is an important life event and relationship status change being reflected in significant identifying documents, which must be altered by interacting with government entities at whatever level (state, federal, I dunno, I've never changed my name).

In listing just a handful of documents that we utilize regularly to prove who we are so we can do stuff like apply for jobs and travel, I've pointed out that our relationships and our genders are imprinted onto the things we use to navigate our lives. Among other things—like the fact that people with non-normative genders and relationships often struggle for recognition on this level—this means that we've accepted a level of governance in our lives where our genders and relationships are *made* to matter. We have collectively decided that these things matter, and we're okay with accepting this level of interference in our lives.

There are exceptions, of course. Not every country works like the U.S. (nor should it), and there are outliers here as well, communities that resist regulations such as those who prefer home births to hospital births, and those that cross borders outside of official means.

I mean, in Britain, the Home Office can accuse people of having a fake marriage and attempt to invalidate it by barging into their homes and seeing whether they sleep in the same bed and in pajamas or not. Or couples can be separately questioned about intimate details of their sex lives, such as which sex positions they've used, in an effort to determine whether their marriage is valid, as reported in *The Guardian* (Taylor and Perraudin).

I'm sure I don't need to list all the reasons why interrogating people about their sexual activity to determine if a marriage is legitimate is terribly invasive; some people don't experience a lot of sexual desire, like asexual folks, and may or may not have much sex as a result, but obviously they can still choose to be partnered. Some people experience sex as painful and opt out. Some people have trauma around sex and would prefer not to. The list of reasons to not have sex while married is long and might be extremely personal, so why is it the government's job to get involved?

There used to be even more rules regulating sex, gender, and sexuality in the Western world. Again, sticking with the U.S. as an example, if this piques your interest, you may want to read *Intimate Matters: A History of Sexuality in America* by John D'Emilio and Estelle B. Freedman. Local, state, and federal authorities have always weighed in on sexual matters, such as how in the colonies, even before there was such a thing as the U.S.A., "the crimes of sodomy, buggery, and bestiality carried the death penalty" (30). Rape technically did too, but lesser punishments were often given instead. Parenting a bastard child was also a punishable offense, with courts in Maryland, for instance, doling "out thirty-nine lashes to parents of bastards" (32). The abhorrent legacy of the transatlantic slave trade has echoes here as well; remember how interracial marriage used to be illegal until 1967 in the Loving v. Virginia case? To protect the financial interests of slave owners, state legislatures in the 1660s and onward levied a series of fines, imprisonments, and/or banishments for white people who married or fornicated with anyone from another race (35).

Another institutional inflection of gender was the multitude of laws and policies forbidding women from the great halls of education, science, and medicine. Women did not enter higher education in the U.S. until the 1870s and 1880s, sometimes due to policies forbidding female students (D'Emilio and Freedman 190). Women doctors were rare, and this actually played a part in early abortion laws, which were unevenly enforced: only licensed doctors could legally practice abortion in the early 1900s, and since only dudes were licensed doctors, it meant that women who provided abortions were quite easy to persecute under the law (more on this in the history chapter on Comstock).

Within medical practice and research, gender and sex can impact things even when perhaps they shouldn't. There are good reasons to take down someone's assigned-at-birth sex when treating them, even though this isn't a perfectly rigid binary system (just talk to any archaeologist about how difficult it is to sex a skeleton when you've only got one; it takes a representative sample to get a sense of how things like pelvic structure and overall body size likely are distributed over a population).

But sometimes weird things happen, as with the trials to approve flibanserin—known as Addyi or "pink Viagra"—a drug meant to treat hypoactive sexual desire disorder in premenopausal women. Like the pathologizing of low sexual desire, it is also a problematic topic, though yes, some people certainly experience reduced sexual desire as distressing, hence worth looking into and treating. One of the safety studies, however, was summarized in an article in *The New England Journal of Medicine* as containing this gem of a sentence: "The study did not definitively delineate the risk in premenopausal women who take flibanserin at bedtime because 23 of the 25 participants were men" (Joffe et al. 102).

Can we spot the issue here? I'll wait.

Yep, a medicine *intended for women* was tested primarily on men. Not just for efficacy, but for *safety*. And this leads to a larger issue: women and people with menstrual cycles have largely been excluded from medical testing and trials because...get this...the fluctuating hormones during menstruation were seen as pesky and inconvenient. As medical student Taytum Kahl summarizes the issue, "The changes in hormones and symptoms throughout the menstrual cycle have often been thought of as a confounding variable, which is what initially excluded female models from research for so long."

And from 1977 to 1993, the FDA declared that most women of "childbearing potential" were to be excluded from participating in clinical research studies. I guess this came from a place of concern because the desire was to avoid drug interactions that could cause birth defects but also, um, this led to a severe lack of knowledge around how life-saving drugs might impact people differently based on factors like body fat and hormones which often cluster according to gender ("Policy of Inclusion").

These issues are improving, but I mention them to drive home the point that medicine and scientific research are often thought of as neutral and unbiased, just reporting the facts of reality while uncovering slightly more detail with each study done. Nope. They can replicate gender bias just like any other social system because they are, *gasp*, part of society.

Also under medicine, and veering into psychology a bit, I'll discuss elsewhere in this book just how weird it is that cisgender people (those who identify with the sex they were assigned at birth) can access gender-affirming care without seeing a therapist or psychologist first...if you're a cisgender woman and want some kind of breast-related surgery, go for it! But if you're a trans woman and that's on your to-do list, there are a bunch of barriers to access literally the same medical intervention.

Similarly, puberty blockers have a "record of safety and efficacy" (Lopez et al. 1432). They are an acceptable mode of treatment to delay the onset of puberty for people born with intersex conditions, also called DSD (differences of sex development), so that these folks can take their time deciding how they want to proceed rather than having invasive and nonconsensual "gender correction" surgery forced on them as infants, which is what used to happen (Dalke). Or a child who experiences precocious puberty—starting puberty very early, enough to be incredibly distressing—can access puberty blockers.

Basically, puberty blockers are generally considered safe to use. Unless you're trans, I guess? Somehow, a person's gender identity impacts their ability to access the same exact medical intervention that is deemed to be safe, and this is yet another way that medical institutions take gender into account in ways that are, shall we say, problematic. The hypocrisy of these policies comes out in stories like the one recently published in *The Indianapolis Star*, a local newspaper I subscribe to, in which teen Shay Orentlicher discloses that they were put on puberty blockers to help with their diagnosis of precocious puberty at age seven...but at age twelve came out as transgender. Indiana Senate Bill 480 forbids the use of puberty blockers in minors to treat gender dysphoria, which Orentlicher finds "particularly ludicrous":

> What about me changed so radically with my gender dysphoria diagnosis that I no longer deserved the medical care that was previously open to me? My reproductive organs would react identically to the blockers (that is, simply not developing until I stopped taking them) whether I realized I am transgender or not.

So even though this section of the chapter was meant to focus on how sex, gender, and sexuality are woven into the medical system, we circle back to the law. Which is kinda a bummer, since lawmakers rarely seem to understand the complexity of how all these topics interact.

Even at small-scale institutional levels, we still see a lot of rules around gender. Individual schools still have dress codes that are gendered. One of my aunts recalls that when she was in college, women weren't allowed to wear pants on campus. This would have been in the 1960s. A century ago, women who wore bloomers rather than skirts faced social censure.

I like to poll my college students about middle school and

high school dress codes, and they report strict rules for what girls could wear and practically no rules, or loose rules, for what boys could wear. While unpacking the gendered assumptions here would practically require another book, we can at the very least observe that this is both sexist and hetero-sexist: sexist in punishing girls with stricter rules so they don't accidentally distract boys from the very important task of learning (to say nothing of how distracting it is for female students to be pulled out of class and told their bodies are sexual and must be covered). And it is heterosexist in that it assumes everyone in the school is heterosexual, which isn't always the case.

And, in a brief "this is why feminism benefits everyone" move, I'd argue that the school dress code policies are sexist in ways that hurt men, too. It's sexist to assume that masculine-type people are horny out-of-control rapists waiting to happen, ready to be transformed into a slobbering horndog at the merest glimpse of female skin. I want to believe better of boys and men, that they have self-control and don't objectify women and girls at every turn (not that all boys and men are into women, either).

Beyond institutions that exemplify non-folkloric cultural ways of saying/doing things about sex, there's a whole vast realm of pop culture that also interacts with sex (and some-times the institutions, too). See, folklore is characterized by its constant variation: there's no rulebook governing exactly how to deliver the punchline of a joke, for example. But in pop culture, when you watch a movie, it's generally the same cut of a movie whether you're seeing it in theaters or using a streaming service...yes, with the occasional exception for when there's a new director's cut or whatever. Similarly, when a publisher releases a novel, it's the same text, word-for-word, whether you're reading it in print or on an e-reader.

So when a pop culture text like a film or book is released, and it has some message about sex...that message is disseminated, widely, in the same way each time it's consumed. That doesn't mean readers or viewers interpret it or engage with it the same way, but these texts are less fluid than folklore texts, which is never good nor bad, but for our purposes it means we're gonna have a pretty stable set of sexual messages to analyze.

One great example of pop culture being influenced by the law when it comes to sexual content is the Hays Code. This was a set of rules that Hollywood filmmakers had to adhere to, beginning in 1930 and running for some four decades, which "restricted portrayals of sexual promiscuity, premarital sex, extramarital affairs, and sexual orientations that fell outside the constructed norm and threatened" the so-called sanctity of marriage (Nurik 533). Non-heterosexual sex clearly fell into the forbidden category. For those times when a movie plot clearly needed infidelity or non-straight sex to work, "the Code demanded that the film offer a morality lesson by punishing offenders" (Nurik 533).

Pop culture and the law weave a tangled web of messages about sex, and one common factor linking them—and setting them apart from folklore—is the presence of gatekeepers. Under the social contract, you can't just decide that a given law sucks and you're not gonna follow it anymore...well, you *can* decide that, but there'll likely be consequences if you do. There's a whole convoluted process to changing the law, and authority figures generally have to be involved.

Similarly, you can't up and decide you're going to make the next Hollywood blockbuster film (I mean, if you're reading this and you can, hit me up, I have some great ideas; we folk-lorists are a seriously under-tapped resource when it comes to storytelling!). Changes in technology have made it such that anyone with a smart phone can make a movie, but will it be a movie that reaches everyone? Probably not, since there are multiple levels of gatekeeping that preclude any rando from getting their film into movie theaters and onto streaming services.

Love it or hate it, institutions have staying power, and that actually gives them a lot of power when it comes to messages around sex, gender, and sexuality. Not only can governments, well, govern us when it comes to these things, but the various branches of institutional culture (education, medicine, etc.) can mold and shape us in our daily lives, extending and limiting options according to what our predecessors have decided is appropriate.

Pop culture, too, exerts a strong if subtle influence on sexual norms, showing us which kinds of people get happily-ever-afters in movies and which kinds of people are the villains (hint: until fairly recently, straight and gender-conforming people got to ride away into the sunset together more often than not, while queer people were demonized, set up to be antagonists or objects of pity or both).

There are always more examples of not-folklore-but-still-culture morals and messages around sex that impact us, but I'm trying to wrap this chapter up so we can move on. This adds up to an interesting paradox: many aspects of sex are both personal and social...and the exact ratio of personal to social is always under debate.

Some things are in-born preferences, desires, and orienta-tions; others are socially shaped. But the roles and representa-tions and behaviors available to us? That stuff is *very* social in nature, and so it behooves us all to better understand the ways in which the various institutions of a given culture nudge us in one direction or another when it comes to sexuality.

Formal culture is a series of shared norms and rules telling us what to do, believe, and think about sex. Informal culture or folklore is *us* telling ourselves what to do, believe, and think about sex. We need both if we're going to have a full understanding of sexuality and society.

References:

Dalke, Katharine Baratz. "Affirming Care for People with Intersex Traits: Everything You Ever Wanted to Know." 2020. https://www.lgbtqiahealtheducation.org/wp-content/uploads/2020/06/12.-Health-of-Intersex-People.pptx. min_.pdf. Accessed 13 July 2023.

D'Emilio, John, and Estelle B. Freedman. *Intimate Matters: A History of Sexuality in America*. Third ed., University of Chicago Press, 2012.

Joffe, Hylton V., et al. "FDA Approval of Flibanserin — Treating Hypoactive Sexual Desire Disorder." *The New England Journal of Medicine*, vol. 374, no. 2, 2016, pp. 101–04.

Kahl, Taytum. "Menstruation Is an Afterthought in Research. Here's Why That Needs To Change." *Ms. Magazine*. 23 January 2023. https://msmagazine.com/2023/01/23/menstruation-clinical-trials-research-women-periods-covid/. Accessed 13 July 2023.

Lopez, Carla M., et al. "Trends in the 'off-Label' Use of Gnrh Agonists among Pediatric Patients in the United States." Clinical Pediatrics, vol. 57, no. 12, 2018, pp. 1432–35.

Nurik Chloé. "50 Shades of Film Censorship: Gender Bias from the Hays Code to MPAA Ratings." *Communication, Culture and Critique*, vol. 11, no. 4, 2018, pp. 530–47.

Orentlicher, Shay. "OP/Ed: Puberty Blockers Were Safe until Indiana Legislators and Governor Said Otherwise." *The Indianapolis Star*, 9 May 2023, www.indystar.com/story/opinion/2023/05/09/puberty-blockers-ok-for-one-group-of-kids-but-not-another-in-indiana/70196663007/. Accessed 13 July 2023.

"Policy of Inclusion of Women in Clinical Trials." Office on Woman's Health. *U.S. Department of Health & Human Services.* https://www.womenshealth.gov/30-achievements/04. Accessed 13 July 2023.

Taylor, Diane, and Frances Perraudin. "Couples Face 'Insulting' Checks in Sham Marriage Crackdown." *The Guardian*, 14 April 2019. https://www.theguardian.com/uk-news/2019/apr/14/couples-sham-marriage-crackdown-hostile-environment. Accessed 14 July 2023.

STIGMA & SEXUALITY

STIGMA IS a classic concept from sociologist Erving Goffman that has become widely used in a variety of academic disciplines. If we define stigma as an undesirable identity that gets attributed to a person (often against their wishes), then it's possible to explore the intersections of stigma and sexual identity, sexual acts, and so on. It's important to note that stigmatized identities are seen as "spoiled" or irredeemably tainted... and that this taint is often perceived as contagious, regardless of whether it actually is or not.

In this chapter, I describe some of these connections, and in a chapter in The Case for Sex Ed section of this book, I'll talk about why the stigma around STI status is such a public health concern (but could be easily fixed with better comprehensive, accurate, and shame-free sex education). Additionally, people who are stigmatized face higher risks of violence, discrimination, and microaggressions (which can add up, even if they're supposedly minor things like slurs and insults rather than acts of physical violence).

So, stigma and sex. Which sexual acts can you think of that are regarded as deviant, wrong, dirty, and polluting? Which sexual identities are seen as tainting someone beyond redemption? Here are a few of my thoughts on these connections:

- STIs are stigmatizing. Unlike other infections, they're seen as dirty, immoral, and/or degrading. I've seen multiple sex educator colleagues point out how irrational this is: nobody thinks you're a disgusting human being for having the measles or the flu, for instance.
- Sex work is stigmatizing. For whatever reason, selling your body under capitalism is fine when you're using your hands to build or clean things, but not when you're giving people sexual pleasure. And this taint is a long-standing one: if someone's outed as a sex worker, it can become difficult for them to find employment, maintain custody of their kids, and so on. As Laura Agustin has incisively written, criminal laws reproduce stigma against sex workers, endangering their lives regardless of what the precise laws are.
- Anything even sex-work-adjacent is stigmatizing; I have friends who take pole dance classes but can't tell anyone in their lives, because pole dance as an art form got its start in strip clubs. While fitness studio pole dancing is rather distinct from its sex-worker-foremother, the taint of sex still makes pole dancing taboo to admit to in certain situations.
- Those who get abortions or have miscarriages face stigma. Cultural silencing of these experiences is harmful and can isolate women when connection

and empathy would help the most (and yet, one of the interesting things about stigma is that since it's social, it can change over time, such that people who got divorced used to be highly stigmatized, and that shame has faded in the last few decades).

- Alternative gender identities carry stigma. It can be difficult for people who don't conform to their expected gender box to date, to use a public restroom without harassment, to keep a job, or to even stay alive (transgender people are at disproportionately high risk for violence and murder). Note that this can affect people who are cisgender (meaning they identify with the gender assigned to them at birth) if they are or appear to be gender-nonconforming as well as people who are transgender, intersex, and so on.

- Alternative sexual orientations are seen as stigmatizing. The fact that gay conversion therapy still exists (though it's mostly discredited) is proof of this. Many other less-mainstream sexual orientations remain poorly understood and often stigmatized; not just bisexuality, but also the asexuality spectrum and those who are pansexual, demisexual, and so on.

- Not to initiate the whole "should these things count as sexual orientations or not" debate, but people in non-monogamous relationships or who engage in kink/BDSM are often regarded as deviant, weird, or broken…hence, stigmatized.

- Being sexually available (a.k.a. "slutty" or promiscuous) carries stigma. There's a double standard for promiscuity by gender, and women's decisions about whether to have uncommitted sex are influenced by perceived negative stigma, as shown in multiple studies, such as one by Terri D. Conley, Ali Ziegler, and Amy C. Moors. The authors concluded, "women are differentially stigmatized for engaging in casual heterosexual sex and that anticipation of this backlash influences their sexual decision making" (404).

- Even people who study sex can be tainted by association. Scholars Natalie Hammond and Sarah Kingston note, "Just as paying for sex lies outside of the boundaries of acceptable sexual behaviour and moral conduct and selling sex is seen as a dishonourable way to earn a living, research into such a topic is also held in less regard" (340).

This is a far from exhaustive list, but hopefully, it's a start. Until recently, masturbation was seen as pretty damning, and some folks still think it should cast shame and stigma on its practitioners (in the history section of this book, I talked about the prompt removal of surgeon general Joycelyn Elders for daring to mention masturbation as potentially a positive thing). Same with premarital sex and having a baby out of wedlock (though this stigma often attaches more to the mother than the father...hm, double standards much?). Other supposedly "weird" sex acts get treated similarly, like role play or phone sex or anal sex. The list goes on and on.

Folklore and culture obviously play a role here; social norms like stigmas don't perpetuate themselves, after all. It takes people to transmit these ideas. And these norms can be shapeshifters, transforming over time to adapt to people's expectations and ideals. For example, I had the dubious delight of learning from my undergraduate college students about the slang term "bodycount"—as in, the number of people that someone has slept with. Did this term exist when I was a youngster? Nope. But it's another way of putting a label on someone's sexual activities, in such a way that traps people either into lying to reduce their bodycount in the minds of their peers, or admitting to having more sexual partners than is considered acceptable (especially for those on the feminine side of the spectrum).

There are so many ways in which deviating from "the norm" in terms of sexual identity, sexual acts, and gender identity/expression can stigmatize a person – and most of these are pretty benign acts and identities when you get down to it. For example, infidelity sucks, but is not the same thing as ethical non-monogamy (like swinging or polyamory) and shouldn't necessarily be perceived or punished the same way. Engaging in a sex act considered icky or undesirable to some shouldn't be an automatic "Here's a One-Way Ticket to Stigma-Land", but I guess sometimes it is, to those folks who cling to judgmental paradigms.

Similarly, sex acts that may resemble one another on the surface need not be judged in the same way if the consent involved differed. There needs to be a cultural conversation around how we treat people who are consent violator repeat offenders or who sexually abuse minors, but that doesn't mean we should lump those people into that same stigmatized group as folks who play with these ideas in consensual adult fantasies, like those who practice a host of things in the BDSM world such as consensual non-consent or age-play.

In short, I think the dialogue around stigma and sexuality needs to be nuanced in a number of ways. We need better ways of talking about actual harm (rather than ontological harm) and better ways of distinguishing sexualities that are common from those that are upheld as normal. What does normal even mean, anyway?! It's high time to stop punishing people from departing from social norms, terms of sexuality, and beyond.

References:

Agustin, Laura. "The sex worker stigma: How the law perpetuates our hatred (and fear) of prostitutes." 17 August 2013. https://www.salon.com/2013/08/17/the_whore_stig ma_how_the_law_perpetuates_our_hatred_and_fear_of_pros titutes_partner/ Accessed 24 February 2023.

Conley, Terri D, et al. "Backlash from the Bedroom: Stigma Mediates Gender Differences in Acceptance of Casual Sex Offers." *Psychology of Women Quarterly*, vol. 37, no. 3, 2013, pp. 392–407., https://doi.org/10.1177/0361684312467169.

Hammond, Natalie, and Sarah Kingston. "Experiencing Stigma As Sex Work Researchers in Professional and Personal Lives." *Sexualities*, vol. 17, no. 3, 2014, pp. 329–47., https://doi. org/10.1177/1363460713516333.

SLANG, STIGMA, & THE CURIOUS CASE OF THE CAMEL TOE

HERE'S one of those "surprise, folklore!" moments around the connections between folklore and sex: so many of the expressions we use to talk about sex acts and body parts and so on belong to the category of folkspeech or slang, figures of speech that are transmitted informally or traditionally, and show variation over time and space.

I don't know whether to blame lack of universal, accurate sex education in America, or the more general sex-negative and sex-phobic lens of mainstream American culture, but based on the proliferation of folkspeech around genitals, it seems to me that people either don't know what's up with their genitals or don't care to know. Things having to do with genitals are largely seen as shameful, and hence, too stigmatized to discuss openly. This is problematic, for a number of reasons.

First, there's a lack of understanding on a culture-wide scale of what genitals are supposed to look like. This leads to shaming people for having otherwise normal bodies.

Exhibit A: camel toe. This is the slang expression for when a woman's vulva, typically the outer labia, can be seen through tight pants or shorts or whatever. Personally, I think this is a silly thing to get worked up about, but professionally, I'm really disturbed about this kind of body-shaming. What it effectively does is say that women with larger labia or more shapely vulvas should not wear certain kinds of clothing. Why on earth would the shape of your genitals matter in terms of what you can wear?!

I'm also disturbed on a feminist level, since I don't see similar shaming directed at men with visible genital outlines; there might be joking or gentle shaming, but nothing as nasty as the vitriol directed at women with certain anatomical configurations who dare to wear tight pants. I don't care if people think tight pants aren't appropriate for every context; I'm not into that level of body policing. People should be able to wear what they want in most situations and not be shamed for it. Full stop.

Next, if you don't know what's normal for genitals (both yours and those of anyone you might be intimate with), you won't know when something's off. Everyone freaks out upon discovering bumps "down there" – but how do you know when it's a sore or lesion from an STI like syphilis or HSV/herpes-2, rather than a zit on one's penis or vulva? The possibility of having a pimple, or rash, or clogged hair follicle exists too, but people might leap to the worst case scenario without having a sense of what a completely normal skin condition looks like because of, horror of horrors, its location on the genitals.

I've also heard STIs such as HPV and HSV/herpes referred to as "acne on your genitals" to emphasize that they are, in their most benign manifestations, just a superficial condition.

Bumps on your genitals aren't necessarily any better or worse than bumps on your face; maybe they're not cosmetically what you're after, but they're not going to kill you, either (again, assuming that there's not something else going on health-wise meaning that you need medical attention, such as when HPV can lead to cervical cancer). I'm still deciding whether I think the metaphor is useful, but if thinking about genital bumps as essentially akin to acne helps de-stigmatize the whole thing, maybe it's worth contemplating?

Finally, there's a pervasive belief that the size and shape of people's genitals has something to do with their sexuality (who they're attracted to, how/whether they express it, which acts they find pleasurable, etc.). Women with large clits are supposedly masculine or hornier than average; men with a large penis are more virile and manly, while the opposite's true of men with smaller genitals, and so on. These stereotypes are toxic and, like camel toe, also need to die in a fire.

I recall some awful (both because they were inaccurate and had the potential to be damaging) images going around the internet in the early 2020s about comparing a woman's labia to a roast beef or bologna sandwich, with the slices of meat thickly layered and protruding from the bread. Which was supposed to be a parallel to how, if I understand correctly, women who have a lot of sexual partners somehow begin to show it in their labia, by the external genital folds getting…I dunno…enlarged, puffy, or something?

One of the ways you can tell how ridiculously this folk belief persists is to hold up a competing folk belief in compari-son: that vaginas actually get stretched on the inside, becoming loose or whatever, when a woman has too much sex. So, which is it? Do the labia enlarge, or do the vaginal muscles retract and weaken? I don't think it can be both simultaneously, not that either is likely to happen in the first place. And yet such misguided beliefs continue to stigmatize femme-type people.

Another important reason to identify and analyze folklore is to get at the assumptions behind it. Because it wasn't just memes going around, there was a whole separate folkspeech item that developed out of it: roasties. This is a term that some men use on the internet to refer to women, "a metonymic reference to female genitalia turned into 'roast beef' by frequent sexual activity" (Burnett 489).

This is an interesting if inaccurate text to analyze, since the use of food terminology by heterosexual men to refer to the potential objects of their lust is a bit predatory to say the least. This phrasing implies that women are there to be consumed, that their flesh is dead, inert, passive. The conundrum also remains that if some of these men, incel-flavored or NoFap-oriented, may want a female partner of their own someday... how to prevent her from attaining "roastie" status once she has participated in penetrative sex with him a number of times? Is there a difference in how "roastie", a set of labia, might get if its owner participates in penetrative sex once each with seven men, or seven times with just one man? We need more data here, people! (kidding, obviously)

Whether folkspeech around genitals is horrifying (as above) or humorous (a "whifflesack" apparently refers to an aged and hence relaxed scrotum, in Randolph 565), it still provides a link to cultural attitudes and is worth investigating. And yeah, that might mean me asking myself why I find "roastie" offensive and "whifflesack" funny, when both refer to (ostensibly) worn-out genitals; I suspect it has to do with how the former is targeting sexually active women while the latter is more about the natural process of aging, but hey, I am human and have biases, too. And ageism exists, sadly.

Having a bigger or smaller or more protruding or less visible set of genitals doesn't mean anything about you, who you like, or what you like. The stigma attached to less-accepted versions of genitals is harmful to sexual self-image, confidence, and body image. As Dr. Emily Nagoski says, all genitals (men's, women's, intersex, trans folks) are made of the same parts, arranged differently (which I cover in a few chapters). Variation and diversity are normal for humans... so why aren't we better at recognizing that?!

When I teach folklore, I like to emphasize that folklore never exists in a vacuum: it often mirrors the values of the group transmitting it. In this case, "camel toe" reflects the normativity of scrutinizing female bodies and female sexuality, while "acne on your genitals" is a bit more subversive: it's not necessarily a dig on a specific person's or gender's body. Rather, it shows the emerging idea that downplaying rather than overemphasizing the link between bodies, sexuality, and morality might be okay. And I find that fascinating!

In folklore (as with human bodies and sexuality), variation and diversity are essential players, and thus I'm not surprised to find folkspeech displaying different attitudes toward the same parts coexisting. In general, I gravitate towards seeing folklore as morally neutral, but with folkspeech items like this one, I hope that we will migrate towards less stigmatizing expressions over time.

References:

Burnett, Scott. "The Battle for 'NoFap': Myths, Masculinity, and the Meaning of Masturbation Abstention." *Men and Masculinities*, vol. 25, no. 3, 2022, pp. 477–96.

Randolph, Vance, and G Legman. *Roll Me in Your Arms: "Unprintable" Ozark Folksongs and Folklore*. University of Arkansas Press, 1992.

SEXUALITY MORAL PANICS IN
FOLKLORE AND POP CULTURE

FOLKLORE MAY BE its own thing (informally transmitted traditional culture) but it doesn't exist in a vacuum, entirely separate from other facets or modes of culture. The existence of moral panics exemplifies this quite well, with moral panics being phenomena that also draw participation in aspects of literature, pop culture, political culture, and more. And, of course, moral panics tend to spring up around sexuality, and they can even influence policies around sex education and sex more broadly, so they're worth talking about here.

First, some definitions. We tend to see a lot of terms like rumor, gossip, moral panic, and conspiracy theory used interchangeably by the general public, but in academic folklore studies we do differentiate these genres of folklore because they tend to look and act a little differently, even if they have some overlap.

- Rumor: an unverified report about something risky or dangerous outside of one's personal experience that is usually not officially documented (Astapova 282).

- Gossip: talk that is of interest to listeners, often because they know the person being gossiped about, or know of them (in the case of celebrity gossip).
- Urban legend: a 3rd person narrative (often attributed to a friend of a friend) that is usually about a bizarre, grotesque, or violent encounter; told as though true and set in the real world, even if it likely did not happen (think: the ghostly hitchhiker, the man with the hook, etc.).
- Personal narrative: a 1st person narrative told by the same person who lived through the event being recounted.
- Ostension: any action or behavior inspired by legends (for example, going to explore a graveyard you have heard is haunted).
- Moral panic: a widespread popular belief in something dangerous and threatening, often disseminated by the mass media or pop culture, reflecting a group identity and boundaries, often with a scapegoat involved.
- Conspiracy theory: built from rumors and legends, this narrative genre asserts that a secret group either already controls the world or is seeking world domination (more on this in a bit).

You can have multiple instances of these genres about the same thing, but that doesn't mean they *are* the same thing. For example, HIV / AIDS is a common topic in urban legends, and there are also conspiracy theories about the secret origins of HIV / AIDS. The urban legends (often about a young white woman who goes somewhere "exotic" on spring break during college, and after being wooed by a man there, comes back with a tiny gift-wrapped coffin saying "Welcome to the world of AIDS") are about enforcing us vs. them boundaries when it comes to risk assessment and who is seen as dangerous (Diane Goldstein discusses this extensively in *Once Upon a Virus*), while the conspiracy theories (such as that HIV originated as a CIA attempt to control undesirable populations, in Goldstein 52-53) reflect widespread distrust of the government.

The other thing about these genres is that they can sometimes hop from medium to medium, but they're still of interest to folklorists (and should be to everyone, as I argue below). Urban legends were sometimes reported in newspaper articles and on the radio, and now, they transition from oral tradition to internet transmission and back again quite readily. Just because a folklore text appears in print or on a screen or has been otherwise adapted into a mass media or pop culture medium doesn't mean it's not folklore, because it can usually shapeshift again pretty easily to resume informal modes of transmission.

I also want to expand on conspiracy theories, because I think they can be co-extensive with moral panics in interesting ways. My folklore colleague Ceallaigh S. MacCath-Moran gives an extended definition of conspiracy theories in her educational blog series:

Conspiracy theories are straightforward cause-and-effect narratives created with threads of information from various sources tied together in a way that looks coherent, but isn't. However, they are told as truthful or factual and carry the authority of truth or fact. Because of this, they express and influence beliefs about the events they describe, and they provoke conversation about how these events might be interpreted. They also affect the behaviour of those who believe them in negative ways by assigning deliberate agency to things that are accidental, unintended, unknown, or unknowable, by expressing a hypercritical suspicion that an evil elite is suppressing the truth about events from the public, and by reinforcing in-group cohesion through the designation of enemies.

What I like about this definition is that it includes recognition that sometimes people are just trying to explain weird events around them, events that might have been accidental or mysterious or unknowable under other circumstances. And when it comes to sexual topics there is a *lot* that remains mysterious or unknown (in part because we still lack decent sex ed, *cough*).

Conspiracy theories and moral panics have a lot in common—both try to come up with an overarching explanation for The Bad Thing, though conspiracy theories often assign more agency to a secret, shadowy group—so I address both in this book. And I think they overlap quite a bit, like in how there's been a moral panic over the supposed sex trafficking of children for over a century in the U.S., but it was expressed quite specifically as a conspiracy theory in the Pizzagate event.

Some moral panics are very old, which is why I mentioned "literature" up top as one of the potential means for conveying them: the *Malleus Maleficarum* is a text that was written in the 1500s as a manual for witch-hunting, and it helped instigate a moral panic on witches. This was in part because it appeared concurrently with the printing press (Frederiksen and Knudsen 5), which helped the ideas contained in the text spread and appear in both secular and religious contexts as a justification for persecuting outsiders believed to be witches.

Changing technologies also change how rapidly moral panics can spread. In the introduction to the book *Modern Folk Devils*, Martin Frederiksen and Ida Harboe Knudsen write, "Moral panics are carried by the speed of media and further stipulate a feeling of belonging among the large majority, by pointing out a deviant and even dangerous minority" (13). To riff off an old saying popular among scholars, form follows function. As in, we get this rapid spread of media moral panics in part to reinforce the sense of group belonging among those sharing an identity while they share the media outlets.

And that takes us to the function, or the why, of moral panics. I thought Frederiksen and Knudsen put it nicely: "By defining the threat to society, society in return is defined by this very threat" (14). Moral panics are not just blips on the radar, but rather defining moments in which a society draws sharp boundaries around who is normal and who is a threat, which in turn influences concrete policies and actions.

What causes moral panics? We're still working on that. One hypothesis is that "serious and disturbing social change and economic upheavals, which create a general atmosphere of uncertainty" can be a major precipitating factor in deciding when moral panics will blossom (La Fontaine 18). And this certainly tracks with some of the post-9/11 moral panics in the U.S. fueled by Islamophobia.

When it comes to moral panics, and especially sexual moral panics, we tend to see that the more things change, the more they stay the same (which, honestly, is a major theme in this book; it is WILD to me that we are freaking out about some of the exact same topics now as we were 100 years ago).

Common topics for moral panics include the following:

- Oh no, someone is doing bad things to children.
- Oh no, someone is sex trafficking our children.
- Oh no, queer people exist and will do bad things to our children.
- Communism!
- Immigrants!
- Women want things beyond being baby-makers and this will lead to the decay of society.

(To be clear, I am being cheeky about these topics and am not dismissive about, say, valid concerns about bad things happening to children, and sadly there are plenty of those, but rather to illustrate just how dang repetitive these are once you start to identify the underlying patterns).

Examples of them over the years are as follows:

- Oh no, someone is doing bad things to children: the blood libel legend in medieval Christian Europe, wherein Jews were thought to kidnap, kill, and ingest the blood of Christian babies (Dundes); the Satanic Ritual Abuse panic of the 1980s and 1990s in the U.S. (Laycock) and in Britain (La Fontaine); the belief that razors or poisons are put into Halloween candy (Grider); the Slenderman beliefs, stories, and subsequent violence (Peck).
- Oh no, someone is sex trafficking our children: the "white slavery" rumors and legends of the early

1900s, which was this idea that "unsuspecting young women," as in, young *white* women, would be exploited and forced into prostitution (Jensen 11-12); Pizzagate.

- Oh no, queer people exist and will do bad things to our children: early versions of the "gay people are pedophiles/groomers" moral panic circulated in the 1990s under the label "gay recruitment" (Irvine 173) and it's been reborn in the 2000s with the "groomer" label (check any news outlet for this).
- Communism!: McCarthyism, 'nuff said.
- Immigrants!: in the aforementioned "white slavery" moral panic, of course the slavers were immigrants (Lord 17), and in the early 2000s in the Netherlands, a cycle of urban legends about Moroccan immigrant teens raping and/or mutilating women arose (Burger).
- Women want things beyond being baby-makers and this will lead to the decay of society: the witch trials of medieval and early modern Europe (Laycock); or, in an ironic twist on this, the "welfare queen" and teen pregnancy moral panics of the 1980s and 1990s, in which women were having children but they were either doing it wrong by doing it too young or doing it wrong by not being white.

You may have noticed a focus on children (and I didn't even mention the supposed "rainbow parties" wherein teens would wear different colors of lipstick and the penis-owners in the group would try to collect all the colors through receiving oral sex; covered in Frank 11-12). To take just one case study and look at some of how these implications ripple out, let's look a bit closer at the Halloween candy thing. As folklorist Sylvia Grider documents, one of the original murder cases dubbed the "Candyman" (because of course there was more than one) involved a father in the early 1970s giving his son cyanide-laced candy. This led to "widespread public service information and education campaigns" that intend to "make children aware of safety precautions needed for trick-or-treat, including not eating candy before it is x-rayed or otherwise inspected" (6). X-rays would not pick up poison, but they would pick up razors hidden in apples, another topic of apparent concern.

The irony of all this, as Grider points out, is that these messages and attempts at institutional control of Halloween "may in fact be at least partially responsible for reinvesting Halloween with a pervasive sense of real danger and threat" (6). Moral panics are interesting to study in large part because their transmission often creates a greater sense of danger than may have existed in the first place.

I'm lingering on this example both because it's fascinating and because it illustrates a major theme of this book: there are some massive fears around the kinds of bad things that might happen to children...and an utter disconnect with what we might feasibly do to protect them. X-raying candy—or holding trick-or-treating at schools or churches or malls or only during daylight hours—would not have prevented the child victim of the Candyman because that was violence that originated in the home. And that is precisely the kind of violence that moral panics seem allergic to acknowledging, preferring instead to focus on stranger danger and the foreign Other.

Like we see in debates around sex education in general, there is a whole lot of "Think of the children!" but not a whole lot of policies that serve actual young people. It's almost as though the fears and anxieties of adults are pandered to the most, whether we're talking responses to moral panics or rules around school sex education.

Coming back to the "why" of moral panics, I think we can usefully examine one of the contemporary examples to see who benefits from this kind of furor among the general public. The widespread accusations that queer people are child abusers and groomers have practically no basis in reality, and in fact a lot of the people making them are hiding skeletons in their own closets.

Like, I don't think there's a single documented case of a trans person assaulting someone in a bathroom, but there are plenty of cases of trans and gender-nonconforming people *being* assaulted in bathrooms. And while plenty of churches are preaching anti-LGBTQ+ hatred and saying that we queer folks are groomers, how many priests are getting away with actual grooming and child abuse?

Moral panics and conspiracy theories can be, when directed by the hands of the powerful, a tool to misdirect and avoid attention. It's far easier to blame convenient and already-marginalized social scapegoats for problems (real or imagined) than to turn the lens on the actual origins of those problems.

To take another example, there is an epidemic of violence against women in the U.S.; according to the Centers for Disease Control and Prevention, half of female homicide victims are killed by their male romantic/domestic partners, past or present. That's a lot of fucking violence and I am personally feeling pretty panicky about it, but it hasn't achieved the status of a moral panic because we're not seeing widespread freakouts about it, fueled by rumors or legends both told interpersonally and in the media. Why not?

Maybe we're not ready to have the conversation yet about how much gender-based violence is the result of a society that doesn't talk about healthy relationships and consent in whatever passes for sex ed in most states. Maybe we're not ready to talk about male entitlement to women's sexual, domestic, emotional, and reproductive labor, the way feminist philosopher Kate Manne does in her excellent book *Entitled*. When half the population is trained from birth to expect affection and adoration from the other half, and told it's valid to respond with violence when denied what they're entitled to, what do you think is going to happen?

But noooo, according to the latest moral panic, it's queer people who are the problem. Or it's those uppity feminists who keep putting fuel on the #MeToo fire who are the problem. I guess confronting the widespread reality of gender-based violence, as well as anti-LGBTQ+ violence, is just too daunting, and we'd rather swallow lies and accusations against those already facing social marginalization and violence.

Rather than confront the actual sexual abuse of women happening so regularly—like to over half of U.S. women and almost one in three U.S. men ("Fast Facts: Preventing Sexual Violence")—we make up ideal victims. Take sex trafficking, for example. Sex trafficking definitely happens, but labor trafficking is a far bigger issue in terms of raw numbers as I understand it, based on the variety of jobs for which people are labor trafficked (domestic labor, agricultural labor, and so on).

So why aren't we talking about labor trafficking more? Could it be that we have an ideal image of the victim (a young, white woman) in mind, and anything that deviates from it is unimaginable or not deserving of attention, activism, or pity?

Hell, this sort of blinders-wearing impacts men as well. 71% of gun suicides in America are white men killing themselves, but we're not talking about that, are we ("Gun Violence in America")? It's a real epidemic of self-inflicted gun violence and it's a real tragedy, but many Americans are oblivious to it because it doesn't fit the narrative of where violence comes from according to widespread conspiracy theories and moral panics.

Stepping off my soap box for a second (sorry/not sorry), my point is that whenever we think we're seeing a moral panic, we should put on our critical thinking hats and ask who is disseminating these rumors and who stands to benefit from them.

I know it can be tough to disentangle the elements of moral panics, conspiracy theories, and their partnered folklore genres. But since these narratives weave in and out of American history, and often point a blamey finger at marginalized groups when it comes to sexual topics, we would do well to try to understand these things when they pop up.

For some of us, it could be a matter of life or death. And if that's not a compelling reason to study folklore, I don't know what is!

References:

Astapova, Anastasiya. "In Search for Truth: Surveillance Rumors and Vernacular Panopticon in Belarus." *Journal of American Folklore*, vol. 130 no. 517, 2017, p. 276-304.

Burger, Peter. "The Smiley Gang Panic: Ethnic Legends about

Gang Rape in the Netherlands in the Wake of 9/11." *Western Folklore*, vol. 68, no. 2/3, 2009, pp. 275–95.

Dundes, Alan. *The Blood Libel Legend: A Casebook in Anti-Semitic Folklore.* University of Wisconsin Press, 1991.

"Fast Facts: Preventing Sexual Violence." Centers for Disease Control and Prevention, 22 June 2022, https://www.cdc.gov/violenceprevention/sexualviolence/fastfact.html. Accessed 10 August 2023.

Frank, Katherine. *Plays Well in Groups: A Journey through the World of Group Sex.* Rowman and Littlefield Publishers, Incorporated, 2013.

Frederiksen, Martin Demant, and Ida Harboe Knudsen. "Introduction: Folk Devils Past and Present." *Modern Folk Devils: Contemporary Constructions of Evil*, edited by Martin Demant Frederiksen and Ida Harboe Knudsen, Helsinki University Press, 2021, pp. 1–24.

Goldstein, Diane E. *Once Upon a Virus: Aids Legends and Vernacular Risk Perception.* Utah State University Press, 2004.

Grider, Sylvia Ann. "Conservatism and Dynamism in the Contemporary Celebration of Halloween: Institutionalization, Commercialization, Gentrification." *Southern Folklore*, vol. 53, no. 1, 1996, pp. 3-15.

"Gun Violence in America." *Everytown for Gun Safety*, 13 February 2023, https://everytownresearch.org/report/gun-violence-in-america/. Accessed 10 August 2023.

Jensen, Robin E. *Dirty Words: The Rhetoric of Public Sex Education, 1870–1924*. University of Illinois Press, 2010.

La Fontaine, Jean. "Hidden Enemies: Evil at the End of the Millennium." *Witches and Demons: A Comparative Perspective on Witchcraft and Satanism*, 1st ed., vol. 10, Berghahn Books, 2016, pp. 13–28.

Laycock, Joseph. "Carnal Knowledge: The Epistemology of Sexual Trauma in Witches' Sabbaths, Satanic Ritual Abuse, and Alien Abduction Narratives." *Preternature: Critical and Historical Studies on the Preternatural*, vol. 1, no. 1, 2012, pp. 100–29.

Lord, Alexandra M. *Condom Nation: The U. S. Government's Sex Education Campaign from World War I to the Internet*. Johns Hopkins University Press, 2009.

MacCath-Moran, Ceallaigh S. "What Is a Conspiracy Theory?" *Folklore & Fiction*, https://csmaccath.com/blog/what-conspiracy-theory? Accessed 10 August 2023.

Peck, Andrew. "Tall, Dark, and Loathsome: The Emergence of a Legend Cycle in the Digital Age." *The Journal of American Folklore*, vol. 128, no. 509, 2015, pp. 333–48.

SEX ISN'T SPECIAL

BUT CULTURE MAKES IT SO

As a CULTURAL CONSTRUCTIONIST, I believe that nothing humans do has an inherent meaning attached to it: culture provides the palate of meanings to choose from, and individuals choose according to a variety of factors in their lives.

This is nowhere more true than sex. Sex has biological facets and facts, but culture makes sex have meaning; sex isn't inherently any more special or meaningful than any other human activity. And yet, people tend to treat sex as though it inhabits some uniquely set-apart realm of human experience, a law unto itself.

I actually just rewrote the last paragraph because initially I had written, "Sex has biological facets and consequences, but..." because I realized, dang, even just saying "consequences" sounds very judgmental, when I was trying to reference certain "If A, Then B" aspects of sexual activity, like how having unprotected penis-in-vagina sex might result in conception, or transmission of an STI. And while those things can technically be considered "consequences," as in, if you do one action, a predictable event will likely be the result of it, simply calling that thing a "consequence" layers on a social level of nuance that comes across, at least in my interpretation, as pretty far from neutral.

When something happens in a relationship between humans that is sexual (rather than a professional or other kind of relationship), the fact that sex is involved doesn't make it unique or special. You're either being ethical and paying attention to consent and health concerns, or you're not, or you're in the gray area of miscommunication that sometimes exists but definitely shouldn't be used to justify or cover up a consent violation. Sex being involved doesn't excuse actions or behaviors that would elsewhere be seen as unethical, reprehensible, or generally shady. This is why we point out parallels between saying someone was "asking for it" in a sexual assault and "asking for it" in a robbery—to highlight the inconsistency in the same rhetoric being applied to abusive/exploitative situations, but where only one is culturally legible. Thanks for that, rape culture.

On the flip side, just because something involves sex, that something doesn't automatically become unethical or reprehensible. This seems obvious to me, but people who are sexually active aren't automatically unprincipled: people do lots of things with their sex lives outside the norm, but those things don't automatically make them irresponsible deviants who should be thrown into jail or reparative therapy.

Unfortunately, even scientists aren't immune to the "specialness of sex" aura. Dr. Emily Nagoski points out in her book *Come As You Are: The Surprising New Science That Will Transform Your Sex Life* that the human nervous system functions on a dual control model: a set of gas pedals and brake pedals that complement one another and govern our responses. This includes sexual arousal (which I cover in a few chapters). However, until about 15 years ago, scientists were still struggling to come up with an accurate model of sexual arousal... and only eventually did they think "hey, maybe sexual arousal works the same exact way that the rest of the human excitation systems work." As Nagoski concludes, this was an embarrassingly obvious conclusion at which to belatedly arrive.

I also maintain that while you may not agree with everything in *Sex at Dawn: How We Mate, Why We Stray, and What It Means for Modern Relationships*, authors Christopher Ryan and Cacilda Jetha make the excellent point that sexual norms and cultural norms are inextricable from one another, and this includes how we interpret historical and scientific findings. There's a good chance that humans didn't evolve in completely monogamous settings, though social pair-bonding has probably been around in one form or another fairly consistently, and yet this remains a pretty taboo topic because, again, adding sex to the topic means we have to treat it as very very special.

And I'm not saying that sex can't be or isn't special to people. I get that it's a compelling way to express your love, affection, commitment, and even spirituality to some. I'm simply stating that none of those things belong uniquely to sexual expression, and that we might not even have these associations if culture didn't imbue us with them.

Unfortunately, my attitude about it not making sense to consider sex apart from the rest of the human realm puts me at odds with many points made by monotheistic religions, which tend to associate sex with procreation and with very specific types of arrangements: heterosexual, monogamous, and so on. I don't think sex is special because it's a mandate from God or any given holy book; I think sex is special when consenting adults engage in it for reasons that make it special to them, and I hope that they're doing so in ways that are in congruence with their own value systems, not simply because culture handed them a set of predetermined values and said "This is the only way to be sexual."

In the end, there are as many ways to be sexual as there are humans on the planet. So long as we're encouraging people to pursue the most ethical, consensual, and healthy ways to be sexual, does the cultural insistence on barricading sex in its own special container really need to exist?

References:

Nagoski, Emily. *Come As You Are: The Surprising New Science That Will Transform Your Sex Life.* Simon & Schuster Paperbacks, 2015.

Ryan, Christopher, and Cacilda Jetha. *Sex at Dawn: How We Mate, Why We Stray, and What It Means for Modern Relationships.* HarperCollins, 2008.

SEXUALLY ACTIVE ≠ UNPRINCIPLED

ONE OF THE ways American culture gets sex wrong is by linking sexual activity with assumptions of being unprincipled, unethical, and perhaps even immoral.

Historically, yes, we can somewhat blame the Puritans for upholding an atmosphere of sexual vigilance, wherein any deviation from heterosexual marital intimacy was violently punished. People who had affairs, or performed bestial acts, were often fined or whipped, or occasionally put to death. But, as John D'Emilio and Estelle Freedman point out in *Intimate Matters: A History of Sexuality in America*, it was still considered normal to want sex within marriage. And people who transgressed social norms were brought back into the fold once they'd been taken to task.

Fast forward to today, when thanks to a number of other cultural shifts, we have more public discourse about sex and less flogging people for stepping outside the lines... but we still have an emphasis on heterosexual monogamous procreative marital sex as the only acceptable sex. And even within those confines, there's such a thing as too much sexual desire, too much masturbation, too much consumption of erotic materials, and so on.

We can trace some of this to the ways in which ideas about sex percolated into public awareness. D'Emilio and Freedman document how "The writings of Sigmund Freud best symbolize the new direction that sexual theorizing took in the twentieth century...Above all, Americans absorbed a version of Freudianism that presented the sexual impulse as an insistent force demanding expression" (223). This impulse could of course be suppressed, but not without consequences, both psychological and physiological. And the proper, moral thing to do in the eyes of many is to sublimate or channel more productively the sexual impulse, because letting it simply have its way could wreak havoc and chaos.

This concept is still with us today, I'd argue, though of course it's not the only way to perceive sexuality. Rather than viewing sexual desire as a raging force of nature that's potentially destructive, it's possible to view sexual desire as a natural part of humanity that deserves healthy expression. To take one example, this occurred around 1917, after the Bolshevik Revolution in Russia, and was known as the "glass of water" theory. Jonathan Zimmerman explains this in *Too Hot to Handle: A Global History of Sex Education*: "Just as people drank a glass of water to quench their thirst, the theory went, so should they have sex to satisfy a different kind of urge; there was no need to complicate the matter with romance or love" (24). This theory didn't last very long, since Lenin didn't like it, but it's an example of how there are many ways to view sexual urges, not all of them negative.

Thanks to the rise of Freudian thought as well as other historical factors, today in America being sexually active or sexually engaged is seen as suspect. Worse, there's a stigma that being sexually active somehow taints the rest of a person, making it seem that because they're so interested in sex, they're somehow incapable of upholding their other agreements or obligations.

This is why we end up with awful things like slut-shaming sexual assault survivors, or saying once you've consented to one outside-the-box thing you've consented to them all. For example, I have seen countless defenses of assault that tried to justify it by saying the victim was an adult entertainer or played some other role that granted consent to a certain type of sexual activity, so they couldn't really have *not* consented to being assaulted.

Just... ugh.

Apart from how it's obviously terrible to say that because someone consented to one outside-the-box sexual act they must've consented to another (because consent is an ongoing conversation, not a universal declaration), we also need to combat the notion that sexuality is this awful dark drive that taints your whole person. We need to be aware of, and actively fight, the implication that once someone has engaged in (consensual) sexual activity, they can no longer be trusted to be reliable in other areas of their lives, such as accurately communicating consent, acting like a professional at work, or being a good parent or a generally principled human being.

Katherine Frank, in her book analyzing group sex throughout the world, argues that sexual excess contaminates both the individual and society: "Losing control sexually is believed to have a domino effect on one's individual morality and sense of self as well as on society as a whole" (15). Which, again, is a strange metric in my view: why not look for social decay in something like how many humans go hungry, instead of assuming that the real moral problem is folks banging too much?

Basically, it comes down to this: no amount of sexual desire or sexual activity is inherently unprincipled or immoral, unless the way you go about it involves non-consent or coercion.

While a lot of examples in this chapter revolve around what's perceived as over-the-top sexual behavior, this applies to less-than-expected sexual behavior too: people who are asexual or demisexual (as in, those who don't experience sexual attraction or those who do only under specific circumstances) are often stigmatized as abnormal too. It's almost as though there's this (totally made-up) happy medium of "normal" amounts and types of sexual behavior, and anything that falls outside what's considered the "normal" center of the spectrum gets dinged as broken, unhinged, unhealthy, and so on. Which is pretty sucky, considering that the spectrum of "normal" sexual behavior is imaginary to begin with.

And this is a huge part of my belief in and effort to act in alignment with sex positivity: promoting views of sex that encourage us to dig a little deeper, to ask why someone doing XYZ Thing Outside the Norm supposedly reflects back on their personality and indeed their entire personhood in such a detrimental way. In my (perhaps overly optimistic) sex-positive view of the world, none of what you're into sexually impacts how I view you, so long as you're going about it consensually. It might not be my jam, I might not always want to hear about it, but I wouldn't judge you for it.

In turn, I'd expect the same courtesy from anyone else... but sadly, there are all too many examples of women who step outside the norm and are punished for it. For example, California congresswoman Katie Hill resigned in 2019 after nude photos were leaked, and there are more details to the story here than I have time to get into, but this is just one instance of a double standard where public knowledge of non-normative sexual behavior leads to severe social punishments for a woman...and that doesn't tend to happen so much to men when their indiscretions become public.

Our views of sexually active people are often conditioned by these kinds of double standards and biases: according to gender, race, and more. But even just learning to identify double standards at work is one step in the process of figuring out where we assign value to people's sexual behavior, whether positively or negatively viewed.

I know that we're socially conditioned to view sexuality according to how our culture perceives it, and I know that cultural norms don't change overnight. But if we get enough people to join the conversation, hopefully we can start to make progress in a more sex-positive, less needlessly judgmental direction.

References:

D'Emilio, John, and Estelle B. Freedman. *Intimate Matters: A History of Sexuality in America.* Third ed., University of Chicago Press, 2012.

Frank, Katherine. *Plays Well in Groups: A Journey through the World of Group Sex.* Rowman and Littlefield Publishers, Incorporated, 2013.

Zimmerman, Jonathan. *Too Hot to Handle: A Global History of Sex Education.* Princeton University Press, 2015.

SEX SHOULDN'T BE ABOUT "GETTING AWAY WITH IT"

BUT HERE'S WHY IT IS

I'VE NOTICED a pervasive attitude or folk idea among Americans: that sex is something we need to "get away with" in order to enjoy it—or have it at all. This can be a problem, or in other cases, it can be absolutely essential.

The linking of religious sin with sexual expression goes way back in America. The specifics have changed over time, as I chronicle in the previous chapter, "Sexually Active ≠ Unprincipled," but the general connotation remains: sex is a sin when performed outside very specific contexts (heterosexual vanilla monogamous marriage, and even so, we've now got the concept of sex addiction for people who want *too* much of that!). But given these connections, it's no surprise that even in emotionally healthy relationships, people might still feel as though wanting sex at all is a problem, and thus whenever they have it, they're getting away with something.

We're not allowed to pursue sexual encounters as young folks (unlike in the Netherlands, where many parents allow their teens to have sleepovers with their romantic partners), so we need to "get away with it" to make those experiences happen in the first place. As one might imagine, this leads to a lot of secrecy and furtive behavior, which might become solidified into habit even as the situation changes when someone turns 18 and/or gets their own place.

Sex ed in the U.S.—when it happens at all—is framed in terms of risks and consequences rather than pleasure. So it's hardly surprising that when we have sex it's with the connotation that we're doing something dangerous, which we hope we emerged unscathed from after. This time: woohoo, didn't get (anyone or myself) pregnant! Another time: didn't wind up with genital sores, awesome! (the stigma of which is its own thing that we're also not talking about enough)

Being able to "get away with" sex sometimes implies that you have to swoop in and convince the other person that they want to do sexy things with you. Hence we run into the problem of consent being perceived as something you have to "get" instead of it being something that people naturally collaborate on as part of a healthy, ethical interaction. Sex educator Allison Moon shines some light on the phenomenon in her book *Girl Sex 101*: "Men, especially, are taught they should 'try to get' as much as they can, and women are supposed to tell them when to stop" (61). Unfortunately there's a gendered dynamic in that sex is commodified as an object that women have and men try to get, which I've referred to in the past as the puzzle box model of sex (as in, insert a token or coin to the puzzle box, and if you do it right, out pops a tasty sex treat!).

Unfortunately, one of the reasons for the "getting away with" aspect of sex that is somewhat transactional as noted above, with men as the seekers and women as the gatekeepers, is rooted in hegemonic masculinity: men's social status rises when they can brag about having had more sexual partners, whereas a woman might be slut-shamed for the same behavior. Attaching social standing to how many people you've slept with, and further, making these two genders into enemies with one trying to get sex and the other trying to play a game of keep-away, is...not a great way for humans to relate to one another.

The whole antagonistic bent to the way in which heterosexual folks are given scripts to act out is a bit odd. I've seen multiple feminists remarking on this exact dynamic: how in patriarchy, men are taught than women are lesser than them, but women are still the desirable thing to pursue and woo, so, er, what do you think happens when roughly half the population is trying to get into the pants of the other half of the population, while simultaneously believing that oh-so-desired population is inferior? Bleh. We can do better than this, people.

There are some legit reasons to want to get away with sex in a different sense of the phrase, such as when you're actually in danger. I'm thinking in particular of LGBTQ+ folks who face discrimination and even violence based on who they're attracted to (or even just perceived to be attracted to). It's a shitty situation, and I'm bummed that we live in a world where people have to weigh the risks of acting on their desires against the potential consequences based on the nasty strains of homophobia and transphobia still alive today.

And then there are situations where getting away with it is part of the experience. When the taboo aspect becomes eroticized or even fetishized, that can add another facet to the desire to "get away with" something sexual. We're still accumulating scientific knowledge about the nature of arousal and how fetishes work, but it seems clear to me based on a lot of sexually explicit materials (from sexual fantasies people write and talk about to erotic materials like porn and erotica) that people are drawn to the taboo, and moreover, that the idea of engaging in the taboo and getting away with it is hot to a lot of folks. See, for example, the large swaths of the romance genre based on taboo attractions between boss and employee, or teacher and student. In my mind, there's nothing wrong with these fantasies, though they are probably too ethically fraught to pursue much in the real world.

Finally, certain forms of sex are criminalized, and thus are necessarily gotten away with. This happens both when the sex is consensual—as with adult sex workers—and when it's not, like with sexual assault/rape (sadly, a lot of people get away with sexual assault). It's odd to me that our society would waste time criminalizing sex that's pursued between consenting adults just because money is also changing hands, and that the people engaging in sex work have to hide it from persecuting parties, but not from the parties they want to be in the transaction with, which is a delicate balance.

At the end of the day, I don't know that the "getting away with it" mentality is in and of itself a bad thing...I mean, if you wanna gamify your life and view it as a series of challenges to overcome and dangers to evade, that's up to you!

But when it's happening in a sex-negative context (as much of the U.S. tends to be), I worry that it could get warped into something unhealthy. By all means, if flying under the radar is your best chance for practicing your occupation or more generally keeping yourself out of harm's way, stick with it! But I wonder whether a more sex-positive society that emphasizes informed consent for all would have quite as much "getting away with it" as we seem to fixate on, so, food for thought.

References:

Moon, Allison, and Kate Diamond. *Girl Sex 101*. Lunatic Ink, 2014.

WHERE'S THE ADVICE TO TEENAGE BOYS?

LADIES—LET'S take charge of our pleasure! ... is a great message, but what's missing?

I love all the talk of empowering teenage girls to learn about sex and relationships on their own terms, for when they're ready, and to make sure pleasure is included in the messages they receive. However, where's the similar advice targeting teenage boys?

Where are the gads of posts reminding them to be courteous to their dates, to brush up on how consent is communicated, to learn about the various links between anatomy and pleasure?

And no, I don't think that the genre of "Rules for dating my daughter" counts as actual advice for teenage boys. Those lists are gross for a number of reasons, among which because they communicate a transactional model of sex (not literally transactional sex) wherein girls are the gatekeepers of sexual activity that boys are trying to get out of them, and wherein fathers are responsible for guarding their daughters' virginity.

The best I've seen so far comes from Emily Nagoski, who wrote a blog post (that is sadly no longer live) responding to a friend's query about what to teach his sons so that they wouldn't learn that it was permissible to assault women (which is basically what rape culture teaches, in dozens of subtle ways).

Nagoski's advice was to teach boys—and indeed, everyone—this:

People get to choose how they touch and get touched.

Obviously this one simple axiom isn't going to end all gender- and sexuality-based oppression in the world. But if we start teaching it to everyone, and we start teaching it young, and we make sure this principle pervades more and more parts of culture, maybe we'll start to make a dent on all the awful stuff happening. In short, Nagoski was imagining a world where everyone agrees that it's not okay to grope strangers or push for sex, or judge people on how much or how little sex they want or have. Shocker, right?

That world's not going to happen overnight, but if we've got a shot at helping it manifest, we need to target everyone—boys and girls and agender and non-binary folk too—with the message that apart from a handful of very specific and likely medical circumstances, you're the only one who gets to decide how your body is touched, and how you touch others.

We *especially* need to make sure that this message reaches teenage boys and young men, who are simultaneously receiving tons of cultural conditioning telling them that they're entitled to intimacy and sex when they're on a date, when they pay for dinner, when they... simply exist. Or think to ask for it. Or simply take it.

So while I'm loving the empowering messages targeting young women (yes, I recall fondly all the Girl Power moments in the 1990s, go Xena and Buffy!), let's ensure that young men are also receiving messages that empower them by humanizing them rather than making them out to be walking boners or almost-rapists, insinuating that not only do they want sex 24/7 but that they'll do anything to get it.

This means normalizing talking about sex, of course. But it also demands that we rethink gender roles, and that is an endeavor that has the potential to benefit everyone.

HOW SEX ACTUALLY WORKS

MEN AND WOMEN: THE SAME
PARTS, ORGANIZED DIFFERENTLY

BINARIES ARE OUT, spectrums are in. We're all uniquely shaped bodies that share a common origin (thanks, homology). I'll go over homology and other things in this chapter, in case this is new territory for y'all, and I'll also talk about some of the very real human rights consequences of sticking with the binary.

On both anatomical and sexual levels, men and women have more in common than not. And I really think it's a bummer that most people don't know this.

As Emily Nagoski writes in *Come As You Are: The Surprising New Science that Will Transform Your Sex Life*, until about six weeks after the implantation of a fertilized egg in the uterus, all fetuses have the same genital tissue. In other words, they're homologues, or traits with shared biological origins but diverging appearances and/or functions. After a hormone wash that most male fetuses respond to, they begin to differentiate. Nagoski states:

Both male and female genitals have a round-ended, highly sensitive, multichambered organ to which blood flows during sexual arousal. On females, it's the clitoris; on males, it's the penis. And each has an organ that is soft, stretchy, and grows coarse hair after puberty. On females, it's the outer lips (labia majora); on males, it's the scrotum. These parts don't just look superficially alike; they are developed from the equivalent fetal tissue. (20)

The really cool thing is that this means that we have to rethink the very concept of having external vs. internal genitalia as a differentiating factor between men and women. In *Women's Anatomy of Arousal: Secret Maps to Buried Pleasure* by Sheri Winston, there are diagrams of the internal erectile tissue that most women have, wherein the legs of the clitoris extend deep inside the pubic area, branching around the vagina. In other words, women have just as much erectile tissue as men do—it's just not always visible.

Homology is also present in nipples. Why do men have nipples if they rarely produce breast milk? Because nature is lazy and decided that it was easier to put nipples on mammals and have them on all sexes rather than putting them on only one sex (yes, I am being a bit glib here, it's a thing).

Intersex folks, and trans or non-binary people on hormones, also have the same type of genital tissues, but remixed somewhat differently, and it's all normal. As Nagoski writes, "There's nothing wrong with their genitals, any more than there's anything wrong with a person whose labia are uniquely large or small. It's still all the same parts, just organized in a different way" (32).

This is why it drives me nuts when people—evolutionary psychologists, pickup artists, certain religious people, whoever—talk about the differences between men and women as though they are absolute, essential, and universal. They're not. They're really not. Apart from a handful of anatomical differences in hormones and what your genitals and reproductive systems can and can't do, men and women are more similar than they're different. And the differences that are really noticeable may well come from a lifetime of cultural conditioning for all we can tell, given that the sex-gender connection is super complicated.

Okay, you want to talk about a few of the supposedly immutable differences? There are a few, but again, I don't think they're completely universal or clear-cut. Based on studies with large, nationally representative samples, Dr. Debby Herbenick has concluded that men's and women's orgasms often work somewhat different, with a lot of men aware of a "point of no return" when they can't stop the orgasm anymore: "This is one distinct difference between men's and women's orgasms, since women's orgasms during sex can be stopped at pretty much any time" (21). But at the same time, both men and women experience coregasms, also known as exercise-induced orgasms, which I discuss more at length in the orgasm chapter.

Differences in when orgasms can be stopped or not are pretty minor in the grand scheme of things, though. And, as with anything human, there are always outliers: both men and women who can have multiple orgasms, or none at all; there are men who can orgasm without ejaculating and women who can orgasm with ejaculating, and so on. So it doesn't make sense to me to treat these minor differences as indicative that men and women are wholly different types of humans from one another.

There are some hormonal differences on top of the configurations of anatomy, too. But I think this nuance gets lots in pop culture, since both men and women have all the hormones, even those considered reproductive hormones! It's not like only women have estrogen (so please shut up about the "soy boy" nonsense, sigh). Are these things patterned by gender? Sure. But we're talking a spectrum, not completely divergent types of humans.

As more evidence of "we're all made of the same parts, assembled differently," trans women also get periods. Their hormones are all in for a menstrual cycle, regardless of what their underlying anatomy may or may not be, which means fun things like cramps, mood swings, and the dreaded period poops. No, I don't have a citation for this, I just talk to my trans friends and listen to their experiences with an open mind. Plus, there's been a fair bit of this chronicled on the internet where people share their personal narratives (another folklore genre that can, for all the individuality inherent in it, affirm just how similar many human experiences are).

Culturally speaking, there have been some interesting shifts in how people think of anatomical sex in the last few centuries. Thomas Laqueur details these shifts in his fascinating book *Making Sex*, taking a trip through medical history (and philosophy, and regular ol' history, and lots more evidence) to demonstrate that for much of Western history, the one-sex model dominated thought and medical practice.

The one-sex model meant that human bodies were perceived to be based on one anatomical model, the male one, with women being a deficient and/or inferior version of it. If this sounds harsh, um, it is.

Westerners since antiquity believed that orgasm on behalf of both parties was necessary for conception (Laqueur 66-67), which fits with the assumption that both male and female bodies are essentially the same, because male orgasm is generally needed for conception. Many of ye olden anatomical drawings depicted a uterus as an inverted penis, with the fallopian tubes as testicles that happened to be inside the body. Weirdly, they weren't totally wrong.

Then came the two-sex model, beginning around the eighteenth century and solidifying in the Victorian era, which asserted that two distinct sexes existed, and these immutable differences showed in women, "in the very nature of their bones, nerves, and, most important, reproductive organs" on which "came to bear an enormous new weight of meaning" (Laqueur 150). Sex differences became a stand-in for gender differences, because golly gee, we just couldn't agree that men and women are basically the same and deserve the same rights during the Enlightenment era birth of human rights discourse, now, could we? (sorry for the cynical tone, I am still annoyed about this)

So, our intellectual heritage has kinda bounced back and forth between acknowledging men's and women's fundamental similarities and denying them. The latter is usually politically motivated.

When it comes to sexuality (orientation, preferences, sexual functioning, arousal, desire, etc.) I follow Nagoski in emphasizing homology above all else: while there are patterns in how men and women react differently to sexual stimuli, we're all coming from basically the same place: "We also find overlap between the two groups, and we find folks who vary wildly from the 'average' while still being perfectly normal and healthy" (35). In other words, it doesn't matter if your sexuality conforms more to what we consider masculine or feminine modes of sexuality, so long as you understand and accept yourself.

This is also why genital shaming is unacceptable (as I wrote about a few chapters back, lamenting the slang phrase "camel toe"). People generally don't have a lot of control over how their genitals look (though these days there are more surgical options than ever before). You really can't infer anything about anyone's sexual orientation or interests by looking at their genitals, so again, let's get used to the idea that everyone's genitals are normal, since we're all made of the same parts assembled differently. Loving your body and culti-vating a positive body image can also have a beneficial effect on your sex life, which Nagoski talks about extensively in her book and her first TED talk, so all the more reason to get on board with the ideas in this chapter.

On a more serious note, binary views of sexual anatomy can take a severe toll on the basic human rights of a couple of groups. Hilary Malatino is among the scholars studying intersex and transgender rights, and in "Medical Ethics and Trans and Intersex Bodies", she documents a series of viola-tions that each group experiences: in the not-so-distant past, many intersex people were subjected to corrective surgery while infants (now widely considered unethical because, ya know, that's what happens when someone is too young to consent to major procedures that are not life-saving). And many transgender people are denied access to very similar treatments, treatments that can affirm gender.

As Malatino puts it,

I've had to think a lot about the way that intersex subjects are constantly positioned as natural errors that can be remediated with the wonders of modern technoscience and restored...While at the same time you have trans subjects being positioned continuously like those unnatural and monstrous threats to the social order who don't deserve rights and don't deserve access to biomedical technologies that might make their lives and indeed do make their lives infinitely easier in terms of their ability to navigate the social environment, their ability to experience pleasure in their bodies, etc.

I want to be very clear: the struggles of intersex people and transgender people are not the same, and in comparing them, I do not wish to minimize the history of each movement. But held up to one another, since Malatino notes that sometimes the same doctors and clinics were working on these technologies deemed to be for disparate subjects, it becomes clear: a lot of people hold a very deep-seated attachment to this idea that our gender resides in our genitals, and if both things aren't binary, that's super bad.

The reality is that bodies always have exhibited and always will exhibit tons and tons of variation. The sooner we can wrap our heads around this simple fact, and make room in our cultures for it, the better off we'll be.

References:

Herbenick, Debby. *The Coregasm Workout: The Revolutionary Method for Better Sex through Exercise.* Seal Press, 2015.

Laqueur, Thomas Walter. *Making Sex: Body and Gender from the Greeks to Freud.* Harvard University Press, 1992.

Malatino, Hilary. "Medical Ethics and Trans and Intersex Bodies." *Journal of the Texas Tech University Ethics Center* 4.2, 2020.

Nagoski, Emily. *Come As You Are: The Surprising New Science That Will Transform Your Sex Life.* Simon & Schuster Paperbacks, 2015.

Winston, Sheri. *Women's Anatomy of Arousal: Secret Maps to Buried Pleasure.* Mango Garden, 2010.

A FEW FACTS ABOUT VULVAS AND VAGINAS

THE LAST CHAPTER should have provided you with some decent facts and food for thought on how a lot of misinformation circulates around genitals, insisting on treating penises and vaginas/vulvas as utterly different types of anatomical structures, when in fact they are made of the same basic tissue, structured a bit differently.

However, there is enough misinformation about vaginas and vulvas specifically that I have decided to insert another chapter here. This is not to say that there's not also worthwhile information to be had about penises, scrotums, prostates, and the like, just that this information is perhaps not as buried as is accurate info about vaginas and such. Well, maybe prostate stuff isn't super well known, but it's easy to find out more both about prostate cancer risks and prostate pleasure with a simple internet search. For vag stuff? You're more likely to find yourself swimming in a sea of misconceptions (sorry, I am trying to avoid puns here, but it's not going so well).

I should also note that this chapter primarily deals with

anatomy as it's often found on the bodies of cisgender women, but I'll include some information about less-binary bodies, too.

Whole books have been written about vaginas and vulvas; I'm partial to *The Vagina Bible* by Dr. Jen Gunter because it's so science-minded and well researched. If you're willing to branch out and be a little more spiritual or woo-woo, I also like *Women's Anatomy of Arousal* by Sheri Winston (and the following facts are found in one or both of these books).

Let's clear up some misconceptions by stating some facts first:

The vagina is the internal anatomical structure that connects the vaginal opening to the cervix and uterus, while the vulva is the external structure (usually thought to comprise the inner and outer labia and clitoris, plus the clitoral hood, urethral opening, and mons if we want to get fancy).

- The clitoral shaft and legs are largely hidden under the skin, but between them, the vestibular bulbs (tissues that surround the vaginal opening), and the urethral sponge (tissue that surrounds the urethra, you guessed it!), women tend to have just as much erectile tissue as men do in the genitals.
- The G-spot (named by Dr. Gräfenberg who apparently discovered it) is actually the urethral sponge, but yes, it's a thing, and for some women it's a bit of tissue that leads to orgasms when stimulated through the front/top wall of the vagina.
- Female ejaculation (one slang word for this is "squirting") is also a thing, and I've seen conflicting studies as to whether it's repurposed urine that soaked through cell walls to get there, or some other liquid that is parallel to male ejaculate, but since it's

processed through the Skene's glands a.k.a. paraurethral glands, which are considered equivalents of the prostate gland in men, it's anyone's guess; Winston hypothesizes that since this ejaculate is "produced by the paraurethral glands and designed to flood the urethra during and at the end of intercourse to protect the urinary system from infection" (135) it serves an important immune function and shouldn't be dismissed.

- The vagina is a self-cleaning ecosystem and there is probably never any reason to douche.
- Most vaginas are 2–4 inches in length when the person is not aroused, and they "tent" to a length of more like 4–8 inches during arousal (Moon 95); they're built to stretch (because childbirth is an option we evolved for) but they pretty much never stretch out, contrary to the fears of people like incels.

Next, let's talk about lube. Using lubricant can be unfortunately stigmatized in sexual encounters, since (see the chapter on how arousal works) there are frequent assumptions about how getting wet = turned on and enjoying. Well, some bodies are like "nah, we're not doing that" for whatever reason (including post-op vaginas on trans women, the vaginas of menopausal women, and so on).

However, if you're going to use lube, please read the label and do a little research! Some lubes have additives in them that are not body-friendly (same with sex toys, really; go with silicone or something non-porous that can be totally disinfected). Glycerin is a common additive but it's a relative of sugar and we shouldn't put sugary things in vaginas due to infection risk. Parabens are also not body-friendly, and any oil-based lube has the potential to destroy condoms that it comes into contact with.

Spermicides are generally not body-friendly either, and their use can increase susceptibility to STIs by disrupting the vaginal ecosystem (Ayehunie et al.).

Furthermore, I remember learning about something called osmolality at a sex education conference. Basically, this refers to how substances can draw water out of cells in order to reach a state of equilibrium. If a substance like a lube is high in osmolality, it can actually dry out the vaginal cell walls, which can be painful and can lead to the kinds of small tears and inflammation that make it easier to contract an STI or related infection like bacterial vaginosis.

You can hit the internet for a list of lubes and their osmolality levels (and pH levels too, since vaginas are naturally quite acidic). Any sex shop worth its salt (like the Smitten Kitten, which has a great web presence and articles you can read on this very subject) will be able to provide you with this information as well. It's not really my intention or expertise to make specific brand recommendations in this book, but I would personally steer clear of Astroglide and K-Y in favor of Sliquid.

Human bodies are characterized by endless variation, and the topic of vaginas and vulvas is no exception. Even if your vulva or labia seem different or weird, they're normal and natural.

Further, Allison Moon's book *Girl Sex 101* has a lot of great info about trans women's bodies and pleasure, along with communication tips (not all women like the same terms for body parts; some might prefer pussy to cunt, for example, and trans women are no different, with girl dick being one term but certainly not the only term).

I could keep going, since there's always more fascinating stuff to talk about in regard to vaginas and vulvas, but hopefully this has given you some food for thought and perhaps corrected some misconceptions. Plus, there are plenty of resources below to check out!

References:

Ayehunie, Seyoum, et al. "Hyperosmolal Vaginal Lubricants Markedly Reduce Epithelial Barrier Properties in a Three-Dimensional Vaginal Epithelium Model." *Toxicology Reports* vol. 5, 2017, pp. 134-40.

Gunter, Jen. *The Vagina Bible: The Vulva and the Vagina — Separating the Myth from the Medicine.* First trade paperback printing ed., Citadel Press, 2019.

Moon, Allison, and Kate Diamond. *Girl Sex 101.* Lunatic Ink, 2014.

Winston, Sheri. *Women's Anatomy of Arousal: Secret Maps to Buried Pleasure.* Mango Garden, 2010.

EVERYONE'S AROUSAL WORKS LIKE THIS—YES, EVERYONE'S

THE AMAZING THING about the new model of arousal I'll explain here is how astoundingly obvious it was, and how long it took science to catch up to social beliefs. No less amazing is the fact that every human works this way.

As you've realized by now, I'm a huge fan of Emily Nagoski's work. This chapter focuses on two aspects of it: the dual control model of arousal and arousal nonconcordance. As in, how do people begin to feel turned on and want sex? How do we even identify being turned on? Why are there some differences between how men and women experience these things? And how can you better understand your own arousal?

To begin, sexual arousal works just like every other part of the central nervous system. It's all got systems of gas pedals and brakes governing its actions. And yet, because of the way that sex is treated as special and unique, scientists didn't figure out the connection til the late 1990s. There have been plenty of other models of arousal, but none of them have been quite this accurate.

In brief, we've got the Sexual Excitation System (SES), a.k.a. the accelerator or gas pedal, and the Sexual Inhibition System (SIS), a.k.a. the brakes. Everyone has this dual control model, and everyone's is calibrated a little differently. The gas pedal notices any sexually relevant stimuli in your environment and sends the message to start arousal, while the brakes pedal notices anything that might impede sexy-times—risk of unwanted pregnancy or STI transmission, shame, trauma, performance anxiety—and says "Nope, don't get turned on."

This is one area where context becomes really important: we're all attuned to context differently, but women in particular have received more socialization reinforcing the significance of context to arousal, as well as more socialization linking sexuality with shame. Bizarrely (to my mind), physiology plays a role as well. Nagoski explains this more in depth in her book *Come as You Are*:

> The "sexy" category in a little girl's mind is populated not with erection-related stimuli but with social stimuli… girls learn what's sexually relevant not because their genitals do something so obvious and new that they can't help learning from it, but rather by paying attention to their *environment*, especially to the other person there with them in the sexually relevant situation. (65)

This type of conditioning, more than any supposedly innate differences between men and women, accounts for more of the disjunctures between male and female sexuality. Remember, as covered a couple chapters ago, we're all made of the same parts, assembled differently. So knock it off with the crummy, essentializing metaphors comparing women to slow cookers or men to matches or whatever (okay, as a folklorist I'm inherently interested in language use, but when it's sexist, it bothers me).

Also, there can be a disjuncture between physiological signs of arousal and subjective signs of arousal; just because you're hard or wet doesn't mean you're enjoying the experience of it!

Wait... there's a difference between being turned on, and enjoying what's happening? YES. Genital response in both men and women means that your body is like, "hey, this is sexually relevant, better get that blood flow going and those juices pumping." It has nothing to do with whether your mind is engaged, on board, excited, teased, tantalized, or aroused.

This is called either arousal nonconcordance or nonconcordant arousal. Either way, it refers to how our bodies and brains don't 100% always get on the same page about what feels sexy.

We can't change how sensitive our accelerators or brakes are; all the science seems to point toward us being born with certain settings. We can, however, rewire what we respond to as sexual stimuli, since we learn what is sexually relevant vs. sexually threatening through experience (direct experience as well as cultural messages).

Similarly, we can work toward becoming aware of what hits our brakes, and thus attempt to lessen the presence of those stimuli in our lives (whether that means removing threats/risks or doing the self-work on negative internal states or perceptions). Nagoski's short answer for how to stop hitting the brakes is "Reduce your stress, be affectionate toward your body, and let go of the false ideas about how sex is 'supposed' to work, to create space in your life for how sex actually works" (68).

These seem like sound goals regardless of whether you're pursuing them in the hopes of increasing your access to sexual arousal, right? And, as I point out in subsequent chapters, none of this is taught as being normal, so people who feel like outliers in terms of how their arousal works can end up with a lot of shame from themselves and stigma from others.

One more thing: most humans sort into having either spontaneous desire or responsive desire. As Nagoski points out, the standard American model of how desire happens is that...it just happens. It's like, bam, out of nowhere, arousal! But for "roughly 5 percent of men and 30 percent of women" (225), desire is more responsive than spontaneous. This means someone may not feel super aroused until they're already in a sexy context, such as their partner cuddling them and flirting with them.

I really like how Vanessa Marin puts it in her book *Sex Talks*: in spontaneous desire, arousal starts in the brain and radiates to the body, but in responsive desire, arousal starts in the body and makes its way eventually to the brain. So a person who experiences spontaneous desire (which gets more air time in our culture, btw) will feel like desire just hits them out of the blue, and it's time for some sexy times ASAP, whereas a person who experiences responsive desire might not think they're turned on or feel turned on until they're midway through a pleasantly arousing scenario.

Both types are normal. Both are fine. But how we *feel* about the way we experience arousal might cause us to feel weird or shameful, so it's also important to figure out what's truly going on when we feel lack of arousal: are we stressed? Feeling unsafe? Dealing with trauma? Those are all valid reasons to not feel sexy, and learning to identify them within ourselves and then communicate about them can make a huge difference.

We all benefit from understanding how our bodies and brains work, and learning about arousal is one important step along the way. This can improve your experience of your sexuality and help reduce victim-blaming, hopefully!

References:

Marin, Vanessa, and Xander Marin. *Sex Talks: The Five Conversations That Will Transform Your Love Life*. Simon & Schuster, 2023.

Nagoski, Emily. *Come As You Are: The Surprising New Science That Will Transform Your Sex Life*. Simon & Schuster Paperbacks, 2015.

SEX IS NOT A DRIVE, SO LET'S STOP SAYING SEX DRIVE

ONCE YOU KNOW THIS, you can't un-know it, and it will bother you for the rest of your life when you see people use the phrase "sex drive." You're welcome!

Let's begin with what a drive is, in terms of human biology. In Emily Nagoski's words, "A drive is a biological mechanism whose job is to keep the organism at a healthy baseline" (229). It's like a series of internal systems to make sure we don't die from preventable things.

Hunger is a drive: if you don't get calories in you, you will die. Thirst is similarly a drive, as is the need for rest/sleep, as is the need for temperature regulation, which we achieve through sweating and/or shivering as signs to address the discrepancy.

A drive is an internal need that pushes you to fulfill it in order to survive.

Sex is not a drive. Yes, it is linked to survival of the species, but you as an individual human will not die if you do not have sex or reach orgasm.

Instead of calling sex a drive, Nagoski goes with the term "incentive motivation system" (230), arguing that instead of being pushed towards sex because omg otherwise we will die, we feel pulled towards it, drawn by a pleasing external stimulus.

Apparently this has been known by animal researchers for a while (Nagoski 231), but it's taken a while to percolate into the study of humans, not to mention pop culture.

And...this next part is important. If sex is considered a drive, and, as discussed in the previous chapter, women tend to experience more responsive sexual arousal whereas more men experience spontaneous sexual arousal, guess what? In mainstream American conversations about sex, that means that men are normal and women are broken.

As Nagoski puts it, if sex were actually a drive, the same way hunger is, we'd look at the many women (and some men) who don't spontaneously crave sex and think, oh wow, these poor people are really sick. We'd want to fix them: "If sex is a hunger and you never get hungry, then there's Something Wrong With You" (231). And thinking there's something wrong with you is also a turn-off in its own right, which can cause the stress response to kick in which is a boner-killer in its own regard.

You see the problem, right? Talking about sex as a drive on par with the other basic human survival drives creates sickness and anxiety where there was none. This happens along highly gendered lines, and I don't think that's an accident.

When the people who primarily experience spontaneous arousal also think of sex as a drive, as a necessary thing to obtain and fulfill, those people (often men) might use this reasoning to justify getting laid by any means. Nagoski notes that "men's sexual entitlement is a primary reason they sexually assault women" (232), and feminist philosopher Kate Manne wrote an entire book about men's entitlement leading them to act violently against women in a number of contexts.

While Manne only devoted a few chapters of her book *Entitled* to sexual violence (and honestly, the fact that there's an "only" in this sentence is pretty horrifying in and of itself), she notes when discussing incels that their stories "are *all* stories, in the end, about the violence wrought by male entitlement" (32). Again, like many feminist arguments, this is not an "all men are bad" statement, but rather an assertion that our society is set up to favor men, to make them believe they deserve lots of things from women, and to dole out rewards and withhold punishments when they take from women.

To stay on the topic of incels briefly, the very notion of labeling oneself an "involuntary celibate" implies the existence of a sex drive. Why would being celibate be so painful unless it were happening in counter to the demand of an overarching sex drive? Manne is once again on point when she notes that if someone's in pain, it's polite/ethical to try to help or be sympathetic:

> But when someone is in pain precisely because he has an overblown sense of entitlement to the soothing ministrations of others, which have not been forthcoming, stepping in to assuage his pain becomes an ethically fraught enterprise. Even expressing our sympathies runs the risk of feeding into his false, dangerous sense that other people—especially girls and women—exist to pander to the incel's needs and to gratify his ego. (29-30)

Is there actually a direct link between the widespread cultural belief in the sex drive and the existence of incels? Maybe, maybe not. But I think it would be harder to defend and sympathize with their positions if we didn't have "sex drive" in our vocabulary.

If you need more reasons to reject the idea of sex drive being a thing, Nagoski has 'em in her book. But for now, let's move on to discussing orgasms!

References:

Manne, Kate. *Entitled: How Male Privilege Hurts Women*. First edition, Crown, 2020.

Nagoski, Emily. *Come As You Are: The Surprising New Science That Will Transform Your Sex Life*. Simon & Schuster Paperbacks, 2015.

WHAT ORGASM IS AND ISN'T

LEARNING what orgasm actually is and reframing its role in sex can be a real game-changer.

As with most sexual topics, my li'l folklorist brain goes "YAY" when we get to look at sexual folklore. So I'll open with a series of folk beliefs/superstitions around orgasm:

- In order to conceive, a woman must orgasm (Whatley and Henken 25);
- Once a man orgasms, he's done for a while;
- Solo orgasms (a.k.a. masturbation) will make hair grow on the palms of your hands or make you go blind (Whatley and Henken 123);
- If a woman orgasms during coercive sex, it wasn't really rape.

Again, the point of studying folklore is not necessarily to identify which folklore items happen to be falsehoods...but in this case, it might be useful (especially in the case of that last, very victim-blamey belief). And it goes hand-in-hand with a neat definition of orgasm that is actually quite revolutionary.

My preferred definition? "Orgasm is the sudden, involuntary release of sexual tension" (Nagoski 267). As you might expect of a book with an orgasm pun in the title, *Come As You Are*, Emily Nagoski spends a fair bit of time on orgasm, both what it is and what it is not. And, again, what it is: a sudden, involuntary release of sexual tension.

That's it. No mention of genital parts, or how they're inserted or arranged. No mention of technique or intensity. No mention of the genders or numbers of people involved.

Heck, there's not even a mention of pleasure. And there's a good reason for that exclusion from the decision, which we'll get to shortly.

In reality, orgasm is just a thing bodies do—some bodies, some of the time, under certain conditions—rather than an indication of an emotional state, a state of consent, or a precursor to other biological things like conception. It just is.

Of course, this fact doesn't help dispel all the (often false) beliefs around orgasm, beliefs which can be quite limiting and even harmful. But there's so much human diversity around orgasm, maybe we can start to broaden our sense of what orgasm is and what's possible to start creating some cracks in these monolithic orgasm beliefs.

First, orgasm doesn't even have to be attached to the genitals. Nagoski summarizes a series of lab studies where, yes, many women (who were asked to masturbate in the lab to the point of orgasm) described their orgasms as connected to "rhythmic, involuntary contractions" of the pelvic floor muscles around the entrance of the vagina...but some women "exhibited no vaginal muscle contractions at orgasm" while other women "exhibited the muscle contractions without orgasm" (269). So there is some variety as to how women perceive and rank the connection of their orgasms to what is actually happening in their bodies.

Research tells us that both men and women experience orgasms completely devoid of a typical sexual context; as Debby Herbenick notes in her book *The Coregasm Workout*, in a nationally representative sample of thousands of men and women, ten percent of them "had experienced orgasm from exercising" while "Even more people have experienced arousal from exercise, or stopped just short of orgasm" (2).

I follow Herbenick and other researchers in asserting that "Genital orgasms are just the tip of the iceberg" (11)! Orgasms can happen through breast stimulation or through fantasy alone, and these aren't "weird" or less-valid orgasms.

And with coregasms (also called Exercise Induced Orgasms or EIOs), two-thirds of the women in Herbenick's study "said they were never sexually fantasizing when they were aroused or when they orgasmed during exercise" (15), indicating that, again, orgasms can happen in a variety of contexts, including ones that don't register as sexual.

Second, orgasms can take a number of shapes and sizes and other descriptors I haven't even thought of, probably. These days, sex educators and sex researchers aren't as concerned with the "type" of orgasm as in the past; I kinda blame Freud for this heightened awareness, since he was among those insisting that women who had vaginal orgasms were more "mature" than women who had clitoral orgasms. One of the many problems with that assertion is that there simply aren't many nerve endings in vaginas, so penis-in-vagina intercourse is only so stimulating. Some women orgasm that way, but not all, so insinuating that it's the pinnacle of feminine orgasm is a little weird.

Third, because orgasms are just a body having convulsions, they don't tell us anything about consent. I talked about this in a previous chapter on nonconcordance, but if we disentangle "visible/embodied signs of arousal" from "someone's actual inner state," we can see that sometimes bodies do show signs of arousal—lubrication, erection or other tissue swelling, even up to orgasm—regardless of what's happening in someone's brain. An orgasm may not be linked to pleasure at all...and that's okay. It's just a thing bodies do sometimes.

At the same time, orgasms may be intensely personal and emotional, very much linked to someone's inner state. A person may orgasm with someone they love...or feel broken when it's difficult to. Our emotions, whether joy or shame, around orgasm can be very revealing in and of themselves. They're all valid because they're what we experience, but we can't assume that they're universal, or that they stem from within us independently of social conditioning.

Some orgasm experiences do fall outside of what's considered normal, and then it's up to the person with those experiences to determine if they want to seek some sort of treatment (seeing a doctor or therapist) to work on or through that. Certain people don't orgasm easily or often or at all; this doesn't mean there's anything wrong with them, though interactions with others could lead them to feel that way.

The good news is, there are lots of ways to engage with orgasm that can lead to more pleasure. Note that I didn't necessarily say "increase your number of orgasms" or "orgasm in every single sexual encounter," since the irony is that the more goal-directed most people are with orgasm, the more fleeting it is. Nagoski has a whole chapter on orgasm in *Come As You Are* so I'll direct you there if you want to know more about her evidence-based strategies, but in brief, taking off the pressure and focusing on pleasure are two great ways to start exploring what makes you feel good in ideal conditions (e.g., a context you control, whether solo or partnered).

And, of course, I couldn't include a chapter on orgasm in this book without talking about the Orgasm Gap, as it's come to be known.

Heard of the pay gap? How in America men are paid more than women, and the differences are exacerbated once you take into account the lesser pay that women of color often experience too? Yeah, it's like that, but with orgasms.

Oh, and because sharing a blast from the past is in line with the major themes of this book, let's recall that throughout much of Western history, it was believed that both parties in a heterosexual coupling needed to orgasm to conceive. This folk belief (admittedly, one boosted by medical doctors, too) was found among the English up through the 17th century, but had vanished by the 19th century, replaced almost by its opposite, that there was something wrong with women who were orgasmic (Knowles 14).

Weirdly, in the Victorian era, talking about one's orgasms or lack thereof became a power move; some upper-class women "knew that masking their sexual desires helped increase their prospects in life" (Knowles 14). Again, in the same way that we see a lot of sexual beliefs and attitudes circling back after a century or two, I see links between this practice and women faking orgasms today, to make their partner feel more adequate or whatever.

Once again, this book is slim on the how-to aspect of sex ed since my main point is how we need to better understand folklore, culture, and history to understand why sex ed and sexuality look the way they do today, but I'll provide some books on orgasm in the resources section if you're curious to learn more. In short, though, let's stop shaming or validating certain kinds of orgasms, or their absence! It can be quite subjective!

References:

Herbenick, Debby. *The Coregasm Workout: The Revolutionary Method for Better Sex through Exercise.* Seal Press, 2015.

Knowles, Jon. *How Sex Got Screwed Up: The Ghosts That Haunt Our Sexual Pleasure. Book Two, from Victoria to Our Own Time.* Vernon Press, 2019.

Nagoski, Emily. *Come As You Are: The Surprising New Science That Will Transform Your Sex Life.* Simon & Schuster Paperbacks, 2015.

Whatley, Marianne H, and Elissa R Henken. *Did You Hear About the Girl Who...?: Contemporary Legends, Folklore, and Human Sexuality.* NYU Press, 2001.

VIRGINITY IS A SOCIAL CONSTRUCT
SO LET'S STOP OBSESSING OVER IT

IT'S bizarre to me that we're still having this conversation, but apparently it still needs to be said: the concept of virginity is just that, a concept, and doesn't necessarily reflect any physiological reality or identity shift.

First, how do we even define virginity? Like, what are the physical attributes of a non-virgin vs. a virgin? How are they measurably different from each other? Humans don't turn a different color or shrink or grow in stature the first time they have sex.

Yes, you may be thinking, but what about the hymen?! Friends, perhaps I am the first to tell you that the hymen is a pretty insignificant scrap of membrane for most people. For some folks, the hymen can be painfully taut and medical attention can help deal with it...but think of it this way. If the hymen were really an airtight seal that needed to be punctured for the very first time by PIV (penis-in-vagina) sex and was totally pristine right up until that moment, how would menstrual blood get out?

The other problem with the focus on the hymen is about gender. It seems like a bit of a double standard to look at the spectrum of human anatomy and decide on a particular outcome of a particular sex act, one that has some potential ramifications for the receiving partner and very few ramifications for the giving partner, and label it as a definitive moment in your identity.

Also, how are we defining "having sex for the first time"? I think a lot of people have PIV sex in mind for this type of act, and sure, many people have that kind of sex. But it's not the only kind of sex. What about oral sex, anal sex, heavy make-out sessions, and things involving different sets of genitals and the people attached to them who may not fit a binary? How do we decide which sets of sex acts get more weight as The One True Virginity-Loss-Status One?

True, certain sex acts carry with them a bit more biological heft, as in, PIV sex can result in pregnancy along with STI transmission. But other forms of genital-to-whatever-body-part contact can also result in STI transmission, so really, pretty much every form of sex should include some conversations about risk factors and the types of protection people want to use (reminder: someone could be on hormonal birth control to protect against pregnancy, but still be susceptible to STIs).

Here, I follow sex educator and Scarleteen founder Heather Corinna in stating the following:

What it means to be a virgin really can only be defined by you, and it has to do with how you define sex... Virginity shouldn't be a standard by which you judge others, or by which you should be judged. It shouldn't be a symbol of status or a lack thereof. Sex—or abstaining from it—isn't something that should be used as a bargaining chip for anything, or used to manipulate anyone. (139)

I love how Corinna encourages teens (and readers more broadly) to not assign value to sex acts or body parts beyond the values we believe to be important. If your family or religion thinks virginity is a priority, sure, that can be a thing, but I would argue it's important to be having conversations in that case as well, because virginity is so ill-defined that even the people upholding it as important may not have a good grasp of what it means!

Once again, bringing folklore to the table can be a great way of analyzing local understandings of virginity. My folklore colleague Niger Sultana wrote an opinion piece in a Bangladesh-based newspaper, and collected personal narratives about experiences of sexuality. She found that some people believe that a woman has two hymens, with the first one breaking during menarche and the second during sexual intercourse (Sultana).

Issues like this one could be remedied by sex education, but again, cultural context is key: Sultana notes that some of her fellow citizens fear that embracing sex education would make them bad Muslims. However, she argues that this would not be the case: "Islam as a religion is open to discussing science. In the holy Quran and some hadith, there are suggestions about man-woman relationships and preparation before intercourse" (Sultana). Sex education need not be inherently anti-religion, and religion need not be inherently anti-sex-education.

And I'll note, I do try to say this with at least a hint of cultural relativism, since there are cultures where virginity still matters in terms of making one a desirable partner. I'm not trying to belittle those cultures or say that we in the West are clearly superior because we're more scientific and understand that a hymen is not a reliable measure of one's sexual activities (in part because plenty of Western people still misunderstand this concept and/or have messed-up ideas about it).

Rather, I think it's worth acknowledging when a cultural notion or folk idea is based on something with an empirical basis or not (in this case, it's a not), and go from there. Plenty of cultures believe plenty of totally made-up shit that is completely divorced from reality, and yes, that includes us. That's fine, it's nothing new. It's when you begin enforcing draconian policies onto people around this topic when it's actually out of their control or hypocritically biased or both that I think it's problematic.

So yes, in cultures that still prize women's virginity to the extent of expecting to see a bloodied sheet on the wedding night, but not holding men to the same standard, and having consequences that probably count as a human rights violation if unmet, then yeah, I think that's kinda problematic. But if it's not my home culture, it's also not necessarily my place to say or do much about it. Other than emphatically tap the "Please stop with the human rights violations, especially the ones targeting women" sign. Which I do a lot anyway.

Virginity is one of the many sex topics requiring more conversation and demystification, in my view. Hopefully this chapter is a good start.

References:

Corinna, Heather. *S.E.X.: The All-You-Need-To-Know Progressive Sexuality Guide to Get You through High School and College.* Marlowe, 2007.

Sultana, Niger. "Why Sex Education Matters: Culturalist Perspective on the Current Debate." *The Business Standard*, 13 February 2021, https://www.tbsnews.net/thoughts/why-sex-education-matters-culturalist-perspective-current-debate-201046. Accessed 25 July 2023.

BODY, BRAIN, AND TRAUMA

WHILE TRAUMA IS NOT NECESSARILY a fun topic, it's one that is crucial to helping us understand a lot of facets of sexuality. It's one I teach at every given opportunity, whether I'm teaching about feminism or first-year writing. Many of the facts about trauma vibe with general lessons about how human sexuality works (such as the complex relationship between our bodies and our cultures), not to mention how prevalent sexual trauma is. So, let's do this!

A couple of caveats first: this chapter talks about triggers and traumatic events and as such may need a trigger warning. Nothing violent will be discussed in great detail. Also, I'm not a neuroscientist or psychologist, I've just spent the past decade-plus studying trauma using my expertise in adjacent fields to help me make sense of the existing research. Some oversimplification of brain stuff follows in my explanations, but I provide citations wherever possible, so please feel free to go down the rabbit hole and draw your own conclusions.

Although many different types of events and situations can

be traumatic, trauma at its basis is defined as an over-whelming event. It's something that physically and/or psychologically overwhelms us, often with elements of help-lessness, loss of control, threat, and existential danger. It can overload our senses because it represents more than what we as organisms are designed to handle.

Some events are easily identified as trauma: assaults and accidents or being a bystander to such things. Being in an abusive relationship. Being part of a war or genocide. And so on.

Other types of trauma are less clear-cut: the pain of rejec-tion by one's peers can be emotionally traumatizing, as can divorce and other forms of social separation and grief. Some types of trauma leave physical scars, while others do not. Different people may experience the same or similar events and come out traumatized to different degrees.

Trauma can also be relative: someone may witness an acci-dent that appears horrifically deadly and be traumatized by it, while the people who survived it might not have experienced the same level of existential threat as a witness, and so they might do relatively fine in comparison to the witness (luckily, it's not a contest to see who is the most traumatized or deserving of care; we all deserve trauma-informed care).

Keeping in mind that trauma can be personal and subjec-tive, our goal is to understand how trauma impacts us in patterned ways, and what that means for our experiences of sexuality and embodiment.

In moments of trauma—sometimes called the traumatic incident—as well as in the aftermath of trauma, many people default to a fight, flight, or freeze response (to add another "f" to the mix, fawn is being discussed these days, too). From what I understand, we don't necessarily get a choice in the matter; our brains may flip a switch, and suddenly, *surprise,* it's the flight response, or the freeze response.

Understanding that trauma responses differ, and are not always chosen by the individual, is one key step to avoiding victim blaming in the aftermath of trauma. See also: why it's not okay to ask the victim of a sexual assault (or any assault) why they didn't fight back or scream or make a ruckus. It's entirely possible that some mechanism took over and short-circuited the response that anyone else thinks perhaps they "should" have had.

From an evolutionary perspective, these responses make sense. The classic example given in trauma workshops is this: pretend you're a prehistoric human, wandering outside your village. Suddenly, a lion rears up in front of you! The fight response kicking in means you're prepared to fight the lion. The flight response kicking in means you're prepared to flee from the lion. The freeze response means, well, it can mean a couple things. It can mean going still and hoping you stay hidden or don't register as food, or (and sorry, this is a downer) it can mean some part of your brain is like "yep, we're gonna die, let's release some chillaxing chemicals and hope it doesn't hurt too much."

I'm going to briefly unpack the freeze response a bit more since it's a newer addition to the fight-or-flight response dyad. Psychiatrist James Gordon explains it thus:

Freezing is mediated by the oldest part of the vagus nerve, deep in our brainstem. It produces physiological collapse and a release of pain-numbing endorphins. When humans freeze, we may experience a self-protec-tive detachment from our helpless, ravaged body, called dissociation. When someone "leaves her body" when she is being raped or beaten, she's in a dissociated response. (29)

Experiencing a freeze response in the moment can spare someone the psychological horror of what they're going through. But that freeze response can continue longer than is needed, because our very complex brains can get stuck in a loop that we can't out-reason or out-think. People whose brains have flipped the switch to go to a freeze response might experience long-term numbness that impacts their lives on multiple levels.

Further, the freeze response is found in all mammals. Emily Nagoski and Amelia Nagoski describe it in some detail their excellent book *Burnout: The Secret to Unlocking the Stress Cycle.* They talk about the freeze response as such: "Your brain was trying to keep you alive in the face of a threat that seemed unsurvivable, so it slammed on the brakes in a last-ditch attempt to do that" (12).

This "slamming on the brakes" could feel like you're numb or dissociated, yes, but also out of control or disconnected from one's body. And in nature, since the freeze response is an option for all mammals, it's common for the creature (human or not) to shake uncontrollably afterward, as one way of releasing the adrenaline and cortisol that had built up in the moments leading up to the trauma. Having a super-active bodily response is one way of completing the stress cycle, almost like an antidote to having been frozen in the first place (discussed in Nagoski and Nagoski 11-15).

If you survive (yay!) then you still might have some trauma triggers left over. Another classic example is the following: say you were in a forest and were bitten by a snake (boo!). But you survive (yay!). But from then on out, when you see a particularly squiggly tree root in the forest, you freak out and can't figure out why. It's because it mimics the initial traumatic event, the appearance of a snake.

Trauma triggers exist because our brains and bodies registered the initial traumatic event and are like, "Well, let's not do THAT again, it nearly killed us!" But whatever got processed at THAT may or may not resemble the actual threat out in the world that almost took us out; it might be an echo of it, or something that looks or sounds similar.

So while trauma triggers serve an evolutionary purpose, hypothetically keeping us safe from future harm, they are also run by super old parts of our brains that we can't just talk to and say "hey brain, can you lighten up on that response? The thing wasn't actually gonna kill me and now I am super jumpy every time XYZ happens."

This is relevant to a modern-day context, because we can't always parse emotional threats from physical threats. Social rejection and emotional abuse definitely suck on their own merit, but they can register as existential threats because in older times, being socially abandoned would likely have been a death sentence. Anxiety-making scary social stuff can therefore trigger a trauma response at times, even if we rationally perceive it to not be a proportionate response to the thing happening to us.

Similarly, other forms of extreme stress on brain and body can act very similarly to trauma; lots of what the Nagoskis describe in *Burnout* applies to trauma as well. In all of these types of situations, the thing that was the stressor might be gone or resolved, but our bodies don't always understand that, and they maintain a heightened stress alert or the aftermath of trauma. Completing the stress cycle (more tips on that in *Burnout*) is thus crucial to our mental and physical health.

I'll say it again, because it's that important: toxic stress and/or trauma can all look the same to the body, and they can all be dangerous. For an excellent overview of how this works, look up ACEs (adverse childhood experiences), or go to my references list for a link to Dr. Nadine Burke Harris's excellent TED talk on this topic, which is a great starting point.

Back to brain stuff: this is a bit of an oversimplification, but our brains are sectioned off into parts that correspond to the functions they serve, and also reflect how old or new they are in terms of our evolution. Our reptilian brain, located in the brain stem, governs automatic bodily functions such as breathing and digestion, stuff you don't have to think about it in order for it to work. This is the oldest part of our brain system. Our mammalian brain, or limbic system, is newer, and governs our responses to emotions and stuff. Bessel van der Kolk considers the reptilian brain and mammalian brain together to be the "emotional brain," which is "at the heart of the central nervous system," governing our intuitive response to situations that might prove promising or dangerous, releasing hormones to spring us into action (57).

In contrast, our prefrontal cortex, also called the neocortex, is the newest development of the brain, and it governs rational thought, language use, and stuff like that. Basically, all the thinky bits that set us apart from other animals.

But in moments of trauma, being triggered, and/or having a flashback, lots of parts of the brain shut down. Portions of the prefrontal cortex go dark, meaning the neurons stop firing and go offline briefly. (side note: we learned this fairly recently using brain imaging technology, because putting a trauma survivor into an MRI machine and telling them to induce a trauma flashback sounds like the kind of thing that is not so fun to experience, but super useful for advancing our scientific knowledge; discussed in van der Kolk 39-47)

Among other things, the part of the brain known as Broca's area goes dark (van der Kolk 43). It's related to speech, so the bummer of it is that during trauma—or a traumatic flashback—a person doesn't necessarily have access to language to say, "Hey, I'm having a flashback, I could use a minute." We also know that certain sensory areas of the brain light up even when there's no visual stimulus present, so the body and brain believe that they are experiencing the thing again in real time.

This brings me to the topic of memory. In general, memories are stronger when there are a few factors present when the memory is made and encoded: the event is an emotionally or personally significant one, and the person is experiencing some kind of emotional high point. So while you might vaguely recall all your birthdays, the ones that were significant (like when you got your driver's license, or did something else important for the first time) or that had strong memories attached (like if one birthday party was particularly disastrous or exuberant) are more likely to stand out more starkly in your memory, with more detail and better recall to them.

As I continue to info-dump about this, hang onto this fact: strongly-felt emotions tend to lead to strongly-encoded memories.

We can generally distinguish between standard or non-traumatic memory and traumatic memory. Standard memories are made the same way and share a few characteristics: they are linear (occurring within the passage of time), generally accessible through language (you can talk about them), and incorporated into your autobiography (you can talk about them as they relate to the rest of your life). Traumatic memories are pretty much the opposite: you can't always access them linearly or through language, nor are they necessarily incorporated into your sense of your life story.

Furthermore, trauma memories are not necessarily ordered: "Trauma is not stored as a narrative with an orderly beginning, middle, and end" (van der Kolk 137). Or trauma memories can be completely repressed for decades at a time. As you might imagine, this can make them difficult to talk about in therapy.

Another significant difference between these types of memory is that standard memory is actually a bit fickle and subject to change. There have been multiple psychological experiments that established the malleability of memory as well as how false memories can also be implanted and manipulated (covered in van der Kolk 177-78, or Google the lost-in-the-mall study by Dr. Elizabeth Loftus). This is part of why the Satanic Ritual Abuse moral panic was so problematic and tricky to navigate: concerned adults actually ended up implanting memories of being abused where probably none had existed.

It is not necessarily either a good thing or a bad thing that standard memories are subject to change. As we grow and experience life, it's normal to look back and revise how we think of things.

But traumatic memories aren't as fluid. I liken them to a jagged shard of glass lodged somewhere in your body that you can't necessarily see: you know something is wrong, and it might feel painful and/or unpleasant, but it doesn't play by the same rules as the other things you're used to. The good news is, one of the goals of addressing trauma in a therapeutic setting is to dislodge those sharp and painful traumatic memories, be able to put them into words or something close enough, and be able to integrate them into your autobiography. More on that shortly.

Now, for a word on language and how it, too, shifts over time. When we call something a trigger in the trauma sense of the word, we mean a sensation or experience that sends someone into a flashback state, as in, that person is triggered. As noted above, unprocessed trauma can feel like it's happening all over again, so being triggered is often an involuntary response that invokes fight, flight, or freeze, and cannot always be consciously or rationally comprehended in that moment.

If you've heard "triggered" being used in the sense of something quite different, guess what: folklore jazz hands! It's folkspeech in action! Rather than a new slang word being coined to mean some new thing, we see instead semantic drift, which is just a fancy way of saying that a word's meaning has been shifted somewhat.

Out in the wilds of the internet, I see people saying "lol I'm triggered" to mean "I'm upset" or "I'm offended," which are valid emotions to feel, but are quite different connotations from "I'm literally having a trauma response to something right now" (though I can see where those things might feel, look, or even be the same to some folks depending on what their trauma is).

I know it's silly to get upset at language for doing what language does—constantly evolving—but I'm a bit miffed that we have a perfectly good term for a physiological response that got coopted and in some ways trivialized. So I am definitely on Team Keep the Original Meaning of Triggered, even though it's probably fighting a losing battle. So I just keep including this section in anything I write or teach about trauma and hope to make people more aware of it.

So if—stay with me here—experiencing a trauma trigger can induce the brain and body to be like "oh shit that same bad thing is happening again" and then go into a fight, flight, or freeze response, and we have all kinds of science backing this up...what is the problem with trigger warnings? Or content notes, or whatever you want to call them? I see people complaining about how anyone who wants or needs a trigger warning is a sensitive snowflake or whatever, but news flash: we all encounter trauma at some point in our lives.

Because trauma is literally a brain and body response, it's pretty much a medical condition. In that sense, I liken giving trigger warnings to warning someone about potential allergens in their food, or letting film viewers know that there might be flashing lights in a movie in case someone has epilepsy.

Giving a heads-up about something, whether an allergen or a trigger, is a basic human courtesy. It's a way of saying "if you have issues with XYZ, you can expect to find it here, and if you know it'll give you a spectacularly bad time, you might want to bow out." Trigger warnings are not censorship. They are not coddling. They are a common-sense call to self-care when possible.

I feel pretty strongly about the importance of this as an educator, even as I recognize that giving a warning for every single potential trigger is impossible since we could try to make a list of all potential triggers and still fail to do so. Trauma, as noted above, can be quite personal. Someone could be triggered by a particular scent or being touched in a specific location on their body. It might not make sense to anyone else, and they might not be able to articulate it to anyone else, and that doesn't matter, I still think we should make a good-faith effort to note major triggers in our course material and art and so on.

In the arts, yes, there might be some concern about spoilers and so on. I think authors and artists can provide a general content note before their work is read or viewed and direct the audience to a more detailed list of triggers if desired. I've seen a number of novelists doing this recently: noting that their book contains some mature and potentially disturbing themes, and directing readers to their website if they want a complete list of potential triggers.

This is crucial for those of us who are teachers, because I know this much: if a student walks into my classroom and is triggered? They're not learning much that day. I know this because I have some mild trauma of my own, and before I spent some time in therapy for it, if I was triggered, there went my day. I might have wanted to get some research or writing done, but I knew my higher brain functions would likely be shot. The same is true for our students: we can't expect them to learn a ton of new material if their brains are telling their bodies they're in a life-or-death situation.

However, I think I can modify that sentiment somewhat to more accurately reflect what might happen in my classroom: the student might not learn the material that day, but they're still learning from *me*. I can do my best to create a trauma-informed classroom and give students a heads-up when we might be dealing with triggering or traumatic material, which teaches them that it's okay to have off days and to need to take a break, and it's okay to not be a perfect learning machine 24/7. Or I can barrel through without any sensitivity to trauma, thereby teaching my students that their responses don't matter and they shouldn't listen to their bodies. Maybe their traumas don't matter. Maybe *they* don't matter.

I'd rather take the trauma-informed route. And if that sometimes means a student lets me know they need to tap out of a video or lesson plan? That's fine. I might have to come up with an alternative mode of assessment, which can be a bit of extra work, but I'm a teacher, it's *my job* to figure out how to assess what and how my students are learning. I'll figure it out.

This may have sounded somewhat doom and gloom thus far, but there's a positive side to all of this: there are multiple ways of healing from trauma. As I've put it in the past, we may not get to choose what breaks us, but we can choose what heals us.

Trauma doesn't always have to hijack the brain and body into a flashback; there are ways of minimizing the aftermath of a traumatic incident. I don't have the space or expertise to get into the weeds here about all the different types of trauma and trauma diagnoses out there, but in brief, not all trauma results in PTSD, or post-traumatic stress disorder. There's also just regular ol' trauma, as well as C-PTSD, or Complex PTSD, which is more likely to result from prolonged exposure to trauma or multiple traumatic events over time, which can have a different and more severe impact than just one traumatic incident.

The type of trauma you've experienced will probably guide the healing process, but what the healing modalities all have in common is that we have to find a way to reassure the brain and body that they're safe in this moment, so the trauma can be unpacked and processed a bit. If someone's always in a hypervigilant fight-or-flight state, it's incredibly difficult to do the processing that helps us respond...hm...not necessarily respond *better* to a trigger, but to have a little more control and agency in that moment so we don't automatically bypass the higher brain functions and go straight to a flashback state.

Ironically, just telling someone to go to therapy isn't always the most useful thing when it comes to processing trauma. Since trauma is so embodied and a lot of therapy simply involves talking to your therapist, there can be a bit of a disconnect there. Furthermore, as we've established, being in a flashback state means the talk-y bits of the brain aren't necessarily functioning in that moment, so not everyone is able to verbally talk through their trauma in the first place.

There are a number of strategies to help heal trauma that various cultures around the world have employed for centuries if not millennia. Prior to Western science coming along and studying this stuff, people have figured out intuitively how to help their peers cope with trauma. I'll mention some of those strategies here.

In order to set the stage for healing, there are a number of things you can do. Learning about emotional regulation is one, so as to not be completely hijacked every time you try to approach the issue. For some people, and in some cultural traditions, this looks like mindfulness practices such as breath work, physical movement, and meditation. In van der Kolk's words, "Practicing mindfulness calms down the sympathetic nervous system, so that you are less likely to be throw into fight-or-flight" (211).

Mindfulness techniques are hard at first, and they're not always fun; I'm one of those people who prefers moving meditations like yoga since I have trouble sitting still. And one time, I remember dealing with a trauma situation that mindfulness practices actually made worse, since I definitely did not want to be in the situation I was in, and being more mindful of the situation only intensified the icky feelings. But if nothing else, applying mindfulness techniques can help you take the temperature of a situation; as van der Kolk points out:

"If you cannot tolerate what you are feeling right now, opening up the past will only compound the misery and retraumatize you further" (211).

Having supportive relationships (with friends, family, a community, a therapist) can be helpful in healing. Support networks come in all shapes and sizes and can be anything that creates a sense of safety. Experiencing rhythmic and synchronous movement in groups also helps, along with physically interacting with the sensations around us and the people around us...again, to whatever degree feels safe and appropriate to you. James Gordon gives strategies for shaking and dancing that have helped many in his workshops (66-79). Sometimes completing the action that would have saved a person from the traumatic incident—being able to fight back, or run away, depending on the situation—can be therapeutic in and of itself (van der Kolk 220-21).

But if you are seeking something specifically within the therapeutic context, there are some trauma-specific therapies that are really wonderful. There are too many to list here, so I'll briefly talk up EMDR (eye movement desensitization and reprocessing, covered in van der Kolk 250-64) and let you do your own research.

Similar to some of the strategies listed above that incorporate embodiment and movement, EMDR involves the person undergoing therapy doing something that uses both sides of the brain and body: they use their eyes to track a light that goes from right to left, or they list to a binaural beat on headphones, or they hold buzzers in their hands that alternate between buzzing just on the right, just on the left, and so on. While doing this, the therapist asks the person to recall a traumatic memory and notice details and associations.

Next, the person might articulate the negative belief associated with the memories. This might be something like "Anyone I let in hurts me" or "I am always left alone." While talking this all through with the therapist, the person is supposed to eventually reach a more positive reframe of that negative belief: "Not everyone will hurt me" or "There are people in my life who support me" (maybe "supposed to" is the wrong phrasing but that was my experience in EMDR). Something about the embodied aspect of EMDR makes it highly successful, which I think is very cool.

No healing method is universal; van der Kolk found that EMDR is more effective for those who were traumatized as adults (257). Neurofeedback seems to be helpful for those with PTSD who also experience substance use issues (329). For other people, practicing yoga under trauma-informed conditions helps (265-78). There is some evidence that Cognitive Behavioral Therapy (CBT) is effective for addressing symptoms of trauma (Gordon 317); Gordon mentions a bunch of other therapeutic modes in the appendix of his book, ranging from Interpersonal Therapy (IPT) to all the "tapping" therapies out there (316-24).

Healing from trauma doesn't mean erasing it. No one has invented a time machine, to my knowledge. Processing it and addressing it means that it's still a part of you, and it's still shaped you...but it doesn't control you anymore. That, I think, is the real beauty of resilience: not "I'm so strong, I never feel pain anymore" but rather "I'm so strong, I don't let my trauma define me."

It's unrealistic to never feel pain. We're human; pain is a signal we're all going to encounter at some point. In turn, everyone is touched by trauma; if not your own, then someone else's. The rare person might exist who hasn't experienced any trauma in their lives, but unless they're living in a cocoon, they surely know someone who has. And if you study history, you run into trauma. Once you start looking, it's literally everywhere.

Okay, so, this chapter has gone on a bit longer than intended, in part because I've been studying trauma for nearly ten years and have a lot of info that I am excited to share with you. But you may be wondering: why is all this in a book about the history and culture of sex education? And why in the "How Sex Actually Works" section of the book?

WELL. Trauma is common to all humans. Culturally, we have different ideas of it, and we may process it somewhat differently, but trauma is a common denominator on some level for all humans, because we all evolved to have bodies and brains that want to protect us and make sure that if we survive bad shit, we'll have a warning system in place to prevent it from happening again if possible.

Gordon writes, "All trauma takes a toll on our sex and love lives", and I'm inclined to agree (195). Trauma is often bound up with sexual experiences, sexual feelings, and our experiences of everything from relationships to gender to our overall identities. Sexual assault remains maddeningly rampant in many cultures, including in the U.S., so we're going to encounter a lot of people with sexual trauma, and it makes sense to have some tools in our toolkits to work with them (or us, as the case may be).

Trauma often happens in contexts that touch on sexuality, even if the trauma was not a sexual assault per se: giving birth can be deeply traumatizing and can result in pelvic and genital pain that impacts how a person feels about being sexually active. Someone can be abused in a romantic relationship even if the abuse is not sexual in nature. Someone who is gender nonconforming can be targeted and traumatized by bigots.

In other words, trauma can happen in an arena that is not explicitly sexual, but it can still connect back to our larger sense of sexuality. Body image and body dysmorphia can reflect back on whether one feels sexually desirable, and bullying or abuse or violence in those aspects of life can add up to result in trauma, for instance.

As noted above, a freeze response can involve dissociation and numbness both in the moment and in the aftermath, and for many people, this can result in feeling disembodied. Which is, you guessed it, kinda the opposite of being present in an intimate encounter, so people with trauma might struggle with that aspect of sexual encounters.

On a slightly more removed note, even if your trauma isn't sexual in nature, it can impact your physiological experience of your sexuality. During one of my recent experiences going down the trauma research rabbit hole (for a new workshop I was teaching for my colleagues at my university, which made me sooo happy because I believe it's so important for educators to be trauma-informed, more on that shortly), I read *When the Body Says No* by Dr. Gabor Maté. It's not specifically about trauma, but it touches on a variety of impactful and negative life experiences that can impact a person's health over their lifetime, which of course can include trauma. Maté found the following:

In a 1990 study of women patients conducted at the gastroenterology clinic of the North Carolina School of Medicine, 44 per cent of the women reported some type of sexual and/or physical abuse. "Those with abuse history had a four-fold greater risk of pelvic pain, two to three times more non-abdominal symptoms (e.g., headaches, backaches, fatigue), as well as more lifetime surgeries." In a more recent investigation at the same centre, fully two-thirds of the women interviewed had experienced abuse of a physical or sexual nature, or both. Again, abused patients were more likely to undergo various surgeries, such as gallbladder, hysterectomies, and laparotomies. They also had "more pain, non-gastrointestinal somatic symptoms, bed disability days, psychological distress, and functional disability compared to those without sexual abuse." (145-46)

This is kind of a big deal, and I don't see many people talking about it. The lifelong impact of trauma on various aspects of our health and bodies, which then can impact our sex lives, cannot be underestimated.

Similarly, there's evidence that trauma can lead to heartburn, ulcers, disruptions throughout the small intestine and colon, and disordered eating (Gordon 34-39). As Maté summarizes the scholarship, chronic pain can accompany trauma as well: "When there are too many 'gut-wrenching' experiences, the neurological apparatus can become oversensitized. Thus, in the spinal cord the conduction of pain from gut to brain is adjusted as a result of psychological trauma. The nerves are set off by a weaker stimuli" (147). Having gut issues and/or chronic pain can definitely impact one's sex life and relationships, and probably other aspect of health and wellness that we are still figuring out.

Bringing this back around to being a trauma-informed educator, there are so many strategies we can use to try to make the classroom less likely to trigger students and hence disrupt their learning process. Since one of the foundational elements of trauma is an involuntary loss of control (that is then often dangerous), giving students some measure of control over various aspects of the classroom, like where they sit and whether they can easily move around, might help. Making an effort to give trigger warnings, and provide alternate assignments where needed, also helps.

In the sex ed classroom specifically, being trauma-informed is quite important, since as noted above, a lot of people have sexual trauma as well as a host of other negative beliefs and experiences that might be linked to trauma: shame, secrets, chronic pain or injury, and so on. I looked at the stats for child maltreatment in the U.S. and they're pretty dismal, so yeah, this is definitely a thing.

Being trauma-informed in the sex ed classroom can mean a few different things, as summarized by Nicole Fava and Laina Bay-Cheng (whom I once fan-girled over at a trauma conference): "an appreciation for the prevalence of trauma, an understanding of its deep effects across development, efforts to avoid re-traumatisation, valuing the person in all aspects of care, non-blaming and supportive language, and awareness of individuals' capacity for resilience" (388). Trauma-informed sex ed doesn't center around treating the trauma (that's for specialists to do), but rather making a safe enough space for everyone, regardless of their degree of trauma.

And for those of us who are educators or otherwise working on the front lines of people with trauma (in health care, for example), we need to be trauma-informed to take care of ourselves. I list the book *Trauma Stewardship* in the references below for this very reason: the authors acknowledge that "Trauma always creates a ripple effect" (Lipsky 17) which we often call vicarious trauma or secondary trauma, and it can have a real impact on people. I also list the book *Healing Sex: A Mind-Body Approach to Healing Sexual Trauma* in the references, which takes a somatic approach to guide women survivors of sexual assault in exploring their sexuality under conditions of their own choosing.

We live in a pretty traumatized world. And if we—educators, nurses, therapists, and more—are going to help care for the people in it, we also need to be caring for ourselves. I know this chapter got to be ridiculously long, but hopefully you learned something useful in it, to help you be more compassionate towards yourself and / or others.

References:

Burke Harris, Nadine. "How Childhood Trauma Affects Health across a Lifetime." *Youtube*, uploaded by TED Talks, 7 February 2015, https://youtu.be/95ovIJ3dsNk.

Fava, Nicole M., and Laina Y. Bay-Cheng. "Trauma-Informed Sexuality Education: Recognising the Rights and Resilience of Youth." *Sex Education*, vol. 13, no. 4, 2013, pp. 383–94.

Gordon, James S. *The Transformation: Discovering Wholeness and Healing After Trauma*. First ed., HarperOne, an Imprint of HarperCollinsPublishers, 2019.

Haines, Staci, and Felice Newman. *Healing Sex: A Mind-Body Approach to Healing Sexual Trauma*. Updated 2nd ed., Cleis Press, 2007.

Lipsky, Laura van Dernoot, et al. *Trauma Stewardship: An*

Everyday Guide to Caring for Self While Caring for Others. First ed., Berrett-Koehler, 2009.

Maté, Gabor. *When the Body Says No: Understanding the Stress-Disease Connection.* J. Wiley, 2003.

Nagoski, Emily, and Amelia Nagoski. *Burnout: The Secret to Unlocking the Stress Cycle.* First ed., Ballantine Books, 2019.

Van der Kolk, Bessel A. *The Body Keeps the Score: Brain, Mind, and Body in the Healing of Trauma.* Penguin Books, 2015.

WHAT I BELIEVE—AND KNOW TO BE TRUE—ABOUT SEX

As AN ATHEIST (AND A FOLKLORIST/SEX educator), the question of the relationship between my faith and sexuality becomes both more complicated and simpler. This chapter originally appeared as a blog post at Patheos, where I was part of the atheist blogging channel, but I've fleshed it all out for y'all to enjoy. This essay builds on many of the points covered in many of the previous chapters in this section, so please go to the appropriate chapter to find citations if you're not seeing them here.

Okay, so while I started out thinking about this topic from the perspective of atheism, technically I'm a Jewish-raised agnostic-atheist hybrid. But I'm functionally an atheist, because I don't participate in any outward-facing faith tradition. I vote like an atheist, in large part because if there's evidence, I definitely wanna see it. And I think theocracies are bad (overgeneralization, I know, but this is my manifesto so I get to say what I want!).

So when I think about what I have faith in, and how that

relates to sex, I have to unpack a faith that is more secular in nature than spiritual. My academic training as a folklorist and my additional research in gender/sexuality studies, feminist/queer theory, and sex education all inform what I believe about the world and the people in it, and in turn, what sex might mean.

And this is relevant for all of us, as we are all sexual beings. To unpack that a bit, this doesn't mean that we're all sexually active beings, nor that we should be.

I follow sex educator Al Vernacchio in asserting that sexuality is a *"necessary and normal* part of the human lifespan from birth to death. We are born with bodies, emotions, and desires —including sexual desires" (10, italics in original). We experience powerful connections with others, some of which are life-enabling like breastfeeding and cuddles from our caregivers. These aren't necessarily sexual experiences in the arousing or orgasmic sense, and that's fine, early childhood experiences aren't meant to be.

But in the holistic sense of how we all have bodies and can use them to experience pleasure and connection, sometimes with an erotic or relational or sensual tinge, yeah, we are all sexual beings. And that's...okay? Normal? Healthy? It's the common groundwork of humanity to be wired for these things, even if our experiences or choices or identities mean we don't engage with them.

Vernacchio and others are clear: just because we're all sexual beings does not mean everyone has to be, or should be, sexually active. And in fact, Vernacchio suggests that if you as a parent or caretaker are not okay "with thinking about your children as sexual beings, let's figure out why" (11). Again, you don't have to leap whole-heartedly into the idea of being sexually active in early or inappropriate ways, you just have to agree that our nerve endings and pleasure centers don't suddenly sprout when we're eighteen, they've been there all along.

For young people, we can acknowledge that they are sexual beings without encouraging them to be sexually active. Same for people who have religious reasons to not want to be sexually active. And for people on the asexuality spectrum, the sexual aspects of their identities and experiences may not be things they want to focus on or that are important to their self-concept. That's valid too.

Having established that we are all sexual beings in some form, let's move on to the good stuff. I hold three things to be true about sex:

- There is no universal, inherent meaning to sex; its many meanings vary by culture.
- There are not essential, universal, hard-wired differences between men and women (other than a few anatomical quirks).
- Both of these assertions—and more—can be empirically demonstrated to be true, because science.

In the rest of this chapter, I'll unpack why I have faith in these three statements, and how they relate to my identity as an atheist and feminist scholar / sex educator.

There is no universal, inherent meaning to sex

ASK ANY FIVE PEOPLE WHAT SEX IS, AND YOU'LL GET AT LEAST FIVE different answers. Are we talking penis-in-vagina? Does that mean only heterosexual people can have sex? Does orgasm need to occur? What do orgasms even mean? And so on.

Every culture conceives of sex differently (see what I did there?). Each individual within a culture, in turn, brings their own expectations and experiences and paradigms to the table. Apart from a handful of biological facts about sex, such as that certain kinds of acts can lead to reproduction, STI transmission, and other physical outcomes, it's all wide open to interpretation.

Culture creates the specialness around sex...and so does religion. As a folklorist, I like to point at how every religion has its own creation myths, and many of these deal with reproduction and gender. Adam and Eve in Genesis? Hello, gender roles. The Greek gods and all their issues, especially with Zeus being unable to keep it in his robes? Also, yes, gender roles. And so on.

Studying the intersections of religion and folklore can give us valuable insights into what people believe is true...and when it comes to sex? People believe some pretty messed-up things, like that the existence and maintenance of a porous membrane determines your morality (as with the hymen). Or that one's religion justifies or even mandates how you treat others sexually, as with the "Quiverfull" Christian movement that encourages their followers to have lots and lots and lots of children.

How we interpret sex is also very much based on culture. Showing physical signs of arousal doesn't mean that someone's enjoying sex, or worse, that they're "asking for it" when an assault happens (we call this nonconcordant arousal, which I covered in more detail a few chapters back, and it's normal). Not experiencing arousal at all, or in limited cases, as with asexual and demisexual folks, is normal, too. But in cultures and religions that expect reproductive heterosexuality from their adherents? Good luck explaining the wide range of natural variation in human sexuality.

In short, wanting (or not wanting) certain kinds of sex doesn't necessarily mean anything about your morality or ethics; casual sex doesn't make you a bad person. Nor does group sex, or kinky sex, or transactional sex, as long as you've got a baseline of consent being met. We get to decide what sex means to us, and regardless of our faith orientation or our cultural background, we should seize this power.

There are not essential, hard-wired differences between men and women

CHUCK THE "MEN ARE FROM MARS, WOMEN ARE FROM VENUS" BS. It's false, as well as offensive.

We'll get to why it's false, but why is it offensive? Well, for starters, binary gender is a fiction despite its prevalence in many religious and cultural traditions. The assumption that gender is a binary erases the experiences of people whose gender is non-binary in nature, whether they're born intersex or are transgender or have a non-binary gender expression or identity in any fashion.

Cross-cultural examples abound. Anthropologists have documented the existence of three and four and more genders in cultures around the world: the hijra in India, two-spirit people in various Native American cultures, and so on. There are *so many* examples of cultures where there aren't just two genders, and I really wanna get into them all but that could be the topic of its own book! (and is, in fact; a good starting point is Joan Roughgarden's *Evolution's Rainbow*).

As far as the truth value, yes, most human bodies conform to one of two templates. Or perhaps it's more accurate to talk about points on a spectrum, while acknowledging that some bodies might diverge from a linear "this or that" model. Again, there's way more complexity than I want to get into right now, but for how human sex is not just a binary, I recommend *Sexing the Body* by Anne Fausto-Sterling, and because humans are a part of nature and nature doesn't conform to binaries either, I'd again recommend *Evolution's Rainbow* (from which I learned that all geckoes are female, aphids reproduce by cloning themselves, some male fruit bats lactate, and lots of fish change sexes over the course of their lifetime).

Human bodies all start from the same fetal stuff (as I covered in more depth a few chapters back), no matter how their eventual anatomical presentation and/or gender expression might evolve. To repeat a line from sex educator/researcher Emily Nagoski, we're all made from the same parts, assembled differently: the penis and vulva both evolve from the same fetal tissue, for instance. All bodies contain a similar amount of erectile tissue, it's just internal in roughly half the cases. The examples continue, and I interpret them to mean that despite many people's insistence on binary genders, we're just not that different from one another.

When it comes to the subjective aspects of sex, the message that we're all basically made from the same parts holds true: all humans experience sexual arousal in similar ways. So forget the "women are slow cookers, men are microwaves" message. Most people exist somewhere on a spectrum between spontaneous and responsive arousal, and both are normal and healthy.

Your gender doesn't predict what your sex life will be like, what (or whom) you'll enjoy, or anything like that (though the gender conditioning you receive can contribute to the contexts in which you're receptive to arousal). And we know this because...human variety? Sexual research? So many friggin' things?!

Gender shouldn't be a box or a prison. Probably the nicest thing I can say about gender right now is that organizing groups according to gender has led to stuff like the feminist movement, and that should help us address historical inequities (I mean, you need the category of women to talk about the gender pay gap, ya know?).

It's fine to have good feelings about your gender, to be proud of it, to be super aligned with it. But don't let that lead you to judge others who are struggling with their gender, or defining it differently, or doing it differently than you.

Science can empirically demonstrate the above statements (and more) to be true

THE SCIENTIFIC STUDY OF SEXUALITY IS STILL A YOUNG FIELD, AND there's a lot for us still to explore (and how to do it both ethically and reliably in terms of the ability to replicate findings remains a thorny issue). However, if you broaden "science" to include the scientific method and the general application of an empirical perspective to the world, you can learn *a lot* about sexuality.

I'm not trying to put science on a pedestal and claim that everything labeled "Science" is automatically true or correct. Indeed, plenty of BS gets passed off as scientific, and researchers are never completely objective.

But the point of utilizing the scientific method, and viewing the world through a more empirical lens in general, is that we're always striving to figure out if our findings can be replicated or not. We're reaching for knowledge that can be generalized, and trying to understand when patterns are context-bound or not, whether we're studying blood flow during arousal or marriage in different cultures. Or, in the case of studies on the sex addiction model, we're looking for whether it can be falsified (spoiler: no, it cannot, and I talk about this in its own chapter in the Taboo Topics section of the book).

And yes, my two statements above are backed up both by scientific studies published in peer-reviewed journals and books, and by the kinds of cultural studies (like ethnographic work) that are "soft" sciences, but still striving for empirical truth. When anthropologists and folklorists go all over the world and find that people have different ideas about gender roles, yeah, that is scientifically valid knowledge too, even if some of our methodologies have improved in the last century.

You know what else scientific findings support thus far?

- That porn is not a public health crisis;
- The effects of fat-shaming and stigma contribute to poor health;
- The sex addiction model does not hold up to lab studies.

So when we're researching sexuality, gender, and the body more generally, we need to keep in mind that there are ways to study these topics that hew closer to an empirical, science-minded approach. Pure objectivity might be a false dream, but we can trust in well-designed studies with representative sampling and replicability to guide us closer to sex knowledge that is worth having faith in.

. . .

What I Believe About Sex

TO TIE ALL THESE THREADS TOGETHER, AND TO CONCLUDE WITH A rumination on what role sex plays in my life, I'll briefly mention that approaching sex from a secular perspective in no way makes it less awesome. Sexuality is still full of mystery, and every time we learn new things about it, it just gets more exciting, in my view.

The fact that I can better understand my body, my gender identity and expression, and my desires using an empirical lens is *amazing*. I don't have to waste time on bigoted or stereo-typical half-truths and shame. I'm free to seek out like-minded people, many of whom, unsurprisingly, turn out to be either atheists, agnostics, or people of faith who are social-justice-minded.

Unfortunately, being an atheist alone is no guarantee of having a gender-egalitarian or sex-positive attitude. I view my feminism and atheism as compatible, but there are atheists out there with real problems with misogyny, homophobia, transphobia, and so on, and I keep hoping they'll come around and realize that we can do better.

My time studying trauma has taught me many things that are true about human sexuality more generally: some things are within our control and some are not. We can't always choose what traumatizes us, but we can choose what heals us. Similarly, we can't always choose our sexual orientation or turn-ons, but we can work with those in playful or challenging ways, exploring pleasure and sensation because it's all just a world of culturally constructed meanings out there, so why not be a bit fluid about it?

The double-edged sword of human connection is that is has both the devastating power to cause harm that seems irreparable, and may sometimes be, as in cases of abuse and assault...but human connection can be just as healing under the right circumstances: a loving family, a deep sexual connection, a long-lasting friendship, and so on.

I'm in camp "can we please stop having to be resilient now? pretty please?" so I'm being careful about using the word resilient as praise...but studying trauma and sex, sometimes together and sometimes separately, has taught me that humans are pretty damn resilient. We can be torn apart by something, and we can rebuild ourselves better and stronger (albeit probably with a few more neuroses and/or coping mechanisms than when we started).

We're resilient because we choose to be. Because we can be. Because we're stubborn as fuck. Because we contain multitudes, meaning that humans interacting with one another and/or with sex can be any dizzying combination of emotions you can imagine.

At the end of the day, sex encompasses experiences that range from romantic to traumatic, mundane to numinous, and serious to silly. Sex can be playful, a way for people to connect, a way for an individual to do self-care, a way to reproduce, and so so so much more. Sex is as diverse and fascinating as all of humanity, and that is a cause for faith and celebration alike in my book.

References:

Fausto-Sterling, Anne. *Sexing the Body: Gender Politics and the Construction of Sexuality.* Second ed., Basic Books, 2020.

Roughgarden, Joan. *Evolution's Rainbow: Diversity, Gender, and Sexuality in Nature and People.* Tenth anniversary edition, University of California Press, 2013.

Vernacchio, Al, with Brooke Lea Foster. *For Goodness Sex: Changing the Way We Talk to Teens about Sexuality, Values, and Health.* Harper Wave, 2014.

THE HISTORY OF SEX EDUCATION

A RELATIVELY BRIEF INTRO TO AND
SUMMARY OF THE HISTORY OF
SEX ED

IF YOU WANT what the internet calls the "tl;dr" version of the history of sex ed, this is it (that acronym stands for "too long; didn't read" as in "didn't read the whole thing" and is meant to be like, okay, here are the highlights, as brief as I could get 'em to be).

I'll provide an introductory overview, a summary of relevant themes, and a tl;dr quick-read version at the end. Then, each chapter in this section will go more deeply into a specific facet of the history of sex education, usually either a time period or a major event. This history is specific to the U.S. which is useful even in other cultural contexts because the U.S. has shaped and continues to shape policy around gender and sexuality stuff worldwide (see: the global gag rule, covered in the 1980s chapter, sigh).

So, to get the obvious question out of the way: how old is sex education and why do we need a written history of it? In terms of a formal school-setting sort of thing, sex education only really dates back to 1913 (an event called The Chicago

Experiment, which we'll discuss in its own chapter). The backdrop of this was the decades following the Civil War and Reconstruction, known at the Gilded Age (1870s–1900) and the Progressive Era (1880s–1920s or 1900–1917, ish).

Basically, the time smushed between the Civil War and World War I in the U.S. saw a ton of expansion of industry, but also corruption. A lot of people migrated from rural areas to urban areas, leading to the explosive growth of cities like Chicago. Public health became A Thing and especially in the Progressive Era, we had reformers (think early activists) focusing on things like labor reform (so people didn't die unnecessarily on the job), social reform (to address things seen as social ills like prostitution, gambling, and alcoholism), and religious reform and revival.

But the reformers were also kinda racist sometimes and so many of the advancements from this time period were a double-edged blade: progressive in some ways, stuck in bigoted nonsense in others. This will be a running theme.

Alongside all these developments, Western feminism was growing and evolving, still considered to be in its first wave because women were still like "um, can we please vote and own property rather than *being* property?" (which, yes, was ironic because early feminism was very centered on white women's experiences, and while not having legal personhood in the same way as men sucked, first wave feminism didn't always account for the people of color who were still enslaved or recently freed)

Women made up a big portion of the social reformers of these time periods, so if you've heard of famous sociologist Jane Addams (who founded Hull House in Chicago to help the underprivileged), that's the kind of thing we're talking about here. More on feminism and its contributions to the history of sex ed in its own chapter. A lot of early sex ed leaders were women, too: Victoria Woodhull, Margaret Sanger, and so on.

One of the feminist topics throughout much of U.S. history has been contraception and abortion, and while not every feminist has agreed on it, most feminists fall into the "let women decide what to do with their own bodies" category. Abortion wasn't necessarily illegal in the U.S. until the early 1900s, falling into a gray area where licensed doctors could pretty much do whatever, so their rich clients benefited from this while poorer women sought black market and back-alley remedies. Discourse and laws around these topics shaped early sex ed, because some of the ways in which sexuality topics could be discussed, including contraception, were made illegal by the Comstock Laws (I use the plural here because there were both state and federal versions of these laws).

In 1873, Anthony Comstock, who was already a moral crusader type of dude, helped write laws at the state and national levels that made it illegal to disseminate obscene materials. Because that's easy to define, right? *eyeroll* Anyway, the U.S. Postal Service was made to be complicit in all this too, and it's a big enough deal that it gets its own chapter.

Nowadays, FOSTA and SESTA (the Fight Online Sex Trafficking Act and the Stop Enabling Sex Traffickers Act) carry on Comstock's work, claiming to protect the innocent by shutting down avenues for sex trafficking, but in reality punishing anyone who is not only sex work-adjacent but also sex education and sexuality-stuff-in-general-adjacent. I cover this in the chapter on the digital age.

The battles of Comstock and his ilk with early feminists and anyone who was in favor of reproductive choice made the early 1900s pretty tense. Also, in case the link between these issues wasn't clear, access to and information about contraception and abortion are not only social justice issues, they are sex education issues, because sex education is all about ensuring that everyone in a population has access to the information about their bodies, and the human body in general, that can impact their lives. Whether or not someone chooses to use contraception or get an abortion can be highly personal, but we all deserve to know how our bodies work and what our options are for medical interventions that can do everything from improve our quality of life to save our life.

What else was happening in the early 1900s? Eugenics. This was/is a movement that cloaks itself in scientific language but is not actually scientifically sound; it takes theories of genetics to a bizarre extreme to speculate about improving the human population through controlled breeding practices. This might sound innocuous on the surface, but it ends up going some pretty dark places, with speculation about and enforcement of policies like forced sterilization.

You know who likes eugenics? Nazis. That should tell you most of what you need to know about how gross it is.

What other thing was happening in the early 1900s, with even earlier roots, that caused some controversy? Moral panics over "white slavery" which is, from a current perspective, pretty damn cringe.

Similarly, President Teddy Roosevelt talked about "race suicide" in the early 1900s, meaning that white people weren't having enough babies and would soon be replaced by people of color and/or immigrants.

Despite all this weirdness, sex education found its first foothold in the U.S. in 1913. One of the earliest women to earn a doctorate, Ella Flagg Young, was a superintendent in

Chicago and was like "heck yeah we're getting these kids some knowledge about their bodies." From what we can tell from the surviving records, the sex ed materials from what became known as the Chicago Experiment were pretty tame from today's standards, very "here's what a period is" and "here's basic human reproduction" type of stuff.

Bizarrely, unless you happen to be quite into military history, World War I was a pretty big "oh crap, maybe we need sex education!" moment in the U.S. See, while venereal diseases (a.k.a. STDs, a.k.a. STIs, which I prefer because illness or infection is less stigmatizing than disease) have been with humanity for centuries, cures have not been. And the U.S. military realized they were losing valuable man-hours to STIs when soldiers would start showing symptoms...but, plot twist, a lot of the men were entering the service already infected from the home front. So it became apparent that there needed to be some amount of sex ed at home, as a matter of national security.

The downside to all this, however, was the American Plan. In brief, some government folks were like "what if we rounded up all the sex workers and women suspected of having STIs and indefinitely detained them in prison-like-structures while also forcibly treating them with crude and harmful interventions like mercury?" So yeah, super misogynist and full of human rights violations left and right.

Once we get out of the Progressive Era, there are a few notable sex-ed-related events: the establishment of Planned Parenthood in 1932 in its early incarnation as the American Birth Control League, the discovery that penicillin can cure bacterial STIs like syphilis in 1943, and oh yeah, the Great Depression, which actually swayed public opinion in favor of birth control, I guess because people were realizing, then as now, that having kids is expensive (D'Emilio and Freedman 247-49).

World War II happened, and with it the subsequent baby boom, and "family planning" techniques, including contraceptive use, continued to rise in popularity (D'Emilio and Freedman 249-52). Ideas about sex were shifting too, with the 1960s counterculture movements and all the questioning of norms they represented. Ironically, as sex became more mainstream due to the lifting of censorship laws and the fact that sex sells and Americans were inhabiting an increasingly commodified society, there remained some ironic contrasts: "a sharp line between what was judged acceptable and what was labeled deviant" (277). Deviance still included anything queer.

As far as I can tell (because I wasn't alive then), the 1950s, 60s, and 70s were pretty chill in terms of school sex education in the U.S. It simply wasn't all that controversial (though it was starting to be). I'm sure, as with all facets of education, that some school districts and individual schools were better at it, and some were worse, and there was a whole lot of middle ground, but it just didn't seem to inflame passions the same way it does now (similarly, you know how both before and after Roe v. Wade passed in 1973, most Americans beyond Catholics just didn't seem all that passionate about abortion one way or the other? It became a major debate and voting point during a targeted right-wing/evangelical campaign to make it into a grassroots movement where none had previously existed).

School sex ed was no longer able to chug along just doing its thing due to some major cultural shifts from the 1960s through the 1980s. Contraception became more widely available with the invention of the birth control pill and its increasing normalization from the 1965 Supreme Court ruling

Griswold v. Connecticut. Which should have been fine, but alas, cue another moral panic about "teen pregnancy" which was thinly-veiled racism that I'll talk more about in the 1980s chapter. Same with another concurrent moral panic, the Satanic Panic and its relatives.

The 1980s also saw the inception of abstinence-only sex education (yep, this is *definitely* getting its own chapter). In 1981, the Adolescent Family Life Act (AFLA) was passed, thereby instituting abstinence-only sex ed as a thing in the U.S. Federal money was, for the first time ever, sent to groups that would use shame-based educational techniques and exercises to discourage teenage sexual activities, sex outside marriage, and teen pregnancies.

Additionally, after 1960s/"Summer of Love"-type shenanigans where having unprotected sex only meant the risk of pregnancy since most STIs could be cured, HIV emerged as a new threat. And to be clear, the threat was mostly ignorance and homophobia and the way the U.S. government left tens of thousands of gay men to die from the unknown disease.

HIV/AIDS changed the way that sex ed was carried out, but often in confusing ways, because there would be states that would mandate HIV education but simultaneously forbid comprehensive sex education.

Though the AFLA was passed in 1981 under President Ronald Reagan (who promoted other conservative and harmful social policies like the belief in "welfare queens" and subsequent tightening of the social support network, plus the slashing of state funding for higher education), it and its future iterations remained popular with a variety of presidents, both Republican and Democrat. The idea of abstinence-only sex ed was here to stay.

Some technological advancements in the last few decades

have also contributed to shifts in society and sexuality educa-tion. The ability to use projectors to show gross-looking images of genitals with STIs as a scare tactic? Yeah, lots of people leapt on that. The increasing availability of pornog-raphy on anything with a screen? Yep, that's contributed to some moral panics around human sexuality and human traf-ficking.

In the 21st century, we get fun stuff like abstinence-only sex still receiving tons of federal and state money despite there being no peer-reviewed studies of its efficacy, continuing attacks on contraception and abortion access, and hardcore anti-LGBTQ+ attacks. Racism and misogyny remain alive and well, too.

What I'm hoping is becoming apparent in this condensed history of sex ed is just how much we're repeating history. We see Comstock reincarnated in FOSTA/SESTA, and "white suicide" in the Reagan era's teen pregnancy moral panic (that was really about getting white people to have more babies, preferably while married). We see doctors who provide contra-ceptive care and abortions targeted once more. All the horrid, dehumanizing language once applied to gay men (to call them predators, etc.) is now being applied to transgender people.

Not gonna lie, I find all this disheartening. Like, didn't we already establish that censorship is bad?! But it's also illumi-nating to write this history and help spread the word in the hopes that others will learn about it and demand change. If nothing else, I would hope we could have new conversations about human sexuality instead of retreading old turf. Or perhaps we can call out politicians who are ignorant to this history and educate them and ask them to please get with the century and focus on problems that people are actually facing (like here in Indiana, where the potholes are so bad they practically have their own zip codes) instead of rehashed moral panics.

And all this is just skimming the surface. There's so much more history and current-day stuff I want to include here, but the point of this book is to be a 101-level introduction, not to overwhelm you with citations. I'm consoling myself with the fact that I can always write a sequel and get deep into the weeds with it all then!

If you want the details and citations on each of the topics introduced here, skip ahead to the next chapters in this section. If you want the list of themes (things like religion, gender, and so on) that appear in the history of sex ed, that's up next, followed by a tl;dr timeline.

SOME RELEVANT THEMES THAT WEAVE THROUGHOUT THIS HISTORY are as follows:

-religion (lots of Christian feels about sex, and any sort of teaching about sex to children, and while Christianity has been a major player in U.S. sex ed it's not the only one);

-censorship (Comstock was one of the first to pass laws to censor sexuality info and prosecute anyone involved in it, but he was far from the last; see FOSTA/SESTA for more recent versions of the Comstock laws);

-feminism (because feminists have largely advocated for the rights of all people to have access to accurate info about their own bodies, but they haven't always agreed on how to go about it);

-war (not only because of heightened tensions around identity and us vs. them politics, but also because the U.S. military created propaganda to protect mostly-white soldiers while overlooking the needs of, and often demonizing, people of color);

-race/ethnicity (because white supremacy and racism in the U.S. dictated different messages for white folk vs. people of color, usually assuming a high level of purity in the case of the former, and corruption/degeneracy in the case of the latter; also, the contributions of non-white sex educators are often unknown and undervalued);

-gender (for centuries now, men and women have been assumed to be completely different kinds of humans with completely different kinds of needs and sex drives, with the result that sex ed policy is aimed at men vs. women in weirdly different ways);

-intersectionality (turns out, if you look at the ways race/ethnicity AND gender intersect and overlap, for example, you see historical patterns in how white men are held up as a "must be protected at all costs" class when it comes to sexual behavior, Black men are made out to be predators and/or lost causes, white women are treated as though they must be bundled in bubble wrap and never told about anything sexual to keep them pure, and Black women are treated as racist stereotypes of whores or sluts, always already irredeemable, and that's just looking at a few of the potential intersections of overlapping identities);

-citizenship (American scientists have deemed it A-okay to

perform unethical medical experiments and sterilizations on non-Americans, and immigrants have often been over-scrutinized and under-served in reproductive capacities);

-sex work (since 20th century stereotypes dictated that sex workers were only ever women, not men, and they were usually already tainted with STIs and fallen morals, and the general *cough* white *cough* population had to be protected against them, we see this resurging today in the moral panic around pornography, where nice normal white guys need to be protected against the supposed ill effects of porn);

-ableism (thanks to eugenics making it seem like a scientifically valid idea to weed out "unfit" populations like the mentally ill and physically disabled, so, these people were more likely to be forcibly sterilized and less likely to be treated with human dignity and given any halfway decent sex education);

-homophobia (being non-straight was seen as a perversion for a good chunk of the 19th and 20th centuries, and sex ed has reflected that by either omitting mentions of non-heterosexual identities/acts entirely, or pathologizing them as a fear tactic);

-transphobia (even before the rise of transphobic hate campaigns and legislation in the 2000s, there was a cultural understanding that people who participated in cross-gender activities were somehow deviant, which is part of why most sex ed curricula don't mention the existence of trans people).

TL;DR:

-The Gilded Age (1870s–1900) and Progressive Era (1880s–1920s or 1900–1917 depending who you ask) were important to the history of sex ed because they were characterized by rapid industrialization and urbanization, which then led to the rise of public schools and the awareness that maybe parents weren't always teaching their kids about the birds and the bees, so public schools needed to handle this.

-The Comstock Laws (on the books from the 1870s until the 1930s in some places) made it super easy for agents at state and federal levels to jail and punish anyone they caught disseminating "obscene" materials, so early feminist proponents for contraception like Margaret Sanger often fled the law's reach by going to Europe.

-The Chicago Experiment in 1913 was the first time sex ed was taught in a public school system in the U.S.; surveys showed that the students loved it and benefited a ton, while their parents hated it (a trend that continues today).

-World War I (1914–1918) and World War II (1939–1945) were also flashpoints in the history of sex ed, because they convinced the U.S. military and government that soldiers needed some form of sexuality education to protect them from potentially disabling STIs.

-The American Plan (1917 through the 1960s in some places) gave state and federal agents the ability to indefinitely detain, without a warrant or accusation, anyone suspected of being immoral or a prostitute, or having/spreading an STI; no surprise, it was only used to imprison and forcibly treat women, and often women of color.

-Scientific advancements like the discovery that penicillin could cure most bacterial STIs (in the 1940s) and the legalization of hormonal birth control (in the 1960s) gave rise to social fears around promiscuity, which led to conservative backlash such as the "welfare queen" / teen pregnancy moral panics.

-The HIV epidemic started in the 1980s and again reframed conversations around sex and sex education.

-Abstinence-only sex ed also began in the 1980s, with the 1981 Adolescence Family Life Act.

-Time marches on, but we're still having a lot of the same conversations we were having 100+ years ago!

SEX ED STARTS IN...THE GILDED AGE AND PROGRESSIVE ERA?!

IF IT'S BEEN a minute since you've taken an American history class, this is definitely the chapter you should start with in this section. This chapter is also for you if you want to be blown away by how much we are repeating history from 100+ years ago in the 20th and 21st centuries when it comes to how we talk about sex and sex ed.

Picture this: the Civil War just ended. It was pretty devastating due to the massive loss of life, the destruction of land, and the shifts in society (mostly good shifts, I should clarify: white supremacy sucks). People were messed up and adrift and kinda like...what's next?

One major paradigm for studying what came next was the search for order: reform-minded individuals responded "to the social, cultural, and economic chaos spawned by post-Civil War urbanization, industrialization, and immigration" (Marten 2). This led to an emphasis on rationality and science and regulation that was, again, somewhat new in the American landscape.

These changes had massive impacts on youth, and while children aren't the main or only focus of this book, a lot of sex education is designed with children in mind, so we need to be attuned to some of this. James Marten, who edited a whole book titled *Children and Youth During the Gilded Age and Progressive Era* (thereby on point for getting us acquainted with this history), paints this picture:

The Gilded Age and Progressive Era saw the United States become "modern" in almost every sense of the word. During this time the country became the leading economic power in the world, producing more steel, coal, and other products than the industrial powers of western Europe combined. And although she had always been a nation of immigrants, the forty years before the First World War saw perhaps twenty-four million immigrants come to the United States, mostly from eastern and southern Europe; the percentage of Americans who were immigrants or the children of immigrants was around 45 percent in 1920. Agriculture would, of course, remain a key industry in the United States, but industrialization was also accompanied by urbanization; by 1920 a majority of Americans lived in cities, suburbs, or small towns. (4-5)

Major themes here are industrialization, urbanization, and immigration on the surface, and racism, xenophobia, misogyny, and eugenics that'll shine through once we know to look for them. Kinda like right now, so get ready to start seeing some eerie parallels.

But first, why the names for these historical eras? Apparently historians remain divided on how accurate the titles are, and tend to consider them as one unit, the Gilded Age and Progressive Era (GAPE—maybe not the acronym I want to use in a book on sex?). The Gilded Age is typically considered rife with excesses such as political corruption, whereas the

Progressive Era was more about reforming and fixing said corruption. Both kinda-also-sorta overlap with the Victorian era (as Queen Victoria ruled the British Empire from 1837–1901), which was a time period notorious for people being prudes and viewing sex as taboo, an attitude that definitely made its way across the Atlantic to the U.S. as well as elsewhere.

I don't have the space to get into all the weird Victorian notions around sex, but just to set the stage, keep in mind that women who seemed too interested in sex were diagnosed with nymphomania, while women who exhibited any anxious or willful or strange symptoms might be diagnosed with hysteria. Other doctors asserted that nymphomania was a symptom of hysteria (Knowles 20-26). Both were sometimes addressed with invasive operations such as a hysterectomy or clitoridectomy.

However, all this time period stuff is a tad reductive. Historians generally agree to lump in the Gilded Age and Progressive Era together as one unit of study, but to take just one example, how progressive was the Progressive Era, and whose ideas of progress got promoted? Christopher Nichols and Nancy Unger, who edited *A Companion to the Gilded Age and Progressive Era*, introduce some of these dilemmas as such:

Progressivism is viewed by some as primarily a white urban middle-class operation designed as a kind of protection against being squeezed out of power by an ever-growing, increasingly diverse working class on the one hand and the expanding power of big business on the other. Others claim the main source of the movement to have been the workers themselves, while still others credit it to business leaders who were seeking to stabilize volatile conditions through regulation. Progressives have alternately been called altruistic reformers bent on improving the quality of American life (especially for the less advantaged, or so-called "unprotected") and selfish condescending meddlers aiming more for social control than social reform. (2)

So, it was a mixed bag. The super-rich, like the Rockefellers, were able to exert tons of influence on society, and in fact John D. Rockefeller encouraged some early sex ed policy under the guise of the social hygiene movement. But there was still room for upstart nobodies to attract a following and change how things worked, as with Victoria Woodhull (more on her in the Progressive Era Feminism chapter).

It was also a supremely xenophobic time, with white American-born citizens not only freaking out about formerly-enslaved Black folk suddenly having rights, but also freaking out about Native American peoples and the influx of immigrants. The Chinese Exclusion Act (1882) happened during this time period and is notable for being the first federal legislation to say "nope" to immigration for an entire ethnic group. I point this all out to plant the idea that a lot of the early sex ed conversations we'll follow were primarily about what was deemed appropriate for white American citizens, in part to protect and differentiate them from these other (apparently awful and/or immoral) groups.

Why did this all set the stage for public school sex ed? Among other reasons, thanks to reformers being like "child labor is bad, yo" and states mandating education up through increasingly higher ages, there were more kids in school than ever before in U.S. history: "between 1870 and 1915 the number of youngsters attending school jumped from seven to twenty million...By 1920, three-fourths of all children were in school at any given time and 20 percent of all teenagers attended high school, especially boys and girls from well-off families" (Marten 7).

Plus, tons of young folks were moving from rural areas to cities, and living on their own, and working, so they had both leisure time and spending money. And unlike in village life, nobody was there to wag a finger over boys and girls mingling freely. More kids in schools + more youth on the streets = more opportunities for young folks to interact and possibly even get it on. The time was ripe for some kind of unified education policy to reach all these young folk.

However, what actually happened during this forty-or-fifty-year time period is that a lot of different groups disseminated a lot of different messages. Many of them were contradictory messages, and there was a battle between the folks who had financial and/or governmental backing and those who appealed to the masses.

Robin E. Jensen wrote a book on this very topic and sums it up thus: "Unfortunately, the ambiguous rhetoric that some Progressive Era leaders used to talk about sex and sex education have since resurfaced to become fixtures in U.S. discourse, thereby shaping what sorts of information was (and is) available to individuals" (xiii). As we read on with this historical backdrop in mind, we'll see some of these ambiguities and I'll also connect them to current day issues.

Finally, to wrap this up, it's important not to view the Victorian era and the overlapping/succeeding Gilded Age and Progressive Era as monolithic. In her book chapter on sexualities during this time period, Leigh Ann Wheeler writes, "The Victorian Era was not as hostile to sexuality as once thought, and sexual modernism brought a mixed bag of new laws, identities, assumptions, and expectations" (111). What's more, many of these attitudes are still with us today: "The Progressive Era has provided surprisingly durable, extending through the twentieth and into the twenty-first century" (111).

Which, again, is part of why I'm spending so much time on history in this book: we are retreading familiar ground even if we're not consciously aware of it. And to echo many of the pro-choice protestors from recent years, we won't go back. Because as we'll see in coming chapters, a lot of the past attitudes about sex were pretty damn harmful.

References:

Jensen, Robin E. *Dirty Words: The Rhetoric of Public Sex Education, 1870–1924*. University of Illinois Press, 2010.

Knowles, Jon. *How Sex Got Screwed Up: The Ghosts That Haunt Our Sexual Pleasure. Book Two, from Victoria to Our Own Time*. Vernon Press, 2019.

Marten, James. "Introduction." *Children and Youth During the Gilded Age and Progressive Era*, edited by James Marten, NYU Press, 2014, pp. 1–16.

Nichols, Christopher M, and Nancy C Unger, editors. *A Companion to the Gilded Age and Progressive Era*. John Wiley & Sons, Incorporated, 2017.

Wheeler, Leigh Ann. "Inventing Sexuality: Ideologies, Identities, and Practices in the Gilded Age and Progressive Era." *A Companion to the Gilded Age and Progressive Era,* edited by Christopher McKnight Nichols and Nancy Unger, John Wiley & Sons, Inc., 2017, pp. 102–115.

ANTHONY COMSTOCK GETS HIS OWN CHAPTER

YES, it's a cheeky chapter title, and I'm hoping it'll piss off Comstock's ghost if such a thing exists, but really, we cannot overstate the effects of Comstock's moral crusader attitude and actions on sexuality professionals of the day...which is being eerily revisited today in new laws like FOSTA and SESTA (a.k.a. recent laws that have contributed to the downfall of Tumblr among other things).

Most of the specific facts in this chapter come from Amy Sohn's book *The Man Who Hated Women*, which is incredibly well-researched and documented, if you want to do your own deep dive into Comstock's life, as well as read about the lives of the women he persecuted. Direct quotes will be attributed, as always, and there are a handful of other good sources that pop up here too.

Anthony Comstock (1844-1915) was an American and Christian who was deeply offended by things he deemed impure. Born in Connecticut, he enlisted in the Union Army and served as a clerk in the Civil War, then moved to New York City.

Before Comstock passed his law in 1873, there was some precedent for obscenity laws. A New York committee passed the Obscene Literature Act in 1868. As Sohn summarizes it,

---

It prohibited the sale, advertisement, or manufacture of "any obscene and indecent book," which included papers, pamphlets, stereoscopic pictures, and more, and any "article of indecent or immoral use, or article or medicine for the prevention of conception or procuring of abortion," as well as advertisement or circulars (advertising brochures) for dirty books, contraception, and abortion. (33)

This new obscenity law, which had parallels in other U.S. states, was notable for two things: including contraception as obscene (when it hadn't been mentioned much in the past) and including the mail system as one route by which one could be found guilty and persecuted for the dissemination of these contraband items.

When this new law passed, Comstock was working as a dry goods clerk in NYC and was an active member of the YMCA (the Young Men's Christian Association). In both contexts, he watched fellow dudes being tempted by "obscene" materials, where "obscene" was interpreted as anything that aroused sexual thoughts, regardless of whether it contained a specific call to action. But if it could be perceived to corrupt an innocent young mind by introducing sexual thoughts where none had previously existed, it was *definitely* obscene (Sohn 34).

Some of the higher-ups in the YMCA agreed that Comstock was right to be ultra concerned, so they created a vice committee to put a stop to the trade in smutty books, and Comstock got in on that. He also benefited from a law that let citizens collect on half of any fines that were levied in these cases, so Comstock could monetize his hobby of going after smut printers (Sohn 62). Again, be on the lookout for parallels to modern-day stuff, as with the 2021 Texas law that would pay a private citizen a bounty for snitching on anyone providing an abortion or aiding someone in getting one.

With some luck, Comstock got a stronger version of the anti-obscenity bill he was working under in front of Congress. He was in the right time at the right place, and the fact that he organized a sex toy show to convince congressmen of how evil and lascivious all this stuff was got everyone's attention (Sohn 79). The law was passed in March 1873, and immediately after, the ads for contraception and abortions disappeared from the newspapers. Multiple states passed laws around disseminating information about contraception and abortion, too. Abortion had not previously been illegal, but new laws at state and city levels made it so.

The government was complicit with the Comstock Laws at multiple levels (and I say Laws, plural, because there were both state and federal versions of the law). Also, in 1873, the New York Society for the Suppression of Vice (full of Comstock's buddies) was recognized by the New York legislature as an independent private society, meaning they would have the power to enforce federal and state obscenity laws with the cooperation of the police. Sending these materials through the U.S. mail was illegal, and the U.S. postal service was instrumental in assisting Comstock and his cronies.

Even though there wasn't anything resembling school sex education yet, married couples still sometimes pursued information about sex for their own reasons. Doctors wrote books with titillating titles such as *Fruits of Philosophy* (1832), *The Marriage Guide* (1850), and *Medical Common Sense* (1858) and these, too, became prohibited, with the coeditor of *Medical Common Sense* being persecuted under the Comstock law to the tune of $5,000 in legal fees which would be $120,000 today (Sohn 92).

Writers, publishers, public speakers, smut printers, smut peddlers, abortionists, anyone selling vaginal syringes or other items to induce abortion or provide contraception—all these different kinds of people could be and were arrested under the Comstock Law. Often, Comstock himself participated in these arrests, assuming false identities to write for mail-order instructions for these medical procedures, or going in person to ask about items to help a lady-friend who was experiencing some difficulties of the feminine sort.

Comstock lost some of his popular support over the years, but he was active in pursuing these supposed vice-purveyors until his death in 1915.

And he legit ruined some lives. He persecuted thousands of people, and at least two—abortionist Madame Restell and sexologist Ida C. Craddock—committed suicide rather than get dragged to jail.

Comstock's rhetoric was also racist at times. In his 1883 book *Traps for the Young*, Comstock presented this whole elaborate equation of light-colored stuff with purity and dark-colored stuff with evil:

Fill a clean, clear glass with distilled water and hold it to the light, and you cannot perceive a single discoloration. It will sparkle like a gem, seeming to rejoice in its purity...So with a child...But put a drop of ink into the glass of water, and at once it is discolored. Its purity cannot be restored. So drop into the fountain of moral purity in our youth the poison of much of the literature of the day, and you place in their lives an all-pervading power for evil. (in Jensen 5)

In addition to these rather obvious racist descriptions, Comstock seemed to take great pleasure in persecuting working-class people who sought to disseminate information about reproduction (Jensen 9). Indeed, reputable doctors who provided their high-status patients with information about contraception and abortion were rarely attacked by Comstock and his ilk.

Among other famous targets, he tried to take down anarchist Emma Goldman, birth control advocate Margaret Sanger, and the first woman stockbroker and first woman to run for president of the United States, Victoria Woodhull. These women took a lot of trips to Europe and Canada, in part to escape Comstock's attempts to imprison them so they would stop saying things like, maybe women shouldn't be forced to endlessly endure pregnancies to the detriment of their physical health, mental health, and financial well-being. Super controversial message, right? And yet.

While the Comstock Laws stopped being enforced in the 1930s, they were nevertheless going full-force for 40ish years while Comstock was alive to be its most enthusiastic enforcer.

This put a damper on the nascent attempts at public discourse around sex, including sex education. Like, I am pausing here to emphasize this point, because how the hell could we have any kind of sex education when it was literally illegal to print and disseminate materials about sex?!

And the federal Comstock Law was never actually repealed, though contraception and abortion were explicitly made legal in subsequent Supreme Court cases (Sanger gets credit for the first chip in this law in 1936 when she won a case allowing a Japanese physician to mail her a box of contraceptives, and even this had to wait until 20 years after Comstock's death! (summarized in Sohn 300).

So the specter of Comstock is still with us, and this vice-obsessed man's legacy pops out to haunt us with every subsequent passage of an obscenity law meant to curtail anything sexual outside the private sphere and even then sometimes intruding into the private sphere...like FOSTA and SESTA, which I cover in the digital age chapter.

References:

Jensen, Robin E. *Dirty Words: The Rhetoric of Public Sex Education, 1870–1924*. University of Illinois Press, 2010.

Sohn, Amy. *The Man Who Hated Women: Sex, Censorship, and Civil Liberties in the Gilded Age*. First ed., Farrar, Straus and Giroux, 2021.

SOCIAL HYGIENE & EUGENICS

THIS IS one of those topics that makes itself out to be very science-y but is ultimately very flawed and bigoted. Fun times, eh?

Eugenics emerged during the Progressive Era because of course it did: people were super obsessed with "modernization, scientific discovery, and the maintenance of human health" (Jensen 17) at that time.

The term "eugenics" was coined in 1883 by British scientist Francis Galton, and it was indeed thought of as very scientific at the time. It went beyond Darwinism (survival of the fittest) to suggest that humans, not just livestock, should follow controlled breeding practices to improve the human race...but it was also super racist and hierarchical, positioning white people at the top of the obviously imaginary ladder of evolution.

As summarized by Robin Jensen in her book on Progressive Era rhetoric around sex, "Eugenicists generally believed that characteristics such as intelligence, physical ability, morality and personality were hereditary traits. In turn, they also came to believe that it would be possible to create a race of people with exceptional abilities" (18) by, you guessed it, breeding only the best of the best.

What about the rest? Not only were they to be discouraged from breeding, they could be forcibly stopped from it. And yeah, we are still talking about human beings here, not livestock.

Since a lot of these eugenicists had the ears of politicians, they were able to sway whole nations. Hardline eugenicists, in Jensen's words again, "equated sex with reproduction and the future health of the nation" (19). So, like, no pressure.

And sometimes it was politicians themselves spouting this rhetoric; President Teddy Roosevelt very publicly reamed (white) women for being too selfish to have enough babies to keep the continent populated by white people. This "New Woman" "married late, had few children, and worked outside the home," leading Roosevelt to claim that she was basically damaging the whole nation by dragging it down while she committed "race suicide" by ignoring what she owed her country as a wife and mother.

This rhetoric is still around, btw.

Anyway, in the early 1900s, the main movement utilizing eugenics-speak regularly was the social hygiene crew. In general, when looking at this time period, you can swap in "sexual" for social, since polite people of course did not talk directly about sex when it could be avoided. And the "hygiene" part of the equation refers to how public health was becoming an increasingly important topic. Social hygiene = sexual health, but when inflected with a eugenics perspective, it was still highly moralistic and hierarchical. Just because they'd moved away from Comstock's moralizing language didn't mean the messages weren't still there, emphasizing the importance of premarital virginity and monogamy and not being queer or a sex worker or anything outside the box.

In the U.S., the founder of the social hygiene movement was Dr. Prince A. Morrow, and he was impacted by European discourse around the dangers of venereal diseases (or VD, now referred to as STDs or STIs). At the time, STIs were thought of as a punishment for immoral behavior, so the move to reframe them as a medical and published health issue was actually pretty revolutionary. To paraphrase Morrow's thinking,

"As long as propriety blocked open discussion of the diseases and their transmission, men would remain ignorant of the dangers of sex with prostitutes, women would enter marriage uninformed about the risks they faced, and doctors would stand by silently, refusing to intervene." (D'Emilio and Freedman 205).

Morrow kicked off a plan to have an early version of sex ed that would "focus on specific topics (e.g., the dangers of extra-marital sex and the ways venereal diseases were transmitted) ...and to omit other topics (e.g., the pleasures of sex and unorthodox topics such as homosexuality)" (Jensen 22). Then he died in 1913.

The next person to take up the social hygiene flag was John D. Rockefeller, Jr. (son of John D. Rockefeller, Sr. whose oil fortune was legendary), who in 1914 helped found the American Social Hygiene Association (ASHA, which again, is still around, as the American Sexual Health Association). ASHA seems to do good work nowadays, but their first president basically thought the consequences of syphilis and gonorrhea were so terrible—which, granted, before the ability to treat them with antibiotics was kinda true—that they should implement sex education to scare the crap out of young people so they would be afraid to have sex outside marriage. That scare tactic is still in use today in some sex ed classrooms.

Social hygiene proponents didn't manage to get school sex ed kicked off yet, so their legacy is a mixed one. Mostly their gambit to make sex into a public health topic worked; they helped lift the stigma around talking about sex in public venues to some degree, even though certain topics would remain taboo for decades to come. They perpetuated messages around men being super horny and women needing to remain protected and innocent.

On the negative side of their legacy, their influence on politicians meant that eugenics policies became the law in many U.S. states. Multiple states made syphilis testing before marriage mandatory. So too with the sterilization of the mentally ill and physically disabled. From the Progressive Era until the 1960s, more than sixty-five thousand Americans were forcibly sterilized (Nielsen 100).

In case you've never had occasion to sit down and ponder why the eugenics style of approach to sex and reproduction is a very bad thing, consider this: eugenics basically says "These people are not fit to reproduce." And maybe you're thinking, well duh, if someone is severely disadvantaged, maybe they shouldn't have kids, maybe that would make their lives harder *and* be hard on their kids.

This was, I gather, part of the reasoning for sterilizing the mentally ill or the impoverished, and denying those with syphilis a marriage license (before the 1940s, when scientists figured out that syphilis could be treated with penicillin, and it no longer had to be a physically painful and disfiguring death sentence, and moreover could be transmitted to one's partners and any children one might conceive).

But consider this: a law that puts constraints on the disadvantaged, when the disadvantage in question is one that can impact any individual at any time, has a perpetually moving target. And that target might someday be you.

This is a point that gets made a lot in academic disability studies and in disability rights and justice spaces, that inhumane laws and treatment of the disabled, ill, mentally ill, etc. populations are a terrible idea, not just because, duh, everyone should have the same basic human rights, but also because any apparently healthy individual could become disabled at a moment's notice due to an accident, illness, or whatever.

So it is incredibly short-sighted on the part of the non-disabled or temporarily able-bodied population to pass laws limiting the rights of the disabled, because we're just one bad time away from joining that population. And I say "we" because most of my life experience has been in a nondisabled body, but thanks to some chronic illness stuff I am slouching my way towards that end of the spectrum, keenly aware that my days of pain-free movement are limited.

I am hoping, really truly hoping, that nondisabled people will listen to others like them, who share their privilege, or at least more or less present in the same fashion, because disabled people have been saying this stuff for decades and it doesn't seem to have sunk in yet.

Also? What does it say about those people making these decisions, that somebody pretty much sat down and muddled through this thought process (if one could charitably call it that) to arrive at the conclusion that eugenics was the better idea?

Like: *Hm, these disadvantaged people may suffer additional hardships when they reproduce, so we could either fix society to give everyone more support when they start families, or we could*

189

keep society the same way it is and forcibly prevent these people from marrying and/or having kids...hmm, yeah, let's not try to improve society to make it more equitable, let's just force hysterectomies and sterilizations on the handicapped and mentally ill. Cool, cool.

One other fairly obvious point from disability studies and activism is that making things more accessible for those with disabilities often improves access for those without disabilities too. Automatic doors aren't just helpful for people with wheelchairs and mobility aids, they're also helpful for adults with children in strollers. Having elevators in every building everywhere isn't just essential for people with mobility-related disabilities, it's also useful when an otherwise able-bodied person breaks a leg and is temporarily in a cast and using a mobility aid. The list of examples goes on and on.

So the fact that eugenicists look at society and think to themselves that it's easier to continue to block out disadvantaged people than to just freakin' fix social issues is a bit disheartening. They're telling on themselves and their prejudices. I hope that we can resolve to do better in the future.

Anyway, back to eugenics in these historical moments. As Kim Nielsen documents in *A Disability History of the United States*, the Progressive Era was a time when scientists gleefully leapt into defining "undesirable" traits, linking them with racial/ethnic markers, and assuming that physical and moral "defects" went hand-in-hand (100). Influenced by early genetic studies like those of Gregor Mendel, these people got *super* excited about improving the human race through selective breeding practices.

These folks also lumped in criminal "degenerate" types with the disabled, and the state of Indiana (where I am, sadly, sitting while writing this) was the first to pass a forced sterilization law in 1907 (Nielsen 113). More than thirty states followed suit.

The Supreme Court weighed in on this issue in the infamous *Buck v. Bell* case in 1927, with Justice Oliver Wendell Holmes stating: "It is better for all the world if, instead of waiting to execute degenerate offspring for crime or to let them starve for their imbecility, society can prevent those who are manifestly unfit from continuing their kind" (in Nielsen 117). He capped it off with the oft-repeated slur: "Three generations of imbeciles are enough" (117).

This decision has never been overturned, so the Progressive Era legacy of forced sterilization is very much with us today. Yes, literally today; look up the forced sterilizations in California prisons, which continued until the mid 2000-teens.

As with a lot of social policies made in white supremacist societies, people of color were disproportionately impacted by these sterilizations. Puerto Rican women were experimented upon without their knowledge or consent to develop the birth control pill, resulting in mass sterilizations (Ross and Solinger 46). African-American women alongside immigrant women were targeted for these coercive practices, sometimes even by the services that existed to help them, with public clinics for low-income clients often forcing these procedures on patients who had just given birth or who spoke little English, hence could not reasonably give informed consent (Ross and Solinger 50-51).

Other ethnic populations were specifically targeted for sterilization; a Native American group estimates that "that on some reservations, the rate of female sterilization was as high as 80 percent," with other estimates suggesting that from 1968–1982, approximately 42% of Native women of childbearing age were sterilized (Ross and Solinger 50). And more broadly, during the early 1900s, the Bureau of Indian Affairs deemed numerous Native American citizens insane, confining them to asylums where they died, thereby practicing another form of genocide of those perceived to be socially unfit (Nielsen 119-24).

Now that we've taken this rather horrifying journey through history together, why is all this relevant to the study of sex education? First, some of the social hygiene dudes from the Progressive Era were also steering local and national sex ed policies. Because putting people with genocidal ideas in charge of education is a great idea.

Next, there is a massive double standard in how eugenics policies were applied, and surprise, it's super racist! Or maybe not a surprise, since most of the people into eugenics were white, and concerned with preserving the white race's perceived superiority (gag). Well, unless you're disabled, I guess. But because of this racist bias, it actually became harder for white women to seek long-term birth control procedures such as sterilization. As Loretta Ross and Rickie Solinger describe the situation in the 20th century in their excellent book *Reproductive Justice: An Introduction,*

A white woman typically could not be sterilized unless her reproductive output satisfied a formula devised by the medical profession: her age multiplied by the number of children she had already given birth had to equal the number 120 or greater. Plus, she needed the permission of two doctors and a psychiatrist before sterilization was approved. Only after meeting all of those conditions would the white woman have satisfied her reproductive duty. (51-52)

And so another double standard emerges: gender. It's historically been easier for men to obtain vasectomies than for women to obtain the equivalent sterilization procedure. Another ironic historical note: the originator of the current vasectomy procedure, Dr. Harry Sharp, also lived in Indiana. He was a vocal proponent for sterilization of "degenerates," which he bragged about in his piece in a 1909 issue of *Journal of the American Medical Association*. If you can get your hands on it, it's a trip to read for sure.

Finally, bringing this back to the modern practice of sex education...does any of this stuff get taught in most curricula? NO. Even though it might be super useful to know that we've got a century-plus of history dictating who can and can't reproduce, even as sex ed programs withhold accurate reproductive info from young people of all ages and races. And then said young people get blamed if they reproduce in any way considered inappropriate, such as too young or outside marriage or whatever. It's pretty messed up, to pretend people have sexual options, not tell them the history of destroying those options, and then punish them for exercising those options.

References:

D'Emilio, John, and Estelle B. Freedman. *Intimate Matters: A History of Sexuality in America*. Third ed., University of Chicago Press, 2012.

Jensen, Robin E. *Dirty Words: The Rhetoric of Public Sex Education, 1870–1924*. University of Illinois Press, 2010.

Nielsen, Kim E. *A Disability History of the United States.* Beacon Press, 2012.

Ross, Loretta, and Rickie Solinger. *Reproductive Justice: An Introduction.* University of California Press, 2017.

Sharp, Harry C. "Vasectomy As a Means of Preventing Procreation in Defectives." *Journal of the American Medical Association,* vol. LIII, no. 23, 1909, pp. 1897–1902.

PROGRESSIVE ERA FEMINISM: SOCIAL PURITY VS. FREE LOVE

FEMINISM HAS WORN a lot of faces over the years. Sometimes they remain relevant and sometimes they end up pretty cringe, and with the manifestations of feminism in the Progressive Era, it's a little bit of Column A and a little bit of Column B.

First, let's recall that U.S. women had very few rights in the 19th century, and even though the mid-20th century, progress was slow. White women got the right to vote in 1920; it took longer for women of color. Divorce laws did not make it easy for women to leave abusive husbands, and if they succeeded, it was difficult to find enough work to make ends meet.

Sex work ended up being an important issue to many early feminists, but as with feminism today, the opinions were divided. Let me state this: I believe sex workers of any gender have the right to engage in this form of work as they choose, and if their choice to do so seems forced because of capitalism, well, that's more of a capitalism problem.

And if we are classifying an entire group of adults (like sex workers) as always automatically victims, that robs of them of their agency to make choices, even if they're choices you might not agree with. I would caution that it's very, very dangerous to conceptualize of a whole group of adults as lacking agency and choice, as feminists then and now have found in their attempts to rescue and reform sex workers who don't necessarily want to be rescued or reformed.

Records show that prostitution (again, I am using language from the source texts; "sex work" is generally the preferred terminology today as I understand it) was on the rise in the 19th century. Part of this was due to the social shifts accompanying industrialization: "prostitution had taken economic root in the late eighteenth century, but commercial and urban growth in the early industrial era created both an enlarged supply of prostitutes and a new demand for their services" (D'Emilio and Freedman 132). Paid work was scant for many women, and when they were runaways or single mothers or immigrants, prostitution might be preferable to a boring or demeaning domestic service position.

Prostitution seems to have been tolerated throughout much of the 19th century, up til, you guessed it, the Progressive Era. Apparently people before that were just like, "Yeah, unmarried dudes gonna sex it up" and "Yeah, soldiers gonna pay for sex with 'camp followers'" and "Yeah, mining towns in the Wild West gonna attract prostitutes." I say this glibly to convey the sense of social acceptance, not to make light of how this was at times a kinda horrific experience; there was definitely a coercive element to many of these practices, as with Chinese women who came to the U.S. seeking employment but were forced to work in brothels (discussed in D'Emilio and Freedman 134-35).

With all this happening, there was a move to regulate prostitution, which I'll talk more about in the chapter on the American Plan, but in brief, public health professionals and doctors in a given city or state would inspect sex workers and offer them certificates of health on a regular basis so they could stay in business.

This is similar to the modern-day move to decriminalize sex work, but it goes further than mere decriminalization (as in, sex work alone will not get you sent to jail, which seems to be a popular option among sex workers) and adds state regulation as an extra requirement to be active. The logic seems to have been something along the lines of how men are more sexual than women, so they need a release valve or outlet beyond marriage so they don't force their frequent and violent desires on their wives. This is messed up because it assumes that some women deserve protection more than others, which we also see in contemporary discourse where some incel will suggest that rapists wouldn't rape if they just had access to sex workers (it is unclear whether they feel entitled to free access to women's sexual labor)...but I digress.

In the Gilded Age and Progressive Era, sex work wasn't as hidden. It was increasingly visible and available in the public sphere, and some cities (like St. Louis) were trying to weigh in on its social acceptability by landing on the "yes, this is acceptable as long as it's regulated" side.

Where this interacts with feminist concerns is...interesting. Because, as noted above, women were often trapped in unhappy marriages, and they cared that their husbands were gallivanting about on the town. And because penicillin wasn't discovered to clear up syphilis until the 1940s, having your spouse bring home an STI was quite a big deal.

In short, Progressive Era feminists found their voice and used it, not just to demand the vote but also to demand an end to men's easy access to sex workers. This branch of feminism was known as the social purity movement. Other feminists were like, no, marriage itself is basically a form of prostitution since women are so lacking in rights, and these feminists congregated under the banner of free love.

Some Progressive Era reformers, yes, wanted to save these "fallen women" and convert them to Christianity. And there was that moral panic over "white slavery" in the early 1900s (Jensen 11). I definitely see parallels to feminists today who lump in all sex workers as victims of sex trafficking, when that's usually not the case (yes, some women are victims of sex trafficking and need help getting out; other adults choose to engage in sex work in some cases because they enjoy it, or for much the same reasons today as in the past: it seems a better option than the other grueling or inhospitable or impossible situations available under capitalism).

A lot of these activist women, however, embraced the social purity movement, called such because these women demanded a single standard of social purity for both men and women. They wanted an end to the double standards whereby men could sleep around with impunity whereas women were punished for the same behavior...and worse, men who had lots of extra-marital sex actually endangered their families at home due to the severity and longevity of STI symptoms.

The majority of social purists were "middle-to-upper-class, white, Protestant women" (Jensen 9) who agreed with super moralizing folks like Anthony Comstock about how unfettered sex was bad, but they thought some sex education was necessary. It would be super tame sex ed by our standards, but the premise was that young women needed to learn about pregnancy and motherhood in order to become good mothers themselves. And more education all around meant more of a chance to impart these lessons to young men, too, and teach them not to be abusive horndogs.

Social purists sometimes played nice with the eugenicists, too. They bought into Darwinian ideas in circulation at the time about how "children who were conceived during voluntary intercourse would be healthier and more intelligent, while those conceived during unwanted discourse might become criminals, idiots, or paupers" (D'Emilio and Freedman 154). I mean, I'm all in favor of any argument against rape, but this seems kinda, er, weirdly wrong, as well as not placing the focus where it should be, on the bodily autonomy of the person in question??? Anyway, social purists used "voluntary motherhood" as a way to be strategically ambiguous as to whether they advocated for contraceptive use or not; they would often say they were against contraception and abortion, but overall this rhetoric paved the way for family planning, which would come to accept contraception as one of its strategies.

One of the stranger elements of this early strand of feminism is how it also fell in line with the temperance movement. According to this thinking, men abused their wives because they had too much easy access to alcohol, so this was part of the activism that led to Prohibition. Social purists thus represented a bit of an uneasy alliance at times, of "women's rights advocates, conservative women, and temperance organizations such as the Women's Christian Temperance Union" (Sohn 13). Their message was family, family, family, and also, men, please stop visiting prostitutes and abusing your wives.

Social purity activists were notable for bringing sex talk to the public sphere, which was a bit ironic given how they were trying to make the point that sex really belonged in the marital bedroom and nowhere else. And it seems like they were trying to improve women's lives despite what would come across as weirdly moralizing language today. They succeeded in raising the age of consent from ten years old to the mid-teens, for instance (D'Emilio and Freedman 153), and that's an ongoing battle still, y'all.

In contrast, free love activists didn't want to work within patriarchal structures like marriage and the family unit: they wanted to challenge them.

Free love didn't mean "anything goes" or a sexual free-for-all as the term might imply; instead, it "referred to the right of all men and women to choose sexual partners freely on the basis of mutual love and unconstrained by church, state, or public opinion" (D'Emilio and Freedman 161). Many free lovers wound up in long-term monogamous relationships, for example. Though it's worth noting, some of the free love rhetoric came out of the earlier utopian polyamorous communities like the Oneida community (Sohn 13).

While the social purists hung out with clergy members and temperance activists, free lovers hung out with anarchists and spiritualists. I know who I'd rather party with!

The free love doctrine was most vividly present in the life and writings of Victoria Woodhull. Married early and unhappily, then divorced and kickin' it with rich dudes, Woodhull broke and spoke out about multiple norms.

Woodhull and her sister Tennessee Claflin, with the backing of legendary industrialist Cornelius Vanderbilt, became the first female stockbrokers on Wall Street. For reference, the New York Stock Exchange didn't officially admit its first female member until 1967, when Muriel Siebert bought a seat on the Exchange (Fisher 40); until then, and apart from Woodhull and Claflin, any women in finance worked behind the scenes in research or secretarial positions.

Woohull also ran for president in the 1872 election, which, yes, was nearly 40 years before women could vote. Her running mate—who was not consulted about the whole thing —was Frederick Douglass.

She also managed to supremely piss off Comstock when she published a lurid exposé on an affair that Reverend Henry Ward Beecher (yes, brother to Harriet Beecher Stowe, the famous writer, who also opposed suffrage even though she was a woman?!) had with a friend's wife. Possibly due to this, as well due to yet another lurid exposé that she'd written, Woodhull spent election night in prison (she didn't win).

Woodhull's publications and speeches on free love illustrate what the movement was all about. In one famous speech, she claimed:

Yes, I am a free lover. I have an inalienable, constitutional and natural right to love whom I may, to love as long or short a period as I can; to change that love every day if I please, and with that right neither you nor any law you can frame have any right to interfere. (qtd. in Sohn 55-56)

For this, Woodhull was depicted as a devil in political cartoons, hounded by Comstock, and written out of her part in the suffrage movement for being too radical.

Speaking of radical, anarchist Emma Goldman was another free love advocate who gave speeches and published articles advocating for women's rights, labor rights, and birth control. She also got into trouble with Comstock.

Margaret Sanger had one foot in the free love movement and one foot in eugenics (unfortunately), and she also drew

Comstock's ire, especially for her activities publicizing birth control from 1913 onward (Sohn 266-67). Goldman and Sanger worked together on some publications, too. For fitting poor women with pessaries (a birth control device like a diaphragm, also used for pelvic organ prolapse), Sanger was jailed.

Her defense was one that resonates with the classist restrictions on health care even today: her attorney "argued that the state Comstock law's medical exception impeded the constitutional rights of poor people by denying them the right to family limitation, but upheld the rights of middle class people with private doctors" (Sohn 293).

And the judge who sent Sanger to prison articulated a sentiment that is also seen today, that women do not have "the right to copulate with a feeling of security that there will be no resulting conception" (in Sohn 293). Again, I point all this out to show that feminists from around 100 years ago (this particular trial was in 1916) were fighting some of the same fights that feminists today are fighting, to separate sex acts from reproductive acts and to assert that consequence-free sexual pleasure should not only be the domain of men.

Most social purity and free love advocates didn't cross paths, but Ida C. Craddock was an odd exception. She worked as a writer for a variety of radical and free thinker publications, deemed herself a sexologist, and also got on Comstock's bad side (to the point where she committed suicide rather than be condemned to jail or a mental institution). She thought both men and women could and should orgasm, and she advocated for contraception in the form of male continence (being able to abstain from ejaculation). So that all seems a bit free-love-oriented.

But in her writing of marriage manuals and such, Craddock "wanted to appeal to respectable people—temperance activists and churchgoers, ordinary Americans seeking no-nonsense advice" (Sohn 178). She didn't seem to see her work as political in the same sense that free lovers did, and she was also anti-masturbation and anti-clitoral stimulation (Sohn 188), which aligned her more with the conservative social purists. I guess the fact that she also called herself a "Lecturer and Correspondent on Social Purity" in her book *Helps to Happy Wedlock* may have been a clue (Sohn 189).

So Craddock was unique for a variety of reasons, among them that she considered herself in a spiritual marriage with a ghostly entity (Sohn 176). Spiritualism was almost mainstream by the late 19th century, characterized by a belief "that certain people, called mediums, could contact the spirits of the dead and transmit their messages about the nature of existence, humanity, and the afterlife" (Bowman 172). Along with other religious revival movements in the Gilded Age and Progressive Era, spiritualism was super popular (Woodhull and her sister were both into it, among others).

Craddock, in her sexological book *Helps to Happy Wedlock*, said a number of very feminist things (Sohn 190): she wanted women to know how to access sexual pleasure, she believed not all sex had to be procreative, and she came down as against marital rape (which, duh, but it wasn't formally made illegal in the U.S. until 1993). Mailing out this book was illegal under the Comstock Act, and Craddock agonized over that a fair bit, which was just one incident that led her to take her own life and blame Comstock for it in her suicide note.

Social purity feminists used ambiguous language to stay out of Comstock's crosshairs for the most part, while free love feminists seemed to enjoy giving him the middle finger. Despite all the differences between them, there were some commonalities between the beliefs of social purists and free lovers: "Both opposed the sexual double standard, which held that women were expected to be faithful but men were not" (Sohn 14). Both were anti-prostitution: the social purists because they felt it threatened good wives at home and/or because they wanted to rescue sex workers, the free lovers because they felt it was just another extension of an unjust hierarchy between men and women (see also: marriage).

Woodhull says it best: "I can see no moral difference between a woman who marries and lives with a man because he can provide for her wants and the woman who is not married but is provided for at the same price" (qtd. in Jensen 14). This is a sentiment I hope modern feminists spend some time thinking about, as some modern feminists are still anti-sex-work in every single instance, which in my mind is a bit short-sighted and doesn't diagnose the correct problem: not sex work, which takes so many forms and can be entered into as consensually as any job under capitalism, but patriarchy and capitalism as coercive institutions.

Whether social purists or free lovers, many of these radical thinkers and writers made their voices heard even when it was literally illegal to publish about sex (thanks, Comstock). Many of them contributed to the suffrage movement and to labor rights and free speech issues, and I hope that learning about these early feminists both sheds light on how we got to where we are today in feminism and helps illuminate some of the perennial issues in American sexual attitudes and beliefs.

References:

Bowman, Matthew. "Religion in the Gilded Age and Progressive Era." *A Companion to the Gilded Age and Progressive Era*, edited by Christopher McKnight Nichols and Nancy Unger, John Wiley & Sons, Inc., 2017, pp. 165–77.

D'Emilio, John, and Estelle B. Freedman. *Intimate Matters: A History of Sexuality in America*. Third ed., University of Chicago Press, 2012.

Fisher, Melissa S. *Wall Street Women*. Duke University Press, 2012.

Jensen, Robin E. *Dirty Words: The Rhetoric of Public Sex Education, 1870–1924*. University of Illinois Press, 2010.

Sohn, Amy. *The Man Who Hated Women: Sex, Censorship, and Civil Liberties in the Gilded Age*. First ed., Farrar, Straus and Giroux, 2021.

THE CHICAGO EXPERIMENT

HERE IT IS: the first recorded instance of school sex education in the U.S.! Hurray!

As with many of the historical topics covered in this book, get ready for some déjà vu. Because the things parents and kids were saying about sex ed one hundred and ten years ago are still being repeated today.

In brief, Chicago had a lot going on in the Progressive Era: massive surges in population due to immigration, horrific public health issues to face (in 1854, 60 people a day were dying of cholera; discussed in Jensen 42), and there was both a thriving underworld and an immense push by reformers to address said underworld problems.

Dr. Ella Flag Young (she completed her PhD in education at the University of Chicago at the age of 55, #lifegoals) became superintendent of Chicago Public Schools in 1909, and having paid attention to some of the social hygiene conversations happening around sex education, she started a committee to weigh in on these issues (Jensen 47).

Dr. Young justified the push for sex education by linking sexuality to other biological facets of being human, which was a move modeled by both social hygiene and social purity activists. She published the following appeal:

The child is told in school that if he doesn't keep his skin clean, his system will fill up with poison, that if he abuses his stomach, he'll suffer with indigestion, if he gathers the contagion of tuberculosis, he'll die of consumption, but never a word of sex organs and the terrible cost of abuses. (in Moran 51)

She also brought the social hygiene and social purity models together by arguing that "scientific facts about sex were not only credible, a position that most Progressive Era citizens already upheld, but that they were also inherently moral" (Jensen 57). The fact that she called these sex ed lesson plans "personal-purity lessons" was another clue to how she borrowed social purity rhetoric to further her goals.

And Dr. Young backed up her words with action: she had doctors come in to give lectures to over twenty thousand high school students.

The lectures would not have been super racy by our standards; they got some anatomy lessons and some superstition-busting, and like today, boys heard from a male doctor while girls heard from a female doctor (Moran 52). There is some survey data from these students, and it's actually pretty amazing, because most of them *loved* the personal-purity lessons and wished they'd had more of them.

One female student complained, "Mother told me about

menstrual periods after they arrived" while another said, "Got my first information from my girl friends. Was very glad to hear lectures and want to hear more, for while my mother knows a lot, she won't tell me a thing" (qtd. in Jensen 37). So much for the ageless argument against school sex ed: that parents will educate their children themselves.

How did Dr. Young get around the Comstock Laws to implement this curriculum? Well, first, she didn't entirely evade the Comstock Laws, which I'll address shortly; otherwise, my best guess is that she managed to fly under the radar by not using a printed textbook nor being centrally located in New York, where Comstock and so many of his agents resided (since the Comstock Laws could only be used to persecute speech if an agent witnessed it).

The problem arose when a medical organization tried to mail transcripts of the personal purity lessons to the parents in the school district. The post office seized these lesson plans and deemed them "unmailable" under the federal Comstock law (Jensen 64), leading to a bunch of national attention and the declaration that if these lesson plans were too obscene to mail, they were too obscene to teach.

This level of national attention surely did not help Dr. Young's efforts. However, as with sex ed efforts today, the main problem was with the parents. While only 8 percent of parents yanked their kids from the first round of lessons, the program was discontinued in part due to calls for Dr. Young's resignation, because she was interfering with "the rights and prerogatives of parents" (Jensen 64-65). So the Chicago Board of Education said "nope" to continuing the lessons the following year.

But the lessons were super popular with the students themselves; according to one study, "90 percent of surveyed graduates found the lessons helpful and worth continuing in the future" (Jensen 64).

Anyway, Dr. Young's amazing accomplishments are chronicled in great detail in Robin Jensen's book *Dirty Words* (that's where I first heard of her), and I'll stop fangirling so I can move on to other topics, but it really is amazing that a sixty-eight year-old woman who was probably considered over-educated for her time managed to be the first one to implement school sex ed in the U.S.

Further, Dr. Young's initial success followed by an immediate downturn gave future sex educators ideas about what to do and what to avoid; scientific rhetoric remains popular to this day, and sneaking sex ed into "health class" or "human biology" is one way to escape scrutiny and fury from those who are eager to deny young people access to information about their own bodies.

References:

Jensen, Robin E. *Dirty Words: The Rhetoric of Public Sex Education, 1870–1924.* University of Illinois Press, 2010.

Moran, Jeffrey P. *Teaching Sex: The Shaping of Adolescence in the 20th Century.* Harvard University Press, 2000.

MASTURBATORY FEARMONGERING
IN AMERICAN HISTORY

THIS TOPIC GETS its own chapter because it spans multiple time periods and it's just so deeply weird yet also impactful. Fear of sex is literally baked into American history—I say literally because of Graham crackers—so it's like, no wonder we're so messed up about sex and sex education!

Using lingo like "male continence" and "chastity," 19th century doctors and health writers advised men to avoid masturbation due to its supposed negative health effects (D'Emilio and Freedman 68-69). I guess they assumed women didn't masturbate unless they were super deviant, since a lot of the writing was aimed at "normal" men and the importance of self-control in their lives.

What kind of negative health effects are we talking about? Before this dialogue reached the U.S., French and British writers argued that masturbation caused acne, headaches, stomach pain, insanity, and even death (Knowles 101-03). And while excessive masturbation might make the penis small in men, it would increase the size of the clitoris in women

(Knowles 107), which just shows how many of these conversations around sexual behavior are inflected by gender norms.

If sending a masturbator to the insane asylum sounds a bit drastic (the British did this for a while), how about food as a remedy? Sylvester Graham and John Kellogg—who went on to manufacture Graham crackers and Kellogg's corn flakes, respectively—believed that bland foods were crucial to help "remove unnecessary physical stimulation that might lead to sexual excitement" (D'Emilio and Freedman 68). Graham was among those who "argued that *all* sexual excitement was physically dangerous" (69).

Graham was active as a preacher in the early to mid-1800s, and among other things, he recommended that a married couple only have sex twelve times a year (Knowles 45). The question of how much sex was healthy and how much was pathological was deeply concerning to thinkers of the past.

In case you were wondering, even the most bizarre-sounding of these premises still gets some traction today. Heard of the NoFap movement? If not, sorry for the weirdness that is about to enter your brain through your eyeballs. There's a group of men nowadays who follow a "NoFap" regimen of not masturbating in order to supposedly increase their testosterone count. There have been a handful of studies, with sample sizes too small to yield significant results, and they did not find much improvement or change in that regard (Kelly).

Similarly, some people today think watching pornography is basically evil and makes you a bad, immoral, and impotent person. This probably-not-actually-accurate take often pairs with the belief that masturbation will ruin your life.

Ironically, people who cease masturbating or take a break from it might perceive themselves to have a better quality of life...but this could be because "stress from prolonged guilt, anxiety, and depression can cause decreases of testosterone and in these situations, abstinence may relieve such feelings and could then theoretically lead to a testosterone increase" (Kelly). Similarly, Nicole Prause's research suggests that it is not pornography viewing, but rather anxiety, that leads to men experiencing erectile dysfunction...but since it's not considered manly to talk about anxiety, some of these men are swayed by reframing their issues with porn or masturbation as a heroic battle.

I don't mean to shame people who are tricked by this rhetoric; clearly, as it's nearly two hundred years old, it works! And if having less or no sexual contact works for you, great. Just don't be fooled into it by someone with a compelling (if utterly unscientific) message.

Also, maybe it's not great that large swaths of NoFap followers tend to align themselves with fascists, specifically antisemitic and alt-right adherents. Scott Burnett analyzed the NoFap discourse online and found that while there were many concerns reflected in the dialogue—anxieties about one's religious faith, for example—this area of the "manosphere" reveals overlapping social problems: "racism, nationalism, and ableism, as well as misogyny" (494).

In some cases, this rhetoric mirrors the centuries-old stuff uncannily, with some of the Internet users Burnett studied specifically talking about how "Conserving semen or sexual energy preserves virility and aggression" (491). This was seen as especially important given the supposed control of the pornography industry by Jewish people who want to keep non-Jewish men "passive and weak" by draining men of their "vital fluid" (491). If you made it through that word salad with your sanity intact, good for you, you're doing better than me.

Also, while I have focused on some of the more incon-

gruous examples here, there's a tragic dimension to the pathol-
ogization of masturbation as well. Some women who were
perceived to masturbate too much were subjected to ovari-
otomy and clitoridectomy, while other women were diagnosed
with hysteria and massaged by doctors to orgasm (Wheeler
103-04).

Kinda funny how for men, it was like "oh dang this might
be bad for you, but don't worry, we'll feed you some bland
food and you'll beat (heh) the urge" whereas for women it was
like "touching yourself leads to madness, so don't worry, we'll
excise your clitoris for you." Which is also why Westerners
sound hypocritical whenever they freak out about other
cultures' genital cutting practices because, um, we have done
that too in the not-so-distant past.

On that note, some historians suggest that circumcision of
American boys became widespread to curb masturbation, and
only after the Victorian-era freak-out about masturbation
ended "did physicians begin to rely on health-related justifica-
tions for male circumcision" (Wheeler 104). So maybe guys
didn't get off easily either, because nonconsensual surgery on
genital tissue isn't great for anyone.

Briefly returning to the overall topic of sex ed, do we get to
talk about masturbation in a no-nonsense, this-won't-kill-you
way in the comprehensive sex ed curriculum? That's a super
complicated question, as former Surgeon General Joycelyn
Elders found out, which I'll talk about in the chapter on the
1990s.

In this historical account of masturbation, pretty much
everyone loses. Kinda like what's coming in the next chapter,
about World War I and the American Plan.

References:

Burnett, Scott. "The Battle for 'NoFap': Myths, Masculinity, and the Meaning of Masturbation Abstention." *Men and Masculinities*, vol. 25, no. 3, 2022, pp. 477–96.

D'Emilio, John, and Estelle B. Freedman. *Intimate Matters: A History of Sexuality in America*. Third ed., University of Chicago Press, 2012.

Kelly, Daniel. "Nofap: Can Giving Up Masturbation Really Boost Men's Testosterone Levels? An Expert's View." *The Conversation*, 29 March 2021, https://theconversation.com/nofap-can-giving-up-masturbation-really-boost-mens-testos terone-levels-an-experts-view-157701. Accessed 25 July 2023.

Knowles, Jon. *How Sex Got Screwed Up: The Ghosts That Haunt Our Sexual Pleasure. Book Two, from Victoria to Our Own Time.* Vernon Press, 2019.

Prause, Nicole, and James Binnie. "Reboot/Nofap Participants Erectile Concerns Predicted by Anxiety and Not Mediated/Moderated by Pornography Viewing." *Journal of Psychosexual Health*, vol. 4, no. 4, 2022, pp. 252–54.

Wheeler, Leigh Ann. "Inventing Sexuality: Ideologies, Identities, and Practices in the Gilded Age and Progressive Era." *A Companion to the Gilded Age and Progressive Era*, edited by Christopher McKnight Nichols and Nancy Unger, John Wiley & Sons, Inc., 2017, pp. 102–15.

WORLD WAR I & THE AMERICAN PLAN

WAR—WHAT is it good for? Instigating some gross misogynist and racist policies of sex education, as it turns out.

Remember the American Social Hygiene Association, ASHA, from the chapter on eugenics? They show up again in World War I, because turns out, STIs don't get put on hold when war is declared.

Leaders of ASHA said a bunch of stuff about how venereal disease has the potential to make or break an army, and they had evidence, too. Dr. Prince Morrow, one of said social hygiene dudes, "estimated that during the American occupation of the Philippines, venereal diseases had robbed the army of millions of work hours, and syphilitic complications had killed four times as many soldiers as any other disease" (Moran 71). And American leaders listened. So, bizarrely, "the war served as justification for providing many of the country's young men with increasingly straightforward education about sex" (Jensen 71).

Fear of STIs wasn't an isolated thing; turns out non-sexual

diseases and infections killed a lot of soldiers prior to the rise of modern medicine and hygiene: "in the Mexican-American War...The army had lost six soldiers to disease for every one lost to a gunshot. But in the Civil War, the Union lost only three to disease for every two lost to a gunshot" (Knowles 8). Dunno about you, but I just sat here for a few moments, haunted by the use of "only" in that last sentence.

Shortly after the U.S entered World War I in 1917, the government established the Commission on Training Camp Activities (CTCA), which oversaw wholesome activities like sports and music for the soldiers. But the CTCA also had the mission of keeping the soldiers as free from venereal disease as possible, so they delivered sex ed lectures to soldiers and...

...oh wait, they only prioritized this programming for white soldiers. Between racist folk ideas and stereotypes about African-American men being unteachable and/or already dirty or diseased (Jensen 81-84) and the fact that training camps were mostly segregated, wartime sex ed ended up super lopsided along race lines.

In fact, these white supremacist attitudes put African-American soldiers into a double bind: they were both treated as ignorant and as already-polluted. To understand that better, we'll need to talk about a precursor to widespread condom use: chemical prophylaxis (oh yeah, and why were condoms hard to get a hold of, as in, kinda illegal? We can thank Comstock for that one, since sending birth control supplies at the time by mail was illegal thanks to his laws).

Jeffrey Moran describes the alternative in great detail:

Chemical prophylaxis at the time involved the laborious process of scrubbing the genitals, injecting a chemical solution into the urethra, and then wrapping the genitals for a while in calomel ointment and waxed paper. Performed competently and within a few hours of intercourse, the treatment was quite effective. (71)

That does not sound particularly pleasant to me. And I can't imagine that everyone who engaged in sexual activities would be thrilled to volunteer that information if they knew they were signing up for a few hours of having their junk wrapped in—I looked it up—a mercury compound. Mercury is toxic. More on that shortly.

So, while white soldiers were receiving at least a little bit of sex ed info in the camps, and being asked if they'd had sexy times before getting a toxic compound slapped on their genitals, African-American soldiers experienced literally the opposite: they "did not get the social-hygiene education that white soldiers received *and* they were punished and treated for venereal diseases, no matter their choices or actions" (Jensen 85) since there were some camps that mandated that all African-American soldiers be given chemical prophylaxis upon returning from leave, no matter what (or whom) they said they'd done.

On the gender axis, yeah, things were similarly messed up. As Jensen notes, "The CTCA's pamphlets for women of 'respectable' ilk worked to ensure, first and foremost, that they did not give in to the 'lure of the uniform' and become conduits for venereal disease among soldiers" (86). Because, ya know, it's not enough to want to protect women from harmful STIs because, like, they deserve protection as human beings on their own merit (this is one of the many places in the book where if I could insert an upside-down happy face emoji, I would).

Women of "respectable" ilk, of course, means white women. Women of color received no similar pamphlets, even though these pamphlets were pretty vague. It wasn't just pamphlets, either, as there were wartime propaganda films by that time period, and some of those sex education films targeting women "framed white women's purity as their contribution to the war effort" (Jensen 87). Which, again, ew.

All of those gross gendered disparities on protecting (white) soldiers from any diseases women were assumed to carry came to a head in the American Plan. I'm going to spend a good chunk of this chapter on it, in large part because it's something I never learned about in school despite almost declaring a history major, and reading most history books I could get my hands on in my own time. I learned about it because I followed the author of the only/major book on the topic on Twitter (may its birdy soul rest in peace).

As Scott Stern documents in his breathtaking book *The Trials of Nina McCall: Sex, Surveillance, and the Decades-Long Government Plan to Imprison "Promiscuous" Women*, governments and citizens have been experimenting with, implementing, and protesting the regulation of prostitution for at least two centuries. In the early 1800s, under Napoleon Bonaparte's rule, Parisian leaders created a new rule requiring prostitutes to register with the police and live in a designated part of the city.

When other nations struggling with these same issues noticed, they referred to this attempt to regulate prostitution as the French Plan (Stern 12-13). Many countries subsequently adopted versions of it, though it rested on a faulty premise: that sex workers were primarily responsible for spreading

STIs. And tracking and diagnosis methods were not advanced enough to disprove this hypothesis, so good ol' stereotyping and stigma made sure it stuck around for a while.

Britain passed their first Contagious Diseases Act in 1864, and as with the French Plan, poor women were more heavily policed, among other flaws in implementation. And to the abolitionists (the kind who wanted to entirely abolish prostitution, not regulate it), the regulationists were contributing to an entire host of social ills: "extramarital sex, sexual infection, and the abuse of women" (Stern 14). Which is kinda what sex workers and allies/supporters of sex workers get told today. Funny, that.

Bankrolled by the Rockefeller Foundation, ASHA was trying to figure out how to handle the problem of young women who were on the path to prostitution, hence corruption and vice and the spreading of venereal diseases. In 1917, spurred to urgency by the U.S. joining World War I, California state health officials adopted a series of regulations empowering them to quarantine and treat anyone suspected of being a prostitute and/or spreading venereal disease.

These new rules allowed health boards to dispense medical examinations and treatments, and to isolate and detain people indefinitely, "without a trial, a conviction, or even a semblance of due process" (Stern 54). The original language was gender-neutral, but only women were ever detained in this fashion. And these resolutions spread, state by state, enforced by police and health officials and members of what would become the FBI, until it spanned all of America. This was the birth of the American Plan. It was entirely legal at the time. And it was devastating.

Nina McCall, an eighteen-year-old girl in Michigan, was one of thousands to suffer. A sheriff reported her as likely diseased, and she was forcibly given a vaginal exam and determined to have gonorrhea and syphilis. She was locked up for three months and treated with mercury, which again, is toxic. Oh, and medicated douches. Those sound fun. The mercury made her arms swell and her teeth loosen, and while locked up in a "women's dormitory," she was expected to do hard domestic labor, such as scrubbing the floor on her hands and knees.

Then, Nina was declared non-contagious and released. Later, she was stalked by a welfare worker who dragged her back in for more tests and more treatments. She eventually sued her captors. And she lost, which sucked, but it meant that we have a rich treasure trove of transcripts, which helped Stern write his book.

The American Plan was notable for making having or being suspected of having syphilis a crime that could get you locked up. It also encoded a bunch of biases and suspicions into law:

...that young women were responsible for the indiscretions of young men; that promiscuity in women was worse than it was in men; that STIs merited jail time for women; that women could not merely serve their time as men did, not that they had to be cured of disease and be "reformed" in order to merit release. (Stern 186)

You see why this is disturbing, yes? Also, on a folklore note, much of what passed as evidence for hauling women into hospitals, prisons, and reformatories was gossip, rumor, or hearsay. These kinds of folkloric materials are not necessarily true or untrue, they're just products of oral transmission...but they probably shouldn't be taken as hard evidence of having an infectious disease, ya know?

The American Plan had many ripples. One of the surgeons general to oversee the American Plan was Thomas Parran. He continued to work with ASHA officials to incarcerate women. But if you've encountered Parran's name before, it was likely because he also oversaw part of the Tuskegee syphilis experiment (which ran 1932–1972), in which U.S. officials allowed African-American men with syphilis to believe they were being treated...but did not treat them. Many of the men died, but not before passing syphilis along to their wives. It was a horrific violation of human rights and an abomination of racist medicine that it happened in the first place, but it also had a lot in common with the American Plan.

Also, to be clear, I'm not trying to equate the horrors that the victims of both phenomena experienced. Nobody wins when we play the Oppression Olympics, but there are definite benefits to looking at the common logic underlying the two things.

Among other reasons, the two main creators of the Tuskegee study "had played active roles in the American Plan," persecuting women nationwide who were believed to be infected. And the two plans had much of the same logic in common, reinforcing "for these physicians their authority and power over those whom they viewed as subordinate and inferior" as well as reinforcing "for these physicians the unimportance of consent when it clashed with their ideas of what was best" (Stern 203). Medicine run amok, practiced unethically on two vulnerable populations? Check and check.

Women were assaulted and detained under the American Plan for decades to come; there are records of cases into the

1940s and 1950s, which is ironic because penicillin was discovered to cure most STIs in the early 1940s, so why the continued need to police promiscuous-seeming women?

In brief: control. The American Plan integrated so seamlessly with the criminal justice system because their values were already in alignment. Women of color and impoverished women were also targeted relentlessly under the Plan, which also makes sense since they were often seen as dangerous populations.

One more fun (read: horrifying, needs a trigger warning) fact: in 1965, now-famous feminist Andrea Dworkin was jailed during a protest while eighteen years old, and assaulted by doctors with a speculum as well as with their hands. She bled for days. This was legal under the American Plan, and the threat of "crude examinations for venereal diseases" at the hands of police was also known among Civil Rights activists marching at Birmingham and planning with the Black Panthers (Stern 251).

To sum up, the American Plan was paradoxically both very American and very un-American. It was American because, let's face it, this country has embraced being a carceral state; we have the highest prison population of any country in the world. We're also still a highly misogynist nation, as evidenced by the gendered wage gap and the extremely high rates of sexual assault. The Plan was carceral and misogynist for sure.

And the Plan was bizarrely anti-American, because in theory, we have the legal right to not be arrested without a warrant or detained indefinitely without an accusation. We (should) have the right to bodily autonomy, to accept or refuse health care. And we think we're so evolved because most American subcultures don't demand a virginity check upon one's wedding night, but damn...try to keep this conundrum in your head: we are a nation still subtly obsessed with female virginity and purity and were handing out forced vaginal examinations to women who were probably virgins on the regular.

So...that was a lot. And it's weird to be writing about this in a book about sex education, because so few Americans know this part of our history, nor does our sex education ever really cover the fact that being suspected of having an STI was enough to destroy your life, at the hands of officials encouraged by the federal government to do so.

In addition to locking up women suspected of spreading venereal diseases, the U.S. government bought into the social hygiene leaders' dire predictions about how controlling STI spread during the war effort would only be so effective if the civilian populace remained ignorant. How dire are we talking? According to Moran, "The surgeon general estimated that five of every six soldiers had contracted their disease *before* entering the service" (73, italics in original).

In 1918, Congress passed the Chamberlain–Kahn Act, which among other things, created some new social hygiene entities and distributed money to colleges and universities to start normalizing sex education (Moran 73-75). Some states and cities also tentatively began bringing sex ed to high school. This whole series of events really helped kick off sex ed as a respectable school endeavor. (among the "other things" the Chamberlain–Kahn Act accomplished were establishing boards and earmarking money to reform the "camp girls" a.k.a. sex workers and adjacent types of women like "charity girls" suspected to be giving American soldiers venereal disease; discussed in Zipf)

Shocking numbers from WWI really helped solidify the

U.S. government's decision to go all-in on sex ed when WWII rolled around as well: the American military lost an estimated "7.5 million working days to venereal disease during World War I" (Lord 84).

And even though the Comstock Laws were still on the books at this point, the fact that the U.S. government and its appointed officials at various levels were now like "It's okay to talk about sex...for the war effort!" kinda meant that any attempt to fully crack down on sexual talk or writing was no longer feasible. The "conspiracy of silence" that Comstock and his ilk worked to reinforce (Moran 81) was over. But it wasn't necessarily smooth sailing from there onward.

References:

Jensen, Robin E. *Dirty Words: The Rhetoric of Public Sex Education, 1870–1924*. University of Illinois Press, 2010.

Knowles, Jon. *How Sex Got Screwed Up: The Ghosts That Haunt Our Sexual Pleasure. Book Two, from Victoria to Our Own Time*. Vernon Press, 2019.

Lord, Alexandra M. *Condom Nation: The U. S. Government's Sex Education Campaign from World War I to the Internet*. Johns Hopkins University Press, 2009.

Moran, Jeffrey P. *Teaching Sex: The Shaping of Adolescence in the 20th Century*. Harvard University Press, 2000.

Stern, Scott W. *The Trials of Nina McCall: Sex, Surveillance, and the Decades-Long Government Plan to Imprison "Promiscuous" Women*. Beacon Press, 2018.

Zipf, Karin L. "In Defense of the Nation: Syphilis, North Carolina's 'Girl Problem," and World War I." *The North Carolina Historical Review*, vol. 89, no. 3, 2012, pp. 276–300.

SEXUAL REVOLUTIONS AND THE CULTURAL DIVIDES OF THE 1950S AND 1960S

SAY "OKAY, BOOMER" all you want, but the Baby Boomer generation has seen and been through some shit.

After World War I, things calmed down a bit with all the panics around sex, and then the Great Depression happened, which hit sex educators in ASHA (the American Social Hygiene Association) pretty hard (Moran 114-15). Plus, sex educators were starting to question the very premise of social hygiene...did the conversation have to be all about venereal disease 24/7?

As World War II happened, a few more things shifted: condoms, which were being manufactured in great numbers since the 1920s, were more accessible due to the lessening power of the Comstock Laws in the 1930s, so suddenly soldiers had better options than the unpleasantness of chemical prophylaxis. Weirdly, as Alexandra Lord notes in her book *Condom Nation*, there was a time in the 1930s when "condoms were illegal when distributed as contraceptive" (because Comstock), but "legal when promoted as a means of preventing disease" (69). How's that for a tidy example of the U.S. government's many contradictory messages around sex?!

Plus, in the 1940s, scientists discovered that penicillin could be used to treat gonorrhea and syphilis, lessening the threats of these STIs. Military leaders focused less on encouraging soldiers to be good and pure and abstinent and more on what we might call harm reduction: if these dudes are looking for a good time, at least make sure they're safe.

And by some estimates, a good time was definitely had, with soldiers buying 50 million condoms monthly during the war (Moran 120). Slowly, STI rates fell in the U.S. armed forces, which Jeffrey Moran attributes to this change in attitude: "By accepting what many considered to be immoral behavior, the army achieved great success in its program to enhance the health and efficiency of the troops" (120). Women perceived to be either prostitutes or just loose were still deemed problematic—and arrested and corralled under the American Plan—but the moral panic around STI transmission had definitely faded a bit.

With the dialogue shifting away from viewing venereal disease as Moral Contamination Forever (That'll Also Kill You and Your Loved Ones), sex education took on a new foe: the "disordered state of youth and the family" (Moran 122). Focusing on the family gave a new interpretation to problems like promiscuity; it wasn't necessarily immoral per se, but could play a role in youth delinquency, which was seen as a rising problem during and after World War II.

Spurred by salacious newspaper reports and other things, "Americans believed, incorrectly, that juvenile delinquency was reaching new levels" (Lord 81). One newspaper ran a story about a fifteen-year-old runaway girl who bragged to social workers about entertaining sailors in her hotel room

(Lord 81). Of course, some of these stories may have been folk-lore, since it's not unheard of for newspapers and radio shows to report urban legends as the truth; Lord suggests that while these stories were "probably often exaggerated and did not reflect the very real decline in crime that occurred during" World War II, such stories "did, however, clearly reflect Americans' fears about the state of their nation" (84).

At some point in the 1950s, a major shift in morals kicked off, in what would be the precursor to the sexual revolution. There were a couple of factors going on here.

One major gamechanger was Alfred C. Kinsey's research, published where the general public could read it and freak the fuck out. His 1948 book *Sexual Behavior in the Human Male* found some things that resonated with previously accepted notions of men's sexuality: "evidence of nearly universal masturbation and widespread same-sex sexual behavior among adolescents of all classes" (Moran 135). But Kinsey's 1953 book *Sexual Behavior in the Human Female* drew back the curtain on an even more taboo subject, leading to protest and outcry.

Other notable events in the 1950s included the debut of *Playboy* magazine, a series of U.S. Supreme Court decisions that reversed earlier obscenity laws (Moran 167), and of course Elvis. Subtler changes involved nixing curfews imposed on female college students, the easing of complete condemnation of women who had premarital sex, and the ability of unmarried couples to rent hotel rooms and buy property together (Lord 118).

Some of the change occurring was not just in events themselves, but in more open discussion around them. Lord writes, "In 1959 nearly half of all American women were married by the age of nineteen, and half of those women became pregnant within the first year of their marriage" (116). But many people were *totally* having affairs, and the "rise in illegitimacy rates and sexually transmitted diseases" (116) became harder to hide. Renewed calls for access to contraception (again, still illegal, even in private married usage) were part of this cultural shift.

I don't have the space to get into all the cultural revolution and sexual revolution stuff of the 1960s, but it was a pretty exciting time to be alive, as I understand it. For our purposes, with debilitating STIs sidelined by penicillin and more contraceptive access than ever, one of the major consequences of the sexual revolution was leveling the playing field between men and women, or at least making some steps in that direction.

I take this point from Kristin Luker, who observes that intimacy has always carried certain risks, say, of being abandoned when you're in love or when you're pregnant...though of course the latter mostly applies to women. And has, historically, for a long time. But "what changed in the sexual revolution was the cultural belief that the party who had more to lose was always and forever the woman" (314, note 7). How much women can and should emulate men's gender roles and sexual behavior has always been debated, and again, this assumes a somewhat heterosexual model to begin with. But I think Luker is correct here, in that this ability for women to act like men if they wanted to (as in, have fairly consequence-free sex) was one of the elements that led to the pushback from conservatives.

This, too, has echoes in history: early social purity feminists thought the best method of birth control was just for men to not have sex with their wives until the wives thought it was a good idea to conceive again, which was a push to equalize the power of these two genders in marriage; in contrast, free love advocate Victoria Woodhull "believed that women had a right to have sex," a right, which if exercised, would make them fully equal to men (Knowles 230).

Meanwhile, in the 1950s ASHA was chugging along with fairly non-controversial school sex ed programming, especially with this new focus on family life education. These classes were sorta like a combo of home economics (household planning skills) and sex-ed-lite, and they were apparently pretty dry and full of "middle-class assumptions and emotional flatness" (Moran 152). Sex ed seemed to be widespread but a bit stagnant.

A new player entered the game in 1963: SIECUS (the Sexuality Information and Education Council of the United States), founded by former medical director of Planned Parenthood Dr. Mary Stiechen Calderone. While working for Planned Parenthood, she was stunned by the "hundreds of letters... evincing a stunning ignorance about sexuality" (Moran 161) that the organization received every year. Again, the education SIECUS workers provided would be pretty tame by today's standards, still emphasizing the importance of marriage for young adults.

SIECUS was able to provide more sex ed in part due to how the sexual revolution of the 1960s put sex on the docket for public conversation and concern. In fact, "many parents began to believe that sex education might be the proper response to the younger generation's moral decline" (Moran 168) as evinced in higher teen pregnancy and STI transmission rates. By one estimate, "nearly 50 percent of all schools were offering some kind of sex education" by 1968 (170). In another sex ed scholar's words, "Americans generally viewed these programs in a positive light" (Lord 3), until some of the late-60s and early-70s nonsense I'm about to detail.

Basically, sex was no longer perceived as a problem because it was evil; if sex was problematic, it was because it was disruptive. And with the Cold War brewing, social disruptions were framed as dangerous due to where they might lead. Because, ya know, Communism. Some folks were pushing boundaries, especially in the 1960s with all of the hippie movement and Summer of Love type of stuff, with other folks primed to push back.

As with a lot of counterculture movements in the 1960s that inspired extreme backlash—think of the framing of the Civil Rights or Vietnam War protestors as anti-American, for example, and the violence that ensued like the killing of protesters at Kent State University and the assassination and/or jailing of multiple antiracist leaders—sex ed was due for its own backlash, which would culminate in the heavy politicization of all sexual topics and the birth of abstinence-only sex ed in the 1980s.

Here is some of that background, with some of the resurgence of "oh no, the wrong kinds of sex are actually immoral/evil" that had seemed to die down for a few decades.

For every "Make love, not war" message being disseminated in the 1960s, there were people who thought sexuality had gone too far. Some of them showed up in California, where conservative parents suddenly began protesting an otherwise tame comprehensive sex education program for junior high and high school students in Anaheim (where Disneyland is). These religiously conservative parents were in the right place at the right time to tap some other conservative networks and get professional activists involved. Gordon V. Drake was a religious muckraker who got in touch with the Anaheim parents and was soon publishing anti-sex-education diatribes for an audience of almost one hundred thousand (Moran 179-180).

What were the shocking allegations? From a folklore perspective, Drake was recounting urban legends, or unverified third-person narratives that nonetheless sound credible. He claimed that students were shown explicit films and that one teacher had applied a condom to a realistic and life-sized human phallus. And there were already other anti-sex-education urban legends in circulation, such as the one where a sex ed teacher strips in front of her classroom to give an anatomy lesson (Moran 181).

Part of what makes legends believable is that they include a decent amount of detail, and they allegedly happened to a "friend of a friend" or at least someone or somewhere recognizable. These legends shared those characteristics and helped whip up a frenzy of anti-sex-education attitudes where none had previously existed. Drake and his fellow activists blamed Jews, socialists, and the Devil for all of this, with talking points familiar to anyone who's tuned into conspiracy theories from the last century (or millennium, really, since the antisemitic blood libel legend, that Jews kill Christian babies and use their blood in rituals, goes back at least 1,000 years).

And, because I can't miss an opportunity to make the point that these moral panics are often recycled, consider that Drake and his cohort "made the false charge that sex educators often forced boys and girls to use same-sex bathrooms" (Moran 191), which would have freaked out conservatives worried about the destruction of rigid gender roles.

Kinda like some conservative todays are freaked out about the loss of gender roles if we, gasp, let transgender people use the bathroom.

Anyway.

Other conservative activists helped put school sex ed on the national stage: Reverend Billy James Hargis and his Christian Crusade and the John Birch Society, which published pamphlets and hosted radio shows and cross-promoted each other's work (Irvine 44). In a pamphlet that Drake wrote for Hargis, which explicitly attacked school sex ed, Drake warned, "[if] the new morality is affirmed, our children will become easy targets for Marxism and other amoral, nihilistic philosophies—as well as V.D.!" (Irvine 51)

These moral panics emphasized communism and depravity as real threats that were all linked to sex education. And, again, they participated in folkloric discourse that draws on urban legends, with one Anaheim activist who opposed the school sex ed program recalling, thirty years after the fact, that "It got so wild that one teacher even went so far as to have intercourse in front of her class" (in Irvine 55). I guarantee that this did not happen, but rather, circulated as a legend. And yet, fearful people ate it up and asked for more.

The intense school board debates that started in Anaheim spread all over the U.S., with the result that "the sex education controversies of the late 1960s were crucial events in the development of the religious right" (Moran 186). Concern (however inflated or false) over the apparently semi-pornographic teachings in normal sex ed curricula united Catholics, who had always skewed somewhat conservative on these issues, with evangelicals who had not necessarily been super involved in politics.

As with other events in the history of sex ed, this is a bit ironic: the vitriolic attacks on SIECUS-style sex ed seem to have missed the fact that the norm in sex education of the day was to condemn teen pregnancies, homosexuality, and other forms of non-normative sexual behavior (Moran 186). I cannot stress enough for modern readers just how old-school and conventional the sex ed of the past few decades was, in contrast to how it was painted as this new and majorly harmful thing.

The 1970s thus saw the entrance of sex education into the sphere of public debate more than ever. There were still some unresolved issues, like how to address the fact that we queer people exist (remember, the Stonewall rebellion happened in 1969, since gay and trans folk were sick of the police preying on them and jailing them for the crime of being not-straight and worse, doing so semi-publicly).

In the 1970s, we also saw the first glimmers of the moral panic over the "epidemic" of teen pregnancies, even though it wasn't really an epidemic and it required some massaging of the numbers to reach that conclusion. This becomes a bigger deal in the 1980s, but between teen pregnancies, the passage of Roe v. Wade legalizing abortion in 1973, and advancements by both the feminist and LGBTQ+ movements, the stage was set for some (more) serious conservative backlash to anything and everything that seemed inappropriately sexual.

And that, of course, included school sex ed, which will morph to include the idea of abstinence-only sex education, as we'll see in the next chapter.

References:

Irvine, Janice M. *Talk About Sex: The Battles Over Sex Education in the United States.* University of California Press, 2004.

Knowles, Jon. *How Sex Got Screwed Up: The Ghosts That Haunt*

Our Sexual Pleasure. Book Two, from Victoria to Our Own Time. Vernon Press, 2019.

Lord, Alexandra M. *Condom Nation: The U. S. Government's Sex Education Campaign from World War I to the Internet.* Johns Hopkins University Press, 2009.

Luker, Kristin. *When Sex Goes to School: Warring Views on Sex-- And Sex Education--Since the Sixties.* 1st ed., W.W. Norton, 2006.

Moran, Jeffrey P. *Teaching Sex: The Shaping of Adolescence in the 20th Century.* Harvard University Press, 2000.

THE 1980S AND THE RISE OF
ABSTINENCE-ONLY SEX ED

THE 80S WERE responsible for more than MTV and the GameBoy: that decade saw the creation of abstinence-only sex education, which is still a hot mess for many disturbing reasons.

Recall that in the late 1960s and in the 1970s, there was beginning to be a conservative backlash to some of the sexual freedoms that came after World War II, some of which were spurred by the discovery that penicillin could cure the once-feared STIs syphilis and gonorrhea, some of which came about in response to the freer gender roles women had enjoyed in the workplace while men were overseas fighting. The hippie generation was doing its free love thing, while various countercultures united to stick it to the man.

Again, sex ed was not necessarily controversial for much of the 1960s, 70s, and 80s. In *Condom Nation*, Alexandra Lord observes: "In 1988, over 80 percent of Americans believed that school should teach sex education, while over 93 percent of

American schools provided this type of education" (165). Then, everything changed when the Fire Nation attacked. Wait, wrong catastrophe.

The people who believed—and who derived power from others believing—that gender roles were strict and natural, that sex anywhere outside marriage was bad, and that homo-sexuality/abortion/whatever-deviant-thing was bad found each other and built coalitions. This was the birth of the Christian Right, or the Conservative Right, or Religious Right, or whatever you want to call them.

Reagan was in power, if that gives you any idea of where this is going: not fun places.

The theme that united the Christian Right and spurred them to activism was chastity: not having sex until marriage (which would lessen that dreaded and inflated teen pregnancy rate), not having sex if you're going to get an abortion (which would lessen the oh-no-now-it's-legal abortion rate), and certainly not having any sort of gay sex (which would prevent you from being a total sinner and also ostensibly protect against HIV, which was about to enter the scene).

This multi-stranded emphasis on the significance, nay, the indispensable essentialness of chastity, led to the 1981 passage of the Adolescent Family Life Act (AFLA) that funded multiple nationwide sex education programs...but only the ones that taught abstinence as the sole strategy for, well, pretty much everything. The AFLA also denied funds to programs that provided abortion counseling or abortions (Moran 204).

We are going to backtrack to the 1970s real quick: there was a 1975 statistic from the Guttmacher Institute (which I usually view as an ally to reproductive rights, but dang, they sure messed up here) stating that there were a million pregnant teenagers a year. This seemed like a huge number at the time and caused a lot of alarm.

However, this was misleading: it included the eldest of the teens, nineteen-year-olds who were also married, along with younger teens (Irvine 109). And, as with many issues in America, it was also not-so-subtly about race, since the birth rates among non-married women were increasing among white women specifically (Irvine 109). It's a weird hill to die on, but a lot of Americans totally freaked out about how white girls were mimicking the behavior of those apparently more degenerate/deviant people of color.

In fact, rates of teen pregnancies would fall in the 1980s and 1990s (Irving 110), and there's also evidence to show that being a teen mother was not the absolute worst life-ending disaster in the world. There's an article by Arline Geronimus I love to assign because it unpacks this assumption, citing numerous studies that do not find "large, negative consequences" to teen pregnancy (883).

What's more, Geronimus found that among African-American teenagers who gave birth, they had better outcomes in infant health and mortality than their older peers. These fertility-timing norms, while not accepted by the mainstream, work within this group in part due to extended multi-generational family support systems...which, Geronimus is clear and I want to be clear about too, are reactions to the deprivations white supremacy has forced upon Black Americans. And it is pretty crappy to enslave a population, then free them but force them to continue living under Jim Crow conditions, and then blame them for their adaptive strategies therein.

The other issue with framing teen mothers as an epidemic is that this framing completely ignores the role of the fathers;

one analysis from the 1980s showed that "men over the age of twenty were responsible for impregnating about 70 percent of all teenage mothers and about 60 percent of all 'school-age' mothers (conservatively defined as under nineteen years of age)" and that similar figures are true for the transmission of STIs to teenage women (Moran 224). Ignoring the gross power imbalance implicit in these numbers for the moment...

Naw, nevermind, let's go there. How wrongheaded is it to give all this federal funding to tell teens to abstain from sex when it's the adults in their lives who are making those decisions and getting away with them, without being blamed for them as well?! It is unlikely that these are all very egalitarian relationships, since adults generally have more power than teens in this culture. I would argue that once again, American policy makers either ignorantly or willfully ignored the real perpetuators of the problem here: adult men. But sure, it's convenient to blame horny teens for all your country's problems.

Again, I am seeing some Progressive Era parallels here: a century ago, there was this focus on keeping (white) women pure and making alcohol illegal rather than holding men to higher standards of behavior. Fun times.

So the teen pregnancy epidemic wasn't really an epidemic at all, just thinly veiled racism and some weird number mushing. But you can't put a moral panic back into its box once it's...sprung? Panicked? Not sure which verb to use there. The point is, the specter of teen pregnancy has haunted us for decades now, forcing increasingly bizarre policies onto the American people.

I also have to briefly mention the global gag rule, which went into effect in 1984 and denies organizations working outside the U.S. access to U.S. financial assistance even if they so much as mention abortion as a thing or provide referrals to clinics that perform abortions. One common misconception is that it prevents U.S. taxpayer money from going to abortions, but that's not true, since the Helms Act already forbade it.

Once again, this is all very Progressive Era, except the U.S. started tossing its weight around and telling women in *other* countries that merely accessing or disseminating information about abortion would not be tolerated (if the organizations serving those women wanted some sweet U.S. financial assistance). The global gag rule has gone through some repeal and then return phases; I believe it is currently in the off position thanks to President Biden.

The other major social issue to mention here is HIV/AIDS, which was initially documented in 1981 and nicknamed GRID (for Gay Related Immune Deficiency). There's good HIV/AIDS education available now online so if what I write next is new to you, please utilize it: HIV/AIDS is *not* a gay men's disease, that's just where it first was noticed.

Sex educators began discussing HIV/AIDS as early as 1985 just to assess the general level of knowledge about it, but soon, public health officials were like "oh crap, we'd better be proactive about this, given that sexual contact transmits this and teens are notoriously sexual" (not an actual quote from anyone, just me facetiously paraphrasing on a very serious topic).

Also, why was this just being talked about as late as 1985? Because the Reagan administration silenced then-surgeon-general C. Everett Koop, forbidding him from speaking publicly about HIV/AIDS (Lord 140). In case you are wondering just how complicit the U.S. government was in straight-up letting people die of HIV/AIDS.

A couple of problems impeded HIV / AIDS education from becoming a serious part of comprehensive sex ed, though. For one thing, it just reinforced old and not-great attitudes about sex that have plagued Americans for centuries: that sex is dangerous and immoral, for example (which was very much how earlier STIs/venereal diseases were framed). Moran points out the trends in HIV / AIDS responses:

AIDS locked sex education even tighter into the instrumentalist model; it solidified the dominance of danger and disease in thinking about adolescent sexuality; and it reinforced the American faith in the schools as a tool for social reform. (205)

While I haven't used the term "instrumentalist" as much as Moran does, basically, it means that sex ed is a tool for achieving social change. Which, sure, it can be...but as I plan to talk about in the concluding chapters, sex education can—and should—be liberation. It should help us understand ourselves on multiple levels (biological, social, emotional, possibly even spiritual), not lock us into rigid little roles. And early HIV / AIDS education followed some of the older and more conservative models of sex ed rather than transforming the conversation as much as it could have.

Another barrier to HIV / AIDS sex ed being truly transformative was, you guessed it, the Christian Right. Congress would allocate money for education and Reagan would cut it, while George H.W. Bush defunded programs seeking to understand teenage sexual behavior (Moran 207-08). The CDC (Centers for Disease Control and Prevention) managed to control a chunk of the budget, but even that was a mixed bag. Most states required sex ed by 1990, and all fifty mandated some form of HIV / AIDS education in schools (Moran 208), but of course there was no agreement on what that education might look like, and in some cases, providing HIV / AIDS education directly conflicted with the abstinence-only education guidelines available in a certain state.

Moving on: the AFLA was distinct in that it not only discouraged all sexual activity, it also "expressly encouraged pregnant women to carry the fetus to term and give the child up for adoption" and "mandated that to qualify for funding, programs involve religious groups" (Irvine 92-93). Somehow, this was not seen as violation of the separation of church and state.

The religious stuff is, you guessed it, one of the problematic aspects of abstinence-only education. And there are more.

And here is where I get a bit ranty, and I'm not going to apologize for that, but I do want to clarify: I am against abstinence-only sex ed as an institution, not against abstinence as a personal choice. I fully support everyone's right to know that abstinence is an option, and to exercise that option as they desire.

The entire concept of abstinence-only sex ed is based in "a moral framework that derives from a particular interpretation of biblical and contemporary Christian texts" (Kendall 4). From there, we can observe a few central tenets, like the privileging of heterosexuality and strict gender norms.

In Nancy Kendall's excellent ethnographic study *The Sex Education Debates*, she identifies a few more central components, including:

The idea that the nuclear family is the basic unit of identity, community, and nation, that the male is the head of the family and adults have authority over children, that these hierarchies are biblically ordained and necessary to the social order, that sex is a sacred act that should be kept private and within marriage, that sex that occurs outside of marriage is socially destructive, and that when sinful behavior is widespread, the sinner, society, and nation all suffer. (5)

Does this sound familiar? It should. *cough* *Comstock and early 20th century moral panics about sexual deviance spoiling children and the (white) nation* *cough*

As Kendall observed in her research (and yes, she was doing fieldwork and writing in the early 2000s, not the 1980s, but most abstinence-only education has used the same tools and tactics for the last few decades), these lesson plans tend to rely on the gender binary...and they also teach lies. Class materials from Florida's "It's Great to Wait" program asserted that HIV was rare in the U.S. while HPV was super widespread and wouldn't be contained by condom use (37-38). And while technically, yeah, HPV is more transmitted by skin-to-skin contact than bodily fluids as with HIV, it's also incorrect to say condoms don't work to help at all.

If you are noticing this weird counterpart to the justifiable "um, let's educate people about HIV/AIDS ASAP!" fuss when it comes to HPV, yeah, that was a thing for a while in the 1980s. Granted, HPV can lead to cervical cancer when undetected and untreated...but focusing solely on that and not other STIs, or solely on that and not the significant mental health challenges teens face, seems a bit myopic.

Kendall speculates, "Because HIV is quite effectively prevented through consistent and correct condom usage, it needed to be downplayed" (136). Which sounds strange—like why wouldn't we hype this up and make sure everyone knows it?!—this is in line with abstinence-only thinking: the only safe sex is (heterosexual, monogamous) married sex, so they're not about to mention the fact that unmarried sex can be made safer by following these few steps. It's simply not an option in their worldview.

Keeping with the topic of STIs, abstinence-only sex ed has some pretty chilling implications. If you only ever frame STIs as "horrifying diseases" and lean into the fear-based approach, you're facing these potential consequences:

First, that the vast majority of people will have an STI during their lifetimes; second, that most of the STIs contributing to high teen STI rates are not only fully treatable, they have no significant health consequences *if treated in a timely manner*; and third, that stigmatizing STIs and those who have them makes it harder for people to quickly and easily receive preventative care of treatment for STIs (Kendall 133, italics in original).

For these reasons and others, shame-based sex ed is no good. And it has measurable negative effects on teens.

What's worse is that abstinence-only educators teach lies in the classroom, and this just offends me on a fundamental level, since I come from a family of educators and am one myself. If you're teaching lies, you shouldn't be allowed to call yourself an educator; you are betraying your students' trust and sullying the rest of us with your misdeeds! (Yes, I feel strongly about this.)

And this isn't just a rant on my part, it's been documented and studied. In a 2004 study of abstinence-only curricula, researchers found that "over 80 percent of the curricula" studied contained "false, misleading, or distorted information about reproductive health" (Lord 182). The introduction of religious morality into public school materials can also be considered misguided and inappropriate, due to how we're supposed to have separation of church and state here in the U.S.

These so-called educators use "CDC data to claim that condoms are unreliable in preventing pregnancy and STIs, and may in fact increase these outcomes by creating a false sense of security" (Kendall 183). That is an outright lie. These so-called educators also assert that traditional families are "protective and productive in society, while alternate family structures (particularly mother-headed or gay parent homes) are socially destructive" (183). These, too, are lies, because the data doesn't back up those assertions, plus, like, there is no study showing worse social or health outcomes from having same-sex parents! That's just homophobia talking.

Among other reasons to loathe and lambast abstinence-only sex ed, it doesn't really work. One study has found that students who take a "virginity pledge" tend to delay their first sexual activity longer than the non-pledgers, but "once they were sexually active, they were equally likely to contract a sexually transmitted disease and less likely than students who had not taken such a pledge to know their STD status" (Luke 258).

Finally, abstinence-only educators actively harass sexuality researchers. William Bailey and Michael Young chronicle their experience in an article, which I'll summarize here: basically, in the early 2000s they sent out a bunch of surveys to deter-mine what abstinence educators mean when they say to abstain from sex. They listed some (potential) sexual behaviors with a request to identify which behaviors would be consid-ered as having sex. For their trouble, they were harassed at

their own university, with their academic freedom and positions threatened by outsiders. Their findings are as follows:

First, we found out that, although hundreds of millions of
dollars have been spent to teach abstinence from sexual
activity, states cannot actually indicate what it is that they
are teaching people not to do. Second, it seems that some
groups that profit, financially and otherwise, from this
conservative abstinence legislation are easily offended by
anyone suggesting that it may have a few flaws in its
implementation. (294)

This is exactly the sort of silencing of sexual research and
speech that I'll talk about in the next chapter, but let's just sit
with this for a moment: researchers who simply want to study
how abstinence-only educators use language faced threats by
said abstinence-only folks. If we can't even research a topic
without being harassed, that's a pretty bad sign.

To start wrapping up this chapter, I want to ruminate a bit
on the weird hypocrisy of how the Christian Right got super
into protesting school sex ed (and in fact these protests may
have helped birth their whole conservative coalition). Like, it's
not just me, right? It is actively weird to protest sex education
when your whole movement has some pretty public-facing
things to say about sex, yes?

Yet another irony of the Christian Right's involvement in
the sex education debates is that they apparently had a pretty
booming sex writing industry of their own (and to be clear, I
think everyone deserves a quality sex life, and I am using reli-

gious labels here because they seem to accurately identify a population that was acting in certain ways, not because I dislike Christians; I dislike hypocrites and bigots, and many of these folks were acting in those ways).

For instance, by the mid-1970s, "evangelicals had generated a boomlet in sex advice material" such as sex manuals, marital advice books, and so on (Irvine 83). The vibe seemed to be that they approved of certain sex acts (the heterosexual married kind), but there were still absolute moral truths about sex that had to be upheld, and anyone on the wrong side of these truths was an evil sinner or whatever.

So that was a strange time, and honestly, I see some parallels with the contemporary Christian Right's attitude towards sex: some of them spend *so much time* telling us how bad porn is or how women's vaginas get bent out of shape by having too much sex that it's like...you guys do realize that your anti-sex position involves talking about sex a lot?! That's one paradox I will likely never get my head around.

In another way, the 1980s were just like the early days of the Comstock Laws. Many of the anti-sex-ed folks staged attacks on the people running SIECUS (the Sexuality Information and Education Council of the United States, discussed in the previous chapter) as well as Planned Parenthood's newly formed (as of 1979) Department of Education. For instance, former president of SIECUS Debra Haffner was accused in an interview on CNN of promoting "necrophilia, bestiality, coprophilia" (Irvine 76). I didn't even know what that last term meant until looking it up on the Internet just now, and so that seems like a pretty good indication that it's not a commonly known enough thing to be taught in schools!

Just like it is kinda weird that American sex ed really got

its start due to World War I, it is kinda weird that a religious coalition gave us the dominant sex ed paradigm (in terms of federal funding, anyway) by suggesting that lots of outlandish sex things were happening...when they were not in fact happening. Folklore genres like urban legends, moral panics, and conspiracy theories buttressed the abstinence-only movement, and continue to sustain it.

And things don't really get much better from here on out. We'll wrap up the history section of the book in the next couple of chapters, but just remember, the 1980s are very much still with us in terms of their sex ed policy legacy, for better or for worse (and if you've actually read this chapter, you'll know that I fall on the "for worse" side of things, big sigh).

References:

Bailey, William, et al. "A Cautionary Tale About Conducting Research on Abstinence Education: How Do State Abstinence Coordinators Define 'Sexual Activity'?." *American Journal of Health Education*, vol. 33, no. 5, 2002, pp. 290–96.

Geronimus, Arline. "Damned If You Do: Culture, Identity, Privilege, and Teenage Childbearing in the United States." *Social Science & Medicine* vol. 57, 2003, pp. 881-93.

Irvine, Janice M. *Talk About Sex: The Battles Over Sex Education in the United States.* University of California Press, 2004.

Kendall, Nancy. *The Sex Education Debates.* University of Chicago Press, 2013.

Lord, Alexandra M. *Condom Nation: The U. S. Government's Sex Education Campaign from World War I to the Internet.* Johns Hopkins University Press, 2009.

Moran, Jeffrey P. *Teaching Sex: The Shaping of Adolescence in the 20th Century.* Harvard University Press, 2000.

IN WHICH WE STILL CAN'T TALK
ABOUT SEX IN THE 1990S

I WASN'T GOING to have a chapter on the 1990s since it wasn't a super eventful decade as far as sex education history goes, unless there is some conspiracy theory involving Lisa Frank Trapper Keepers I haven't heard of. But then a couple of facts caught my attention, and I thought I'd weave this into the overall narrative.

As abstinence-only sex ed continued to worm its way into schools across the U.S., and as pop culture got sexier than ever before (does anyone else remember watching some of those music videos on MTV?!), there was also an institutional silencing of sexuality conversations that had a chilling effect.

First, the U.S. government adopted the "Don't Ask, Don't Tell" policy in the early 1990s, allowing non-straight people to serve in the armed forces if they remained closeted. This was an extension and clarification of an earlier policy basically forbidding LGBTQ+ people from being in the military, and while yeah, it might seem like an improvement from an outright ban, requiring people to be in the closet is still not great (the ban was lifted in 2011, but the question of transgender people in the military remains unclear).

In a related move, in 1996 Congress passed the "Defense of Marriage Act," which defined marriage as between one man and one woman, thereby opening the door for any given state to *not* legalize same-sex marriage (D'Emilio and Freedman 365-66). While that part just applies to states, it also impacted how federal laws could be implemented, with the result that "Veterans pensions, social security benefits, joint filing of tax returns, and the many hundreds of other entitlements that federal law provided would not extend to gay and lesbian couples" (D'Emilio and Freedman 366).

And honestly, while this might seem like it came out of nowhere, there's a pretty compelling argument that the U.S. as a nation has been absolutely obsessed with policing homosexuality for about as long as we've existed. Jennifer Terry chronicles this in her book *An American Obsession: Science, Medicine, and Homosexuality in Modern Society*, positing (and backing up with over 500 pages of evidence) that homosexuality is "symbolically central" (9) in the U.S.: it has become a defining element of our scientific, medical, social, and political discourse.

Second, Surgeon General Joycelyn Elders made a public comment about masturbation that would infamously cost her her job. It was World AIDS Day on December 1, 1994, and Elders said that masturbation "is part of human sexuality and it's a part of something that perhaps should be taught" (Lord 1). In context, yeah, trying to reach the public health goal of reducing unwanted pregnancies and STI transmission might mean destigmatizing masturbation and mentioning it as an alternative option to partnered sex.

But that's not how it was interpreted. There was "a very

public outcry" over it, and within two weeks, Elders was forced to resign (Lord 176). I have to imagine that she was targeted in part because of her identity as a Black woman; she was also the first African American and the second woman to serve as surgeon general, like, ever.

Finally—and this is somewhat minor news compared to my previous two examples, but still indicative of enough people's attitudes during this time period—in 1990 there was supposed to be a survey on Americans' sexual behavior. Congress apparently was all for it, so that the data could be used to guide public policy...but enough conservative outcry killed it (Lord 164-65).

Even just the suggestion that Americans briefly and candidly talk about sex for information-gathering purposes got people saying stuff like how the survey would "sway public opinion to liberalize laws regarding homosexuality, pedophilia, anal and oral sex, sex education, and teenage pregnancies" (Lord 165), in the words of one California representative. In case you were wondering why we can't have nice things.

The patterns of silencing discussed in this chapter are chilling but familiar if you've been paying attention during the previous history chapters. One would think a small but vocal minority of people insisting it's filthy and harmful to even talk about sex wouldn't get their way in a democracy, but here we are.

References:

D'Emilio, John, and Estelle B. Freedman. *Intimate Matters: A*

History of Sexuality in America. Third ed., University of Chicago Press, 2012.

Lord, Alexandra M. *Condom Nation: The U.S. Government's Sex Education Campaign from World War I to the Internet.* Johns Hopkins University Press, 2009.

Terry, Jennifer. *An American Obsession: Science, Medicine, and Homosexuality in Modern Society.* University of Chicago Press, 1999.

THE DIGITAL AGE: MORE RISK, MORE CENSORSHIP, MORE REPEATING HISTORY

Now that we're in the 21st century, sex education is…still not great or universally available? Wait, how did that happen?! Get ready for a couple of "big picture" moments in just how much we're repeating history. Here's a highlights reel before we get into the details:

- Comstock may be dead and gone, but his ideas about needing to protect innocent children from the dangers of immoral and overly visible sexualities are still around.
- The moral panic over "white slavery" is a century old, but we're still seeing a lot of conflation of adult sex work with minors being sex trafficked.
- Most STIs won't kill you or ruin your life, but we still see a lot of panicky messaging around them, especially with HPV.

How did we get here? So glad you asked!

Basically, while organizations and individuals offering comprehensive, medically-accurate, and inclusive sex ed are still fighting the good fight, conservative politicians and advocacy groups have been trying to drag us all back in time a century with them. And their victory would be a lot more impressive if I thought any of them had an accurate grasp of the historical contours of the Progressive Era that they're retracing, but I don't suspect that many of them are that knowledgeable.

We know that the general American public still supports sex education; a 2000 study conducted by the Kaiser Family Foundation "revealed that an overwhelming majority of Americans are still calling for more aggressive sex education" (Lord 187). And we know that abstinence-only sex ed continues to yield impressively bad results, with 88 percent of teens who took abstinence pledges engaging in premarital sex (Lord 189). These teens also are less likely to use condoms or seek medical care when they contract STIs, as compared to their peers who have received comprehensive sex ed (Lord 189).

This is according to data from the mid-2000s. More recently, these numbers are mostly holding true, even across different populations. One 2017 study found that among African-American adolescents, abstinence-only education was correlated with less condom use and were more likely to have unprotected sex than their peers receiving comprehensive sex ed (Shepherd et al.).

But abstinence-only sex ed keeps getting money.

As Nancy Kendall concluded in her book *The Sex Education Debates*, catering to abstinence-only sex ed is actually, like, bad for our society for a number of reasons. Among them is that the ideology underlying abstinence-only sex ed is "fundamentally oppositional to liberal democratic ideals of equality, respect for diversity, and participation in governance" (226). Which is a polite way of saying that abstinence-only sex ed is often misogynist, homophobic, and transphobic.

Plus, abstinence-only education is based on biblical ideals, with its practitioners and programming coming straight out of "the New Christian Right" (Kendall 228). I've said it before and I'll say it again: this stuff doesn't belong in public schools in the U.S. because of the (ideal-world) separation of church and state.

And—I know I talked about this two chapters ago but it bears repeating—abstinence-only sex ed teaches lies. Despite the fact that many teens will encounter STIs, and most of those STIs can be treated with medical care, abstinence-only sex ed continues to distort the facts, thereby causing irreparable harm. In one of Kendall's mid-2000 case studies, in a Wisconsin sex ed classroom, a teacher utilized slides misrepresenting the number of women who die annually from cervical cancer caused by HPV and the severity of HPV infections that for the most part "are asymptomatic and resolve without negative health effects" (97). It's almost as though the fear-based sex ed from the bad ol' days when syphilis and gonorrhea *were* super dangerous and the moralizing that accompanied it never really died out in the minds of the more conservative people in the U.S.

Even more worrisome, however, is the fact that what might be considered decent comprehensive sex ed continues to fall short in multiple ways. As Kendall points out, it's more inclusive and democratic-leaning in theory, but many lesson plans and models continue to assume that all students are "white, middle-class, straight, rational individual decision-makers who had the right and the responsibility to control their environment and their sexual encounters" (229). LGBTQ+ people are still rarely mentioned in mainstream sex ed materials, and that was before the swath of "don't say gay" bills debated or passed in the early 2020s.

It's really disheartening to realize that comprehensive sex ed, which is in theory medically accurate and inclusive, can perpetuate stereotypes about gender and sexual minorities. It can overemphasize the rational decision-making part of sex, which can end up coming off as victim-blamey to people who have been sexually assaulted.

This is indicative of a more general cultural trend, in which patterned attitudes from previous years continue to stay with us. As John D'Emilio and Estelle Freedman observe in one of the new chapters that closes the third edition of their history of sex in the U.S., our society remains sharply divided along gender lines. Among other pieces of evidence, "Pregnancy prevention still remained women's responsibility" and every insurance company covered Viagra over ten years before they would be forced to cover birth control (383). And don't even get me started on the orgasm gap (the phenomenon whereby heterosexual women report far fewer orgasms than hetero-sexual men).

What *is* new? Technology. The digital age has opened up a lot of new avenues for conversation and communication, for folklore transmission, and for people to connect. In some ways, this is amazing and revolutionary: "Lesbian and gay teenagers have been able to explore the meaning of their sexual desires through the relative anonymity of the internet, while transgender activists have effectively used the web to overcome isolation and disseminate their views" (D'Emilio and Freedman 386). In the decade since D'Emilio and Freed-man's update to their book, the internet has continued to help plenty of alternative gender/sexuality folks find one another, from those pioneering neo-pronouns to...more than I can feasibly ennumerate, really (also I ran through a small list of gender and sexual minorities in my head but didn't want to sound like I was conflating any of them, so, no list for us).

What sex educators should truly be focusing on, in this moment of ever-increasing access to technology, is teaching digital literacy skills. Gasp, right? Shocker! But even getting this kind of lesson plan past parents and school boards can be tough, and despite the ever-present arguments about how parents should be the ones handling their own children's sex ed, they rarely do, thanks to shame and a variety of other social factors.

As Al Vernacchio writes, "electronic communication and social media are undoubtedly changing the ways kids talk to one another about sex, fall in and out of love, even how they argue" (210). This extends to topics like sexting, watching porn on the internet, and more.

When I ask my college students about the type and quality of sex education they received, some of them (like me) received decent sex ed that provided some accurate and helpful information, and at the very least, wasn't actively harmful for them. The majority of my students received some form of abstinence-only sex ed and recall the shaming messages they heard, and sometimes internalized. So it's still not great out there.

But, back to the internet! Where people are connecting, there's often an avenue where sexually active adults will want to do their thing. Which is fine, but yes, it raises questions of how to make sure the adult content stays, well, among adults.

I get that this is what laws like FOSTA and SESTA are meant to protect against, but, shocker, even porn stars don't think kids should be watching porn. Yeah, we'll get into that shortly.

There is precedent for saying minors shouldn't have access to obscene material on the interwebs, such as the Communications Decency Act of 1996, which basically said internet service providers and content providers were "generally not liable for content" (Cowen and Colosi 285). They should probably still block or remove stuff that violates copyright or seems offensive, but they couldn't be held responsible for content that might not be suitable for children.

Then FOSTA and SESTA were passed in 2018. SESTA stands for Stop Enabling Sex Traffickers Act and FOSTA stands for Fight Online Sex Trafficking Act. Sounds like a good idea in theory, right? If that was the primary effect of the laws, sure...instead, they "explicitly extended liability for criminal prosecution to online platforms by removing their safe harbour immunities as common carriers" (Cowen and Colosi 286). This has had a ton of consequences, like shutting down websites such as Backpage where adult sex workers were able to connect with clients in a fashion that offered them much more protection than doing so on street corners. This also led to Tumblr's demise.

Are these new laws actually helping to do what they say on the label? Not really. One master's thesis on the subject reports that "the evidence is inconclusive that FOSTA actually helped trafficking victims" (Mantle 20). In fact, service providers who might have previously reported suspicious-looking interactions to law enforcement may fail to do so, rightly fearing "civil or criminal liability for having failed to immediately shut down part or all of their platforms upon discovering the illegal activity" (21). Another legal analysis submits that "though the stated purpose of FOSTA was to reduce trafficking, the legal effects do not in fact contribute to a reduction in trafficking and may even make it more difficult to identify traffickers and find trafficking survivors" (Albert et al. 1091).

Another side effect, however unintentional (though in cynical moments, I think these politicians aren't apathetic to sex workers and might actively want to punish them for having sex outside the boundaries of conventional morality, and what's more, making money from it), is that sex workers are being negatively impacted by these laws. Numerous sex workers report that now that they can't advertise safely online, they are being forced back into unsafe situations with pimps, or are having more violent encounters with law enforcement (summarized in Cowen and Colosi 294).

Yes, laws meant to save sex trafficking victims are making those engaging in sex work less safe. And I'm not the only one noticing the irony here: "Ironically, FOSTA/SESTA may effectively turn consensual sex workers into sex trafficking victims by forcing them to turn to pimps for managing the complexities of the sex trade without the benefit of online platforms" (Mantle 23).

And all this is leading to increased state surveillance, which, as we've established in previous chapters, does not usually bode well for marginalized people. As Musto and colleagues summarize the problem,

---

An overarching critique of anti-trafficking efforts tied to the criminal legal system

is that it transforms seemingly protective laws into a gendered and racialized pipeline to criminal legal system involvement, a trend that expands the criminalization of youth and adults who trade sex, irrespective of whether they self-identify as "trafficked" or not, while enhancing law enforcement authority to surveil and control groups deemed "at risk."

But that's not the angle that is being covered in the main-stream news. If anything, the fact that adult content creators and adult industry folks are vocally being like "Um, no, we have pretty much always guarded our content and communities to make sure no child is being sexually involved" is pissing off the conservative folks even more and making their attacks harsher (in my reading of the situation, anyway). Before it was shut down, "Backpage was able to supply evidence used to prosecute bad actors such as human traffickers when it was in operation" (Cowen and Colosi 296). So why shut it down, if not for pure moral rage and vindictiveness with maybe a sprinkling of ignorance?

Further, the First Amendment implications of FOSTA/SESTA are chilling. People who engage in legal forms of work that are sexuality-adjacent—like us sex educators—sometimes get our content taken down or banned for seeming too sexy, since now the internet providers don't want to be liable in case we turn out to be secretly doing illegal things or whatever.

This sets a really bad precedent for another sexuality-adjacent field too: pornography. As noted by Jennifer Musto and her colleagues, "Just as networked anti-trafficking predates FOSTA/SESTA, the law presaged and created the ideological and sociotechnical blueprint for more recent platform and payment processer responses to sexual humanitarian efforts framed as anti-trafficking measures—anti-porn efforts, for instance." PornHub is being targeted now too, though from what I understand, the porn industry makes an effort to self-regulate in a variety of ways and does not for the most part encourage or allow child sexual abuse to be filmed or disseminated, because nobody wants that kind of jail time.

It's all a huge tangle. And for our purposes—wrapping up this history of sex education in the U.S.—it's reflective of past trends, while also shaping our future. Because there are wonderful sex education sites out there, like Scarleteen, that may someday be threatened if these laws continue their scope creep, thereby depriving teens of comprehensive and inclusive sex ed that they're not receiving elsewhere.

The prospects for sex ed in the U.S. remain muddled and murky, in my opinion. As I write this chapter (in the summer of 2023), a library down the road from me is removing YA (Young Adult) novels from the YA shelves. One of the Hamilton County libraries removed John Green's *The Fault in Our Stars* from YA shelves, spurring Green to take to the internet to protest this kind of blatant censorship of his work. The issue is gaining traction, and it seems (for now) that censorship won't win.

Unfortunately, the ways we legislate and regulate sexuality remain deeply tied to centuries-old attitudes of fear and judgment around sexuality. We can change and challenge laws all day long, but if we still have a large chunk of the population believing sex-negative things, our overall culture won't change.

So as I wrap up this chapter and indeed this whole history section, we should consider just how much of the past is still with us: the fear-mongering about STIs, the assumption that teens must be protected from any and all sexual topics at every cost, and the mishandling of federal laws and resources to enable censorship while throwing marginalized people under the bus. Our ideas about sex ed are still more about what adults think than what kids need, and until we learn to reframe, and until we learn some lessons from our history, I worry that we're doomed to keep repeating these mistakes.

References:

Albert, Kendra, et al. "FOSTA in Legal Context." *Columbia Human Rights Law Review* vol. 52, no. 3, 2021, 1084-1158.

Cowen, Nick, and Rachela Colosi. "Sex Work and Online Platforms: What Should Regulation Do?" *Journal of Entrepreneurship and Public Policy*, vol. 10, no. 2, 2021, pp. 284–303.

D'Emilio, John, and Estelle B. Freedman. *Intimate Matters: A History of Sexuality in America*. Third ed., University of Chicago Press, 2012.

Lord, Alexandra M. *Condom Nation: The U. S. Government's Sex Education Campaign from World War I to the Internet*. Johns Hopkins University Press, 2009.

Mantle, Desmond, "Sex, Money, and Free Speech: The Many Harms of FOSTA/SESTA" (2022). *CMC Senior Theses*. 3170.

Musto, Jennifer, et al. "Anti-Trafficking in the Time of FOSTA/SESTA: Networked Moral Gentrification and Sexual Humanitarian Creep." *Social Sciences*, vol. 10, no. 2, Feb. 2021.

Shepherd, Lindsay M, et al. "Comparison of Comprehensive

and Abstinence-Only Sexuality Education in Young African American Adolescents." *Journal of Adolescence*, vol. 61, 2017, pp. 50–63.

Tripp, Heidi. "All Sex Workers Deserve Protection: How FOSTA/SESTA Overlooks Consensual Sex Workers in an Attempt to Protect Sex Trafficking Victims," Penn State Law Review: Vol. 124: Iss. 1, Article 6, 2019.

Vernacchio, Al, with Brooke Lea Foster. *For Goodness Sex: Changing the Way We Talk to Teens about Sexuality, Values, and Health*. Harper Wave, 2014.

TABOO TOPICS

BINARY GENDER IS A FICTION

NO MATTER WHAT YOUR GOD SAYS

A LOT of my PhD coursework was in gender studies. This qualifies me to say that binary gender—the idea that there's men and women and that's it in the world—is bullshit. While this chapter takes aim at the idea of binary gender as often parsed through religious viewpoints, it's not inherently anti-religious; I don't think religions or their believers all have to be bigoted and narrow-minded about gender. In other words, if you feel targeted by what's going on in this chapter, maybe you should examine why you're so attached to an imaginary binary in the first place.

Oh, I should briefly define gender. Let's go with sex educator Heather Corinna's definition:

... a man-made set of concepts and ideas about how men and women are supposed to look, act, relate and interrelate, based on their sex. Gender isn't anatomical: it's intellectual, psychological and social (and even optional); it's about identity, roles and status based on ideas about sex and what it means to different people and groups. (74)

Gender is often mapped onto sex (one's biological/anatomical traits like chromosomes, anatomy, hormones, and secondary sex characteristics) as though they exist in a one-to-one relationship. But they don't always.

Culturally, gender feels very real. And people's experiences of it are real. But gender is a cultural construction. It varies between societies, regions, and eras. There's very little about gender that's universal, except maybe for people with wombs being more likely to be considered potential mothers, and super generic stuff like that.

But specifically, the idea that gender only exists in a binary, or a dichotomy, or a dualism...that's very Western. Many cultures have a third gender, such as the hijras of India. The Navajo recognize four (or five) genders depending on which sources you use. The list goes on and on.

The other way of evaluating whether the gender binary exists is to ask biology. While I'd urge you to read the work of scholars like Anne Fausto-Sterling, I can also briefly sum up some of her research here:

- The Intersex Society of America defines intersex as a "variety of conditions in which a person is born with a reproductive or sexual anatomy that doesn't seem to fit the typical definitions of female or male. For example, a person might be born appearing to be female on the outside, but having mostly male-typical anatomy on the inside. Or a person may be born with genitals that seem to be in-between the usual male and female types—for example, a girl may be born with a noticeably large clitoris, or lacking a vaginal opening, or a boy may be born with a notably small penis, or with a scrotum that is divided so that it has formed more like labia. Or a person may be born with mosaic genetics, so that some of her cells have XX chromosomes and some of them have XY."

- Some estimates suggest that between .01-02% of Americans are intersex, while Fausto-Sterling estimates that it might be as high as 1.7% of the population.
- There are real human rights violations with how intersex people are treated in society, including problems with attempts to "normalize" anatomy that deviates from the binary by undertaking nonconsensual genital surgeries on infants, for example.

So, no, the gender binary is NOT upheld in the scientific record. Most people's bodies do appear to conform to a binary of sorts, but even within male or female bodies there is a giant amount of variation: in hormone levels, in size (of primary and secondary sex characteristics like breasts and facial or body hair), and so on. Assigning people to the binary of either male or female is a flawed enterprise from the start. I certainly don't want my conformity to femaleness or femininity measured by the size of my breasts, the lack of hair in "unac-ceptable" places on my body, or other traits that I apparently should or should not have. At the same time, I follow many feminist scholars in asserting that gender isn't 100% culturally constructed, and we're still coming to understand just how much of gender and sex are biologically determined vs. socially programmed… but that statement doesn't conflict with gender not being a rigid binary.

Religiously? I get that most creation myths—a prevalent form of narrative folklore—are about the creation of humankind, specifically in the forms of man and woman. So perhaps it feels like a bit of a betrayal to learn that there are other kinds of humans out there, who don't identify as male or female, or who have physiological traits of both or neither, or who started as one and ended up as the other.

Someone told me that humans are made in the image of God, and God doesn't make mistakes, so intersex people can't exist… except in the case of sin/the devil… or something like that? As an atheist I don't believe in God or the concept of sin, and at any rate, if your religious/cultural ideas are incapable of mapping onto the empirical existence of the world around you, they seem like not-so-great tools for understanding the world (and isn't that the point of religion and culture anyway? to help us make sense of the universe around us?).

But here's the thing: if you use any technology whatsoever, you've got to give my line of thinking a chance. If you're reading this book chapter on a screen of some kind, or you happen to enjoy electricity and cars, those things were brought to you by the scientific method, and technological experimentation/innovation. Those same exact processes have brought us a more nuanced understanding of gender and sex at both the cultural and biological levels, and it'd be disingenuous to enjoy your smartphone while discounting the information brought to us by the scientific method about other facets of life.

At this point? It's not relevant if you believe people are made in the image of your deity/God, because gender and sexual variance is a part of humanity. It always has been and always will be. If you're refusing to acknowledge this, you're going counter to a body of information that runs parallel to other important medical, historical, and technological innovations that have been crucial to modernity. Which, I mean, I guess you could do. But it really doesn't make any sense to me.

References:

Corinna, Heather. *S.E.X.: The All-You-Need-To-Know Progressive Sexuality Guide to Get You through High School and College.* Marlowe, 2007.

Fausto-Sterling, Anne. *Sexing the Body: Gender Politics and the Construction of Sexuality.* Second edition., Basic Books, 2020.

"What Is Intersex?" *Intersex Society of North America,* https://isna.org/faq/what_is_intersex/. Accessed 4 September 2023.

PORN IS NOT A PUBLIC HEALTH CRISIS

SAYS SCIENCE

NEWSFLASH: maybe instead of demonizing someone's private experience of sexuality, we should be worrying about other things right now.

The 2016 GOP platform declared porn a "public health crisis" (yep, just Google it, plenty of articles from 2016 will come up) and while that's not even the most problematic thing on there, it's the one that sparked some ideas for me.

Basically, as the peer-reviewed studies are beginning to roll in, we're finding that porn use is unrelated to risky sex practices, to misogyny, to supposed "porn addiction," and to erectile dysfunction (for this last point, see Prause and Binnie). Which is what sex educators and researchers have been shouting for years, but I guess some people think porn is just too convenient to have a sex-negative scapegoat to point at.

Here's the thing: the science doesn't care if you like or dislike porn. It's still not addictive. I may not be that into porn myself, but I defend its existence as free speech, even as I acknowledge there might be some problems with it. Like yeah, it can promote unrealistic beauty standards as well as unrealistic expectations about how quickly a plumber will arrive at your house. Yes, we should talk about fair labor practices in the adult film industry, and yes, there are probably still some misogynist, racist, homophobic, and transphobic depictions happening (in general, though, adult content creators are adults, and they generally have an incentive to make their corner of the workplace a nice and ethical one, so I see no reason for outsiders to police them).

Porn is definitely not meant for kids, and it shouldn't serve as a stand-in for sex education. As my sex ed colleague Reid Mihalko says, trying to learn to have sex by watching porn is like trying to learn to drive by watching *The Fast and the Furious*. In other words, we shouldn't conflate entertainment with education!

...but porn as a public health crisis? Give me a break. This is as ridiculous as politicians and religious leaders taking a stand against dildos...oh wait, except that happened too, as when Texas had an obscenity law that made the sale of sex toys illegal.

Let's dig into some of the research...and the weird, icky vibes surrounding it.

First, to talk about porn as a public health crisis we have to talk about porn addiction, which is adjacent to the idea of sex addiction. This emerged in the 1980s, but in multiple literature reviews, it was not found to be supported by enough empirical data to be considered an actual diagnosis (Hall).

The American Association of Sexuality Educators, Counselors and Therapists (AASECT for short) has published a position paper affirming that there is not "sufficient empirical evidence to support the classification of sex addiction or porn addiction as a mental health disorder." The APA (American

Psychological Association) does not recognize porn or sex addiction in the current edition of the DSM (the Diagnostic and Statistical Manual of Mental Disorders). So if the two major players on the scholarly field don't think this is a thing, why do so many individuals believe in it?

Clearly, someone can experience their sexual desires and behaviors as problematic, compulsive, and/or disordered. But does that subjective experience line up with what is technically an addiction?

So far, it looks like no.

Nicole Prause is among the scholars working in this field, and she concludes based on the existing scholarship, "Neuroscience reviews also concluded that sexual behaviors currently are not accurately characterized as addictive" (2270). Prause uses EEGs and other tools to see what's actually happening in people's brains when they watch porn and/or masturbate, noticing that people (mostly men) who consider themselves hypersexual and/or porn addicted can achieve orgasm from mental fantasy alone, which addiction models would consider impossible due to the absence of the supposedly-addictive item (2271).

Is there a way to prove that porn is addictive? Also no. Prause notes: "No randomized, controlled trials for sex or VSS [visual sexual stimuli, a.k.a. porn] addiction exist" (2271). This is made all the more problematic when therapists claim to be able to treat it, often to the tune of hefty dollar signs. Another relevant finding, in another article by Prause (coauthored with Timothy Fong), is that in an addiction model we'd expect a tolerance component. But in regard to viewing porn, "evidence indicates that those who believe they have a problem with their VSS use actually exhibit higher sexual arousal in response to the same VSS viewed by others" (436). In other words, subjectively reporting that one has a problematic relationship with porn doesn't yield the kind of evidence that would show one has built up the kind of tolerance expected in an addiction situation.

Again, a person could definitely experience their use of pornography or other sexual materials as challenging or problematic. That's one reason I like the out of control sexual behavior model developed by Douglas Braun-Harvey and Michael Vigorito: it's not an addiction-based model and it offers sex-positive tools to address unhappy-making behaviors beyond just, like, going cold turkey (this book and others are discussed in the excellent guest blog post series that my therapist colleague Lucie Fielding wrote for me a few years ago, linked in my references section).

Now that I've mentioned the idea of having to fully quit a substance to free oneself of addiction to it (or go "cold turkey" on it, to use an amusing folkspeech term), that's another reason why sex addiction just isn't a thing: a person could quit an addictive substance like alcohol, and reasonably have a shot at living their lives without it. But how does one quit human intimacy and/or sexuality? It doesn't make any sense.

But wait, there's more: both porn addiction and sex addiction are considered to fall under the general header of hypersexuality...which is also ill-defined. Scholars disagree on what constitutes hypersexual behaviors and how these things work: more like a compulsion, or more like a substance addiction (de Alarcón et al.)? It's pretty unclear.

Oh, and then there's supposedly reverse porn addiction. Porn addiction is a sketchy concept... but to try to flip it and shame women who like being looked at? Nope. That's a whole bag of nopes.

I was, you might imagine, pretty shocked to find out that

this was a thing. I first saw it on a blog, Life Over Coffee, wherein author Rick Thomas defines it as when "a person intentionally attempts to lure the gaze of another person through physical manipulation, either by what he/she is wearing or by how he/she looks." But don't be fooled by the gender-neutral language here.

This (supposedly) applies to women who get "addicted" to the sensation of others looking at and admiring them. There's also a bunch of religious mumbo-jumbo about lust and visual adultery and... it just falls apart from there.

Obviously this concept isn't going to resonate with me because it's inflected with a lot of Christian language that I find off-putting, but also, let's recall that porn addiction and sex addiction aren't real things.

So if porn addiction may not exist in the first place, why on earth would backward porn addiction be a thing? And why would that phrase have the word "porn" in it when it's not actually related to making or viewing porn? The implication is that a woman showing any amount of skin, or trying to look sexy for someone's gaze, is pornographic. *But it's not.* Porn is notoriously difficult to define, but a person wearing kinda-sexy clothing in a context where they're not engaging in sexual acts for a viewer or camera just doesn't strike me as being pornographic...unless, of course, you're coming from a twisted perspective that labels women's bodies as always already sexual.

And I think that's exactly what is happening here. Some people are so intent on controlling women that they'll invent terms and diagnoses to keep women from feeling good about themselves, and to keep people of all genders from realizing that sex is not inherently sinful or harmful.

I know I get on this soap box a lot, but if we had decent sex education and more money going into sex research in the U.S., we'd have informed citizens who know that porn addiction is something to be looked at askance, and who know that it's okay to want to feel good about your body in both sexual and non-sexual contexts. Is it possible to go to extremes with these behaviors? Of course. Is it as widespread as to be considered an addiction or an epidemic? No.

So just... don't. Don't believe the hype about porn addiction, or backward porn addiction, or sex addiction more generally. Do us all a favor and push back against these concepts, because they're neither scientifically valid nor useful in larger cultural conversations.

Porn isn't destroying the world; corporate greed is. And bigotry. And so on. Furthermore, framing anything sex-related as an addiction continues to participate in the rhetoric that sexuality is dangerous and must be constrained to narrow arenas, which makes it harder for us sex educators to do our jobs. If a sexual behavior is problematic because it's nonconsensual, say that. Or if it's causing someone to feel shame, say that. Don't spin falsehoods that distract from the real issues at hand, because eventually, enough people will notice and hopefully demand that we do better with our science and our advocacy.

References:

"AASECT Position on Sex Addiction." *The American Association of Sexuality Educators, Counselors and Therapists (AASECT)*, https://www.aasect.org/position-sex-addiction. Accessed 4 September 2023.

de Alarcón, Rubén, Javier I. de la Iglesia, Nerea M. Casado, and Angel L. Montejo. "Online Porn Addiction: What We Know and What We Don't—A Systematic Review." *Journal of Clinical Medicine* vol. 8, no. 1, 2019.

Fielding, Lucie. "Dreams of Black Swans: Falsifying Sex Addiction." *OnlySky*, 12 September 2016, https://onlysky. media/jjorgensen/dreams-of-black-swans-falsifying-sex-addic tion/. Accessed 9 September 2023.

Hall, Paula. "The Moral Maze of Sex & Porn Addiction." *Addictive Behaviors* vol. 123, 2021.

Prause, Nicole. "Evaluate Models of High-Frequency Sexual Behaviors Already." *Archives of Sexual Behavior*, vol. 46, 2017, pp. 2269-74.

--- and James Binnie. "Reboot/Nofap Participants Erectile Concerns Predicted by Anxiety and Not Mediated/Moderated by Pornography Viewing." *Journal of Psychosexual Health*, vol. 4, no. 4, 2022, pp. 252–54.

--- and Timothy Fong. "The Science and Politics of Sex Addiction Research." *New Views on Pornography*, edited by Lynn Comella and Shira Tarrant, Praeger, 2015, pp. 431-46.

Thomas, Rick. "Backward Porn Addiction: Drawing Attention to Yourself." *Live Over Coffee*, https://lifeovercoffee.com/back ward-porn-addiction-when-women-draw-attention-to-them selves/. Accessed 4 September 2023.

GENDER IS NOT A CRIME

WAY BACK IN 2016, I wrote a series of blog posts about how bathroom access is a public health issue that disproportionately affects women, transgender people, and other people who are agender or non-binary.

At the time, I was incensed about Indiana's Senate Bill 35, which makes "it a Class A misdemeanor if: (1) a male knowingly or intentionally enters a single sex public facility that is designed to be used by females; or (2) a female knowingly or intentionally enters a single sex public facility that is designed to be used by males."

In case you didn't know, a Class A misdemeanor means that you can be punished by spending up to one year in jail with a fine of up to $5,000.

...all for using the bathroom? This is clearly ridiculous. But that's the transphobic agenda these days, sigh.

Below is the text of a letter that I sent to my state representative about this issue. And below that, I ruminate on how these things have gone in the intervening seven years, with attention to how bills like this one have found increasing support for all the wrong (read: bigoted, fear-mongering, moral-panic-creating) reasons.

DEAR STATE REPRESENTATIVES,

I'm writing to urge you to vote against Senate Bill 35.

Mandating bathroom usage by gender disadvantages and discriminates against the following groups:

- Parents who must escort a child into a bathroom, especially when the child's sex or gender does not match that of the parent's, or does not appear to match
- Children who must escort a parent into a bathroom, especially when their sex/gender does not appear to match
- Other family members or professional caretakers who must escort a sick or disabled (in whatever way) person into a restroom
- Women who are ill, pregnant, or for whatever other reason urgently need to use a restroom when there is only a men's restroom nearby
- Men who are sick or for whatever other reason urgently need to use a restroom when there is only a women's restroom nearby
- Transgender people whose official ID does not match their gender identity
- People who do not visually conform to a given gender

This bill is based on the following faulty premises:

- That gender identity, gender expression, and biological sex all neatly line up, which multiple academic researchers have proven to not be the case
- That other people can and should become authorities of the gender of people they don't even know (because who else is going to call law enforcement on folks using the bathroom?)
- That sexual assault already being illegal is not enough of a deterrent to keep it from happening inside public bathrooms (sadly, it does happen sometimes, as in this story from earlier in 2015, but as the perpetrator was hiding inside a stall, it seems unlikely that he would've peacefully left if someone had initiated a conversation about gender with him)
- That people whose gender expression doesn't match their assigned-at-birth-gender are likely to be troublemakers and/or perpetrators of assault, sexual or not, when in reality, transgender people are far more likely to be victimized than to be the ones visiting violence against others (the Office for Victims of Crime estimates that one in every two transgender people will experience sexual assault and/or physical violence in their lifetime)

Let me strongly restate this last point: there are no cases of transgender people committing assaults in bathrooms. There are no reported cases of this happening in the U.S. None. I would think that government legislation should address existing problems, not imaginary ones, yes?

To briefly dwell on another of the above points, it is senseless to make every citizen into the gender police. Trust me, I study gender professionally, and gender is complicated enough merely on the level of how you perceive yourself, express your gender identity, and struggle with conforming to gender norms! Trying to gauge how someone else perceives you on top of all of that is endlessly complicated, and whether one person successfully passes or presents as a given gender should not be dependent on someone else's snap evaluation of them.

Speaking of passing, as many people have stated, bathroom rights ARE civil rights: it wasn't that long ago that some public restrooms were marked with "whites only signs." Further, bathroom policies can have concrete effects on transgender people, which is no surprise, as social groups suffering the effects of stigma often experience other negative impacts to their physical health and mental health. While this law is impractical to enforce and very silly in my eyes, it could also do significant damage to people who are apprehended under it. I for one do not want to see anyone have to deal with the police, or worse, go to jail or face fines, simply because they had to use a public restroom.

I'm also displeased about how the senator who proposed this bill, Jim Tomes, claims to be against big government... but what, exactly, is this bill about, if not the government taking an unseemly interest in who uses which bathrooms? Sadly, conservative legal advocacy groups exist that contact schools and lawmakers across the country to promote their policy (which is against letting transgender students use the bathroom that corresponds to their gender identity), and I can't help but wonder how much these groups have a hand in shaping local policy according to their goals, regardless of the needs of the local folks. In my decade-plus spent in Indiana,

I've met a lot of very tolerant open-minded people, and a lot of people who claim to be in favor of smaller government, so I have to wonder who, exactly, this bill serves.

Even considering this bill makes it look like Indiana's legislators care more about reinforcing arbitrary definitions of gender and waging a larger-than-local ideological war than the following problems citizens of this state face:

- The fact that Indiana already has one of the highest sexual assault rates among states in the U.S.
- How 12% of Hoosiers live in poverty and struggle to put food on the table
- The education system is being characterized as a "mess" by outsiders looking in
- It's even more ludicrous to waste time and money on this bathroom bill in light of Indiana's sexual assault rates as stated above, because the same conservative politicians trying to pass SB 35 are also responsible for laws contributing to the lack of comprehensive sex education and assault information central databases that contribute to the state's alarmingly high assault rates. Tangentially related, but worth mentioning, is how domestic violence survivors in Indiana are needing more and more help, but are unable to get it. And disturbingly, child abuse in Indiana was on the rise in 2015 … abuse which was perpetrated by caregivers and those close to children, NOT strangers they might encounter in a bathroom.

Indiana has plenty of problems with sexual assault and child abuse, but these problems require quite a different approach than an impractical law policing gender in public restrooms. I would urge the lawmakers considering this law to closely examine the other policies in place that are creating the conditions under which sexual assault and child abuse proliferate, such as poverty, lack of education (general education and sex education), and underreporting.

In sum, trying to legislate the gender of bathroom-users is absurd. I have to wonder whether the conservative groups claiming to be in favor of small government are actually walking the walk, or whether they are, as plenty of others have suggested, swept up in a nationwide backlash against transgender people gaining access to equal rights.

Do we want Indiana to be part of a shift that makes citizens into the gender police, invites the governments into bathrooms, and diverts attention from other more pressing issues that Hoosiers face? I remember how the RFRA rhetoric was starting to go, and it was nasty and bigoted. Or do we want to firmly make a statement of non-discrimination, based on empirical research about gender and culture, not giving in to fear but rather promoting evidence-based policies and tolerance? I know which side I stand on, and I entreat others to join me.

I DON'T KNOW IF MY LETTER WAS PARTICULARLY COMPELLING, BUT Senate Bill 35 did not end up passing. Instead, we got a whole bunch of other shitty legislation that year.

Now, the state legislature is back at it with a host of ridiculous bills, such as ones mandating that schools notify parents if their children decide to use a name other than their given name...which affects cisgender kids with nicknames, for instance. The entire thing is ludicrous enough to almost be funny, if these new laws weren't actively harming people.

Also, in case you're wondering why I'm including this in a book about sex education, it's because if more people received halfway decent sex ed that explained "hey, gender is more complicated than the binary" and "hey, trans people already experience a lot of exclusion and violence, maybe you have better things to do with your time than pile on", maybe we'd see fewer of these asinine bills.

But then again maybe that's me being hopelessly optimistic, since education is a tool to fight ignorance...but some people, given tools, figure out how to turn them into weapons, because it's a lot harder to eradicate hate in people's hearts than to simply check to see whether someone's learned some new facts.

AS A CISGENDER WOMAN, I GAIN NOTHING BY EXCLUDING TRANS WOMEN

You know what baffles me? The thing where cis women say stuff like "natural-born women only" or "female bodies only" or whatever. It's gone through a few iterations since I first wrote these thoughts as a blog post a few years ago, too.

What is even the point of that? Are we gonna check for XX chromosomes at the door? Do we even know if someone might be intersex, or what their hormone levels are? How many years of feminine socialization are required to make one truly a woman?

However, I know what the result of this kind of rhetoric is: the kinds of douchey, exclusionary, essentializing policies that have been levied against women for so long that you'd think we'd know better than to enforce it on others by now.

Because here's the thing: if you're worried about letting someone into a safe space who's going to mansplain and be a jerk and interject "well actually" about their own experiences all the time, derailing left and right... they'll get kicked out for being a jerk and interjecting and derailing all the time, not for having the "wrong" body for a given space.

So I'll go ahead and say it: I'm a cis woman, and a feminist, and I don't believe I gain anything by explicitly excluding trans women from women-centered spaces.

If you need a safe space for women who've had certain kinds of experiences – survivors of sexual assault, or miscarriage, or intersectional oppression – then say that. But as Julia Serano has so cogently pointed out in her book *Whipping Girl*, feminine-seeming boys receive venomous backlash, the kind of misogyny that is "normally" reserved for women. So if we're going to play the "well how much feminine conditioning have you received?" card, well, we might not like the answer. "Woman" is not a monolithic category.

There are many reasons why this kind of rhetoric has emerged and become popular, and they don't all portray us (cis, and maybe cis-het, women) in the best light.

Maybe this is just an instance where cis women have been conditioned to believe that trans women aren't women, and it's on us to change our conditioning.

Maybe cis women are so thoroughly conditioned to please others that when we get a whiff of someone having less power relative us, we're eager to seize that power and say what we will and will not allow (it's tiring to have to be nice and polite and pleasing all the time, I get it, but that doesn't mean we should be jerks as soon as there's a turnaround).

Maybe we're so used to being judged and shamed for what we wear that as soon as we get the change to enact those same standards on someone else, we go for it.

Maybe cis women are still pretty ignorant of what trans women go through to arrive at that identification. Anyone who's been through the difficult experience of questioning their gender and understanding that they're a woman despite possible contradictions from biology and/or socialization probably experiences cognitive dissonance at the reminder that they're "originally male" or "were born" male and thus wouldn't bring it up.

Remember, trans people aren't sick, the entire fucking patriarchy is. I'm not saying that to discount the suffering and lived experiences of trans people, but rather to say that the medical model is flawed and comes from a place of relative privilege. Sometime I believe that the diagnosis for gender dysphoria would look pretty different (e.g. way less pathologized/stigmatized) if we didn't place such a high importance on binary gender as one of THE defining traits of identity.

As a feminist I believe we can do better than this. Creating spaces that welcome women of all stripes – including trans women – doesn't take anything away from us. It's sad that we ever got to the point where we believed that it does.

References:

Serano, Julia. *Whipping Girl: A Transsexual Woman on Sexism and the Scapegoating of Femininity*. Seal Press, 2007.

YOU CAN'T MAKE OR UNMAKE
SOMEONE GAY, SO STOP TRYING
AND STOP FEARING US

PART of my plea for universal, comprehensive sex ed and less-shitty laws involves getting cisgender heterosexual folks to stop fearing the LGBTQ+ community. Which is weird, because some of those (totally bigoted and unfounded) fears are rooted in this idea that one's sexual orientation can suddenly change..and that is not really a thing.

If, like me, you've spent any time in Indiana, you'll know that former U.S. vice president Mike Pence is from here and is also super anti-queer, to the point of supporting conversion therapy. Conversion therapy is a form of torture that tries to change someone's sexual orientation from gay to straight, in brief. Torture was illegal and considered a universal human rights violation, last time I checked.

Newsflash: conversion therapy does not achieve its stated aims of converting people from gay to straight. But by the same token, there's (obviously) no "gay agenda," nor is there a way to MAKE someone gay. In fact, according to the American Psychological Association,

There is no consensus among scientists about the exact reasons that an individual develops a heterosexual, bisexual, gay or lesbian orientation. Although much research has examined the possible genetic, hormonal, developmental, social and cultural influences on sexual orientation, no findings have emerged that permit scientists to conclude that sexual orientation is determined by any particular factor or factors. Many think that nature and nurture both play complex roles; most people experience little or no sense of choice about their sexual orientation.

Intriguingly, it seems that there are fairly consistent levels of non-heterosexual orientation among different cultures. In all the research I've seen, the numbers are pretty consistent: less than 6% of the population has usually experienced or acted on same-sex attraction, but it's at least 1–2% of a population. The Williams Institute out of UCLA, for instance, puts the percentage of LGBTQ+ people in the U.S. at around 3.5% of the population, but higher numbers have expressed at least some same-sex attraction. As with all cross-cultural research, different languages and values make these topics difficult to pin down precisely (not to mention the difficulties in trying to study how a marginalized community publicly identifies or presents itself).

While the existence of gender and sexual diversity is pretty well a universal thing across cultures, if expressed differently in different contexts, researchers are still working to understand how much a constant these factors are in the lives of individuals. One 10-year longitudinal study found heterosexuality to be a mostly-stable identity for most participants; sexual minority women apparently experienced more fluidity in how they identified than any other category (Mock and Eibach 2011).

Is it a "kids these days" thing to have more teens than ever before identifying as non-straight? Possibly...but it's also maybe just safer now to be out than it was in the past.

Furthermore, a 2011 paper published in the *Archives of Sexual Behavior* found that there was no rapid shift in sexual orientation during adolescent years. Some folks left queer or unsure populations for the heterosexual side of things, while other folks joined in...but they were overall small shifts, with women being more likely to be more mobile in how they identified sexually than men (Ott et al.).

So, yes, sexual orientation is a tad fluid. Depending on how we measure it, the general population might at any time have between 1 and 5% of folks who don't identify as straight. That's a pretty small number still, and even if there's some flux with who belongs in it, it's not, like, an alarmingly big migration of folks in and out of this population.

Which returns me to the point of this chapter: even with the potential fluidity of sexual identity within different cultural (and generational) populations, we don't know how to predict what causes people to change how they identify. And that means we can't force it to change.

In brief: you can't un-gay us. And we can't gay you. If people are going to experience changes in sexual orientation, that'll happen due to a variety of factors that scientists haven't figured out yet, not because a library had some books featuring queer people as characters or because a sex ed class happened to mention that not being straight was a possibility. If we had better research funding and better sex education in schools, this might be more common knowledge.

But for now? I'll settle for relegating conversion therapy to the annals of shameful and unethical medical interventions. Hopefully you'll join me in recognizing the humanity of LGBTQ+ folks and speak out against it when people attempt to treat us in dehumanizing ways.

References:

"How Many People are Lesbian, Gay, Bisexual, and Transgender?" *The Williams Institute*, April 2011, https://williamsinsti tute.law.ucla.edu/publications/how-many-people-lgbt/. Accessed 4 September 2023.

Mock, Steven, and Richard Eibach. "Stability and Change in Sexual Orientation Identity Over a 10-Year Period in Adulthood." *Archives of Sexual Behavior* vol. 41, no. 3, 2011, pp. 641-48.

Ott, Miles, et al. "Stability and Change in Self-Reported Sexual Orientation Identity in Young People: Application of Mobility Metrics." Archives of Sexual Behavior vol 40, no. 3, 2011, pp. 519-32.

"Understanding Sexual Orientation and Homosexuality." *The American Psychological Association*, 2008, https://www.apa. org/topics/lgbtq/orientation. Accessed 4 September 2023.

THE CASE FOR SEX ED

INTRODUCING THE CASE FOR SEX ED

At risk of being labeled Captain Obvious, all humans deserve access to comprehensive, medically accurate, inclusive sex education.

I started writing this as a blog post series out of a sense of frustration that the state of sex education is just so bad in the U.S. today, and I continued to refine these ideas out of a sense of spite, including them here for your reading pleasure and to maybe help bolster your own ability to make these arguments.

You may not convince every person you're arguing with, but there may be others in the audience or on the periphery who are listening. Debating bigots may not change their minds since they're often too far gone down the rabbit hole of logical fallacies, but doing so informs listeners that you are not falling for the same bullshit, and you will advocate for those who are vulnerable or victimized by these kinds of situations.

Besides, framing sex ed as a public good yanks the terms of the debate away from those who believe that non-normative sex is straight-up evil. We should not cede the framing of these discussions to those who want to impose their religious beliefs on the entire population. So hand out citations like candy, and demand them in return, because even though reasonable people can disagree on a variety of details of implementation, we should be advocating for a move towards policies that benefit everyone...and that includes the people who would want to take away the options from us, ironically.

As you've no doubt gathered by now, I'm a scholar, and all of the empirical evidence points to comprehensive sex ed being beneficial. I'm an educator, and I'm offended at the bullshit that is being passed off as abstinence-only "education" in schools today. And since I had a decent sex education experience of my own, I'm full of mixed feelings—offense on their behalf, pity, and so on—for those kids who are receiving crummy, shame-based sex ed that is causing them damage now and down the line.

We can and should do better. Here are the talking points for why and how.

So read on for a series of essays that will give you more arguments and evidence to keep in your arsenal for when you fight the good sex ed fight.

COGNITIVE DISSONANCE & ABSTINENCE-ONLY EDUCATION

THE CASE FOR SEX ED PART 1

THIS FIRST CHAPTER is about the cognitive dissonance inherent in abstinence-only educational programs (not to lose sight of the fact that these programs are filled with lies and religious propaganda but are still somehow federally funded and taught in public schools!).

The cognitive dissonance I want to discuss here arises from the fear-based tactics that abstinence-only-until-marriage (henceforth AOUM) programs employ to "teach" about premarital sex. AOUM educators use biased metaphors about sexual worth, comparing a person's value to chewing gum or sticky tape (both of which get grosser the more they come into contact with). AOUM educators have tons to say about the social, psychological, and spiritual risks of premarital sex, while withholding factual information about the physical risks or potential ways to prevent specific outcomes like pregnancy and STI transmission.

However, when it comes to marital sex, apparently it's fine to introduce pleasure as a concept... just not in any great detail. As Nancy Kendall writes in her ethnography of sex education in four American school districts, "All sex before marriage in inherently dangerous and wrong, and the moral risk can never be reduced. In contrast, all talk of sex after marriage was glowing and full of pleasure; no AOUM [education] program presented any information about the risks of STI transmission or unwanted pregnancy after marriage because such discussion would be ideologically flawed" (132).

I wonder how young adults (or hell, any adults) are supposed to mentally flip on a switch that says "okay, now that I'm married it's acceptable to start learning about sex – from anatomically accurate body part names to how desire and arousal work – *but not one second earlier!*" My mind reels with the cognitive dissonance of this enormous task: suddenly, upon getting married, being faced with the need to learn *everything* there is to know about how to have a happy, healthy, and successful sex life with your spouse (because even if you learned a little bit in an AOUM program, it was a long time ago, and might be factually suspect).

I mean, that's a lot of knowledge to catch up on! As sex educators generally acknowledge, adults need more sex education, too. Kate Kenfield, one of my colleagues, asserted in a blog post that no longer exists (alas), "Adults need sex ed just as much as young people do. Sexual desires, needs, and physical functioning evolve over time and because of this, we humans need information to help us navigate those changes." She believes that it's important "to normalize the idea that adults need opportunities to expand their sexuality knowledge too."

So if people's experiences of their sexuality are constantly evolving and changing, such that even adults need sex education, what must it be like as a young adult who hasn't had *any* substantial or accurate sex ed who's now married and is expected to know the ropes? What kind of disappointment, guilt, and shame are we setting up our young adults for, when it could be so easily prevented by giving everyone evidence-based comprehensive sex ed?

For what it's worth, comprehensive sex ed isn't anti-abstinence; often, abstinence is presented as one more tool in the toolbox of sexual safety and decision making. But the way AOUM education is done is the U.S. has become a warped mockery of actual sex education: it passes off moral judgments as facts; refuses to take into account peer-reviewed scientific facts about, well, most things (including its own efficacy); and does a poor job of preparing our next generation for making informed decisions about their own sexual lives.

Let's prepare our next generation for a healthy future, and let's reframe the debate so that heterosexual monogamous reproductive sex within marriage isn't seen as the only healthy (or inevitable) outcome. Sure, it's one that many people will be drawn to, and let's support them in seeking information to make the best of their married sex lives. But let's also recognize that human sexuality is vastly diverse and richly varied, and so let's empower our young and old alike to have access to enough sexual information that they're not stuck with cognitive dissonance, shame, or any other totally preventable icky effects of living in such a sex-negative culture.

References:

Kendall, Nancy. *The Sex Education Debates*. University of Chicago Press, 2013.

A BODY-LITERATE SOCIETY

THE CASE FOR SEX ED PART 2

IN CONTINUING my series making a case for sex education, I'd like to make the point that we need sex ed in order to ensure that we live in a society where everyone knows how their bodies work. This includes anatomical functions like puberty and pregnancy, STI transmission, orgasm, and much more.

As a folklorist, I'm aware that there are narratives and beliefs informally circulating in every society that may not be scientifically accurate. This is only a problem when there's not an evidence-based program to rigorously counter these narratives (often urban legends) and beliefs. The book *Did You Hear About the Girl Who...? Contemporary Legends, Folklore, & Human Sexuality* by biologist Mariamne Whatley and folklorist Elissa Henken (which I cited heavily in the first section of this book) documents and interprets many of these folklore items which are currently in circulation.

For example, teenage and college-aged girls listed beliefs about how not to get pregnant – by urinating after sex or having sex during her period – which are patently false. Other folks listed beliefs about how one can get HIV from mosquitoes or toilet seats. Narratives about STI acquisition, the effects of masturbation, and insect infestations of vaginas also abound.

My stance as a sex educator and scholar is that we need to do better at providing accurate, shame-free sex, body, and relationship information to our fellow American citizens (and citizens of the world, really).

This is especially crucial since we live in a democracy, and our citizens vote on policies that affect all. If anyone remembers the "legitimate rape" debacle in the U.S. a few years ago, wherein Representative Todd Akin said "if it's a legitimate rape, the female body has ways to try to shut the whole thing down," then you'll understand why it's important to make sure both our voting citizens and our politicians have an accurate grasp of both the biology and the social trends around sexual violence, pregnancy, and more.

Put quite simply, I don't want to live in a world where my neighbors might think that you can get AIDS from a doorknob, or believe that only a stranger can commit rape (and further, in the Akin case, that a female body is incapable of becoming pregnant from rape). I can't campaign for the elimination of folklore, because then I'd have nothing to study, and it's not like all folklore is untrue; rather, folklore gives us amazing insights into the anxieties, fears, and hopes of people in a culture, and it's incredibly useful in that regard.

Additionally? Last time I checked, we live in a democracy. I believe that, just as voting adults should be educated about how our government works, all of us inhabiting bodies (rather than just being brains in jars I guess?) should have a decent understanding of how our bodies work. It's not like they come with a driver's manual, so that's where sex ed can step in to fill the gap in knowledge.

Our current sex education is not up to the task. As Nancy Kendall documents in her ethnographic study of sex ed in the U.S., *The Sex Education Debates*, abstinence-only classrooms tended to deemphasize the importance of condoms in preventing HIV transmission (and other STIs as well). She quotes from her fieldwork, observing an abstinence educator saying the following: "They say condoms protect you, at least physically, but actually condoms don't even do that well" (132).

Um... no. According to the CDC, correct and consistent condom use reduces the risk of STI transmission, including HIV. I'm really unhappy with the fact that classroom educators (often federally funded—your tax dollars at work!) can make erroneous statements like the one above to students who may not know where to look for correct information.

For many abstinence-only folks, sex is at heart a moral issue, and thus it's reasonable to ignore the biology behind STI transmission and strategies for risk reduction. Kendall writes,

Reduction of STI and pregnancy rates is not a reasonable concept to [abstinence-only until marriage] supporters, because it is the sex act itself that is immoral. ...Since sex within marriage is morally acceptable, these unwanted health outcomes are not in and of themselves a problem. (132)

Does everyone realize how problematic it is to assume that

marriage confers such a sacred status to sex that it obviates the need for accurate information around how pregnancies and contraceptive methods work as well as how STIs can be transmitted and prevented? Sexual assault can be a problem within marriage too. So can gender and sexual identity crises. So can substance addiction.

We need more accurate sex ed in our culture so that everyone can understand the physical dimensions of bodies and sexual acts, but also so that we have a framework in which to make sense of pervasive issues like sexual violence, and what marriage can and cannot do for you (unlike the magical, wishful thinking that abstinence-only folks seem to be displaying).

And yes, it is correct to draw a connection between folks who receive less sex education and folks who are engaging in behaviors that will lead to higher teenage pregnancy rates and higher STI transmission rates. Dr. Debby Herbenick discusses these connections in her TEDxBloomington talk, "Making Sex Normal" (which I *highly* recommend if you haven't seen it). There's also definitely a social justice angle to this issue, since demographics that are already disadvantaged (by living in poverty, being a person of color in a racist culture, by being LGBT) are even more vulnerable to systemic harms, but I talk about that elsewhere in this book.

I mean, if you want to live surrounded by people who are by no fault of their own ignorant about the workings of their own bodies? Go find a time machine. Ignorant people are more easily controlled and instilled with fear. I'd rather live alongside citizens who are empowered by knowledge when it comes to their bodies, their sexuality, and their ability to make informed choices.

References:

Kendall, Nancy. *The Sex Education Debates*. University of Chicago Press, 2013.

BECAUSE TEACHING SEX ED IS NOT THE SAME AS ENCOURAGING SEX

THE CASE FOR SEX ED PART 3

I'VE GLANCED at a lot of sex ed curricula in my time in this field; most of them are pretty unremarkable in my view, in that they give anatomical overviews and talk about reproduction and stuff. None of this should be incendiary for human beings to learn about, and yet here we are.

In Western culture, we generally assume that the purpose of school is to prepare children for life. Sexuality is a huge part of human life, encompassing everything from procreation, marriage/relationship expectations, emotions, fantasy, desire, and illness-prevention, as well as related topics like gender identity, feelings of acceptance, and body image. Since kids aren't necessarily getting sex education at home or from the other parts of culture that they come into contact with, it makes sense that schools would fill this vacuum.

Kids learn all kinds of things at school, and it's pretty much only in the realm of sex education that people freak out about kids wanting to reenact what's been presented in the classroom. Do parents wig out about their kids wanting to enact historically-inspired rebellions, or wanting to suddenly inject mathematical equations into every dinner conversation? Do they worry about their kids suddenly speaking in iambic pentameter? Yes, those are silly examples, but surely there are other dangerous things that kids learn at school—physics and chemistry among them, I mean, c'mon, you have to wear safety gear in those classes!—that aren't seen as being quite so threatening as sex education.

Furthermore, we do have specific evidence from studies that show that having sex education does not increase the likelihood of engaging in sexual activity. As Kristin Luker summarizes several meta-analyses, they compared people who had received comprehensive sex education with those who had not, and found that receiving sex ed does not seem to impact one's chances of having sex (255).

Teens are overall getting better at using contraception such as condoms more often (Luker 256), and so even if the results of sex ed curricula are hard to measure, we do have some positive indications that sex ed is not causing young people to engage in risky sex because sex winds up dominating their minds and ruling out all rational thought due to the sex ed classes they take.

In the end, it seems to me that the greatest fears of kids being information sponges and imitators revolve around behavior to which we attach moral value and stigma. I'm not saying that we should divorce moral value from sex or sex education, but rather that it seems a tad disingenuous to me to pretend that school is all about preparing kids for life, *except in this one really important area where they're not easily able to get accurate information anywhere else.* And it also seems a tad hypocritical to assume that kids will only be "monkey see, monkey do" about sex and not about any of the other dozens of subjects they'll learn about in school.

Finally, kids are pretty darn observant. It's not like they don't notice all the secrecy and shame around sex topics. By modeling how to talk about sex in a shame-free, common-sense sort of way, schools could help demystify it. Once sex is talked about in the same tone as trigonometry or subject-object agreement, it'll lose a lot of its taboo status, and we needn't worry that teens will be soooo intrigued that they just can't wait to try it out in secret.

References:

Luker, Kristin. *When Sex Goes to School: Warring Views on Sex-- And Sex Education--Since the Sixties.* 1st ed., W.W. Norton, 2006.

WE NEED TO DISENTANGLE GENDER FROM SEX

THE CASE FOR SEX ED PART 4

IN THIS CHAPTER I analyze how concepts of gender and sexual activity intertwine in contemporary American culture to the detriment of many, and how accurate sex education can help.*

When I originally wrote this as a blog post, I'd just taught Dr. Nancy Kendall's *The Sex Education Debates*, an ethnography of sex education in 5 different U.S. states, so the book was very much on my mind. One of the chapters is devoted to how gender is represented in abstinence-only and comprehensive sex ed curricula.

Building on her own classroom observations as well as the interpretations in Kristin Luker's book *When Sex Goes to School*, Kendall describes how gender roles and sexual behavior have become intertwined from both progressive and conservative standpoints. Perhaps surprisingly, the abstinence-only (and usually socially and religiously conservative) folks talk more of empowerment for girls and women than the comprehensive-leaning (and progressive/liberal) folks tend to. Part of this is because comprehensive sex ed curricula tend to lean heavily on neoliberal ideologies that paint each individual as a rational actor, making free choices in a context where all else is equal. This viewpoint ignores influences like class and economic disparities, trauma histories, gender socialization, and so on.

However, the type of "empowerment" preached by ab-only educators is anything but. As Kendall writes, "It is not empowering of women's voices, desires, decision-making, or freedom of choice. It is not supportive of structural equity. It restricts women's power, tying it entirely to their ability to control those with greater physical and social power—men— in order to assume their only rightful places in society as mother and wife" (162).

And this is where the connection between gender identity and sexual role emerges. Abstinence-only teachers (and to a large degree, comprehensive sex ed teachers) do not question this connection between proper femininity and masculinity, and the right way to be sexual as a man or as a woman. While there's a difference in the messages "no sex til marriage" and "if you're gonna do it, here are some ways to protect yourself," both approaches to sex ed largely convey the same gendered messages, telling women that they are the gatekeepers of sex, that they need to not tempt men by dressing or acting certain ways, and that it's their fault if they get raped.

To quote Kendall again, she makes this observation of abstinence-only approaches, but it applies pretty well to many of the comprehensive sex ed curricula she observed, too:

This model of empowerment also denigrates men's capacities and choices, and silences male voices and expe-

riences concerning emotional connections in relationships, responsibility toward women and children, and
desires for gender egalitarianism in relationships. Just as
it figures women as weak, emotional, and manipulative,
it figures men as unaccountable, animalistic, and incapable of deep spiritual or social connection. (162)

This, incidentally, is why I tell everyone (especially men)
that I'm a feminist: because normative gender roles suck for
everyone. They suck in different ways, and to different
degrees, and they certainly suck intersectionally, too. But as
sex blogger Cliff Pervocracy writes in their classic post "The
Myth of the Boner Werewolf", "If someone started telling
stories about how my gender was controlled by our genitalia
and sexual arousal turns us into rapist automatons, I would be
outraged. I would explain in very small, very loud words that I
am a person and I can goddamn control myself."

In other words, gender role and sexual behavior are deeply
intertwined in our culture in a way that impacts everyone, yet
it's mostly feminists and other sex-positive folks calling into
question this connection. However, it's deeply problematic,
and it needs to be interrogated by/for all. A comprehensive
AND sex-positive AND critically analytical sex education
classroom could accomplish these goals, maybe, under the
right circumstances (a teacher who's trained in sex education,
given enough time in the curriculum, and who wasn't being
monitored by a paranoid school board or parents who'd rather
condemn their kids to ignorance than have them learn things
that could save and/or improve their lives).

If our educational system and our cultural discourse prioritized conversations about gender that neither revolve around false dichotomies (I'm looking at you, "men are from Mars/women are from Venus" bullshit), nor incorrectly superimposed sexual norms atop gender roles—if we had realistic conversations about gender as a social construct, and how that gets layered with sexuality—then maybe we'd have a shot at raising a healthier generation. Disentangling gender from sex acts and from sexual orientation is a huge task, but the benefits (reduced victim blaming and slut-shaming, greater tolerance for non-gender-conforming and non-heterosexual folks, more life options for all) seem to be worth it to me.

*THE TITLE OF THIS CHAPTER, ABOUT DISENTANGLING GENDER from sex, is not a new concept in feminist and queer studies. Theorists from Simone de Beauvoir up through Gayle Rubin and Judith Butler have done great work on it. For a cultural history of how gender has mapped onto biological sex, see Thomas Laqueur, *The Making of Sex*. What I'm suggesting here is that more attention to the gendering of biological/anatomical sex and sexual acts is a crucial part of the mission of contemporary sex education.

References:

Kendall, Nancy. *The Sex Education Debates*. University of Chicago Press, 2013.

Luker, Kristin. *When Sex Goes to School: Warring Views on Sex--And Sex Education--Since the Sixties*. 1st ed., W.W. Norton, 2006.

Pervocracy, Cliff. "The Myth of the Boner Werewolf." *The Pervocracy,* 29 April 2012, http://pervocracy.blogspot.com/2012/08/the-myth-of-boner-werewolf.html. Accessed 4 September 2023.

HOW ABSTINENCE-ONLY SEX ED ERASES CONSENT

THE CASE FOR SEX ED PART 5

RoleReboot blogger Lynn Beisner beat me to the theme of this chapter with her post "On Josh Duggar And Why It's Time To Do Away With Abstinence-Only Sex Education." But there are some ideas in her post that I'd like to unpack further and give some background for here (and as of the time of this writing in 2023, there's a new documentary out about the Duggars, *Shiny Happy People*, and the abuse therein; I haven't had the bandwidth to watch it yet).

Beisner explains that Duggar's behavior (and the family and local church's response) makes sense in the larger context of Independent Fundamental Baptists (IBF) beliefs. Overlapping social groups that share many of these beliefs include the Quiverfull movement, the Christian homeschooling movement, the purity movement, and the Religious Right.

At their core, Beisner asserts that the reason these groups have such a big sexual assault problem is that their "main thing" is a set of beliefs about sexuality and purity. Those beliefs are not just based on selected scriptures, they are grounded in an incredibly damaging moral logic that is dismissive of the ethic of consent and that discourages compassion for victims of rape and other forms of sexual violence.

What else do these groups overlap with? The abstinence-only sex education movement.

Beisner claims to see links between the religious groups and the abstinence-only group in her blog post, but she doesn't explicate those links in much detail, so I will.

In her book *The Sex Education Debates*, Dr. Nancy Kendall articulates the central tenets of abstinence-only sex ed. Some key points include:

The idea that the nuclear family is the basic and ideal unit of family and community life;

The male is the head of the family (and the differences between men and women are absolute and should be upheld as such);

Adults have authority over children (and such hierarchies are socially and religiously important);

Sex is a sacred act and belongs within marriage only;

Sex outside marriage is a destructive social (and perhaps spiritual) force;

Sexualities that are not straight, monogamous, or vanilla (when acknowledged at all) are dangerous;

Teaching these values will help resolve the nation's STI epidemic and other social ills.

Looking over this list after typing it, I'm struck (as usual) by just how much this does *not* resemble anything like a sensible sex education curriculum. And yet it passes as such, and even receives federal funding ($250 million from 2010–14).

The teachings of the fundamentalist groups that Beisner discusses are as follows:

"All sexual sin is caused by a spiritual deficiency";

"Women are naturally pure" (until properly awakened into sexuality by romantic love within marriage);

"Love is what not only awakens a woman's sexuality, it is also what keeps her sexuality in check";

"We are responsible for the sexual thoughts and feelings that we create in others";

"All of the pain caused by sexual misconduct or violations will be instantly erased if the person forgives their attacker and surrenders to the will of God";

"The ethic of consent does not carry any serious moral weight and is rarely considered. In fact, failure to gain consent can be seen as sparing the other person since you are not leading them into the sin of sexual desire."

It's not so hard to connect the dots between the religious doctrines and the slightly-more abstracted abstinence-only principles discussed above. In both, consent is obscured, because if everyone's acting the way they "should," with women being demure and unobtrusive, and men gallantly waiting for the right partner to wed, then there shouldn't be consent violations, ever.

This moral framework—and abstinence-only sex ed IS a

moral framework, much as it pretends not to be—occludes the very possibility of consent as a worthwhile topic of discussion. That is no small thing.

We already know that abstinence-only sex education is not effective in preventing teen pregnancies or STI transmission. It erases LGBTQ visibility and upholds outdated, toxic gender norms. But, as Beisner suggests, it also spreads a poisonous rhetoric about consent and sexual assault. This is what we need to combat with comprehensive, fact-based, consent-oriented sex education.

To take another example, directly from a school class-room, Alice Dreger's blog post about sitting in on her son's sex ed class reveals a particularly horrifying lesson about consent. A presenter said, "You'll find a good girl. If you find one who says 'no,' that's the one you want."

Obviously it matters that kids are being told that "no" doesn't actually mean "no." The media's passing along that message too, with ignorant, misleading news coverage of rape cases as well as Hollywood films and TV shows where consent figures in little. Abstinence-only sex ed is full of this kind of rhetoric, as Dr. Kendall documents in her book with ethno-graphic examples from classrooms all over the U.S. Girls are told that it's their job not to dress provocatively so as not to drive boys to rape, and rape by an acquaintance or date or within one's marriage is not even discussed as a possibility.

It is no surprise that assault proliferates in environments that are silent around topics of sexuality and consent. I remember seeing footage of the Steubenville rape trial and how one of the teens present at the crime said that it didn't appear violent, so it didn't come across as rape. I suspect this is one of the many ways in which boys are not taught about rape at the same frequency that girls often are (out of necessity).

So what we need, among other things, is sex education that emphasizes consent, that talks about what sexual assault is and isn't, and that disentangles sexual behavior from the tangled—and hypocritical—web of morality that it's become part of in this country.

References:

Beisner, Lynn. "On Josh Duggar and Why It's Time to Do Away with Abstinence-Only Sex Education." *Role Reboot*, 25 May 2015, http://www.rolereboot.org/culture-and-politics/details/2015-05-on-josh-duggar-and-why-its-time-to-do-away-with-abstinence-only-sex-education/. Accessed 4 September 2023.

Dreger, Alice. "I Sat in on My Son's Sex-Ed Class, and I Was Shocked by What I Heard." *The Stranger*, 15 April 2015, https://www.thestranger.com/features/2015/04/15/22062331/i-sat-in-on-my-sons-sex-ed-class-and-i-was-shocked-by-what-i-heard. Accessed 4 September 2023.

Kendall, Nancy. *The Sex Education Debates*. University of Chicago Press, 2013.

WE COULD REDUCE STI STIGMA & IMPROVE PUBLIC HEALTH...BUT WE'RE NOT

THE CASE FOR SEX ED PART 6

In Bruce Link and Jo Phelan's article in *Lancet*, "On Stigma and Its Public Health Implications," they describe the ways in which stigma negatively impacts multiple public health outcomes. Here are a few of the effects:

- The stress of belonging to a stigmatized group can worsen a health condition;
- People with stigmatized conditions may delay seeking treatment, not comply with treatment recommendations, or avoid treatment altogether (e.g., "I'm not one of *those* people, I don't actually need to see a doctor");
- Stigma can create an environment that feels hostile even when the goal is for someone to seek help there (who wants to go somewhere they feel pathologized or like they might be locked away?);
- Stigmatized conditions may receive less research funding over time, especially if it's difficult for

people to disentangle attributed moral causes from actual causes of a disorder or condition.

When the stigmatized condition in question centers on having an STI, this issue becomes especially sticky, thanks to the longstanding moral implications of acquiring a sexually-transmitted disease. As I've discussed regarding venereal disease in the history section of this book, the moral taint of the STIs like syphilis was a major factor in cultural innovations meant to disguise and deal with it. People went out of their way to hide their shame in any way they could. And unfortunately, public thought about STIs doesn't seem to have changed much.

Multiple educators have pointed out that stigma is essentially a public health issue, with people less likely to engage in risk-reduction and harm-reduction behaviors due to shame. Since shame and stigma are related phenomena, and since people are often shamed for contracting an STI, it's worth considering how our public dialogue around STIs influences people's decision-making processes.

We know that half of all people will have an STI at some point in their lifetime. Further, a significant number of teens will contract an STI (I've seen figures ranging from one in four to one in two)—and most STIs have fairly minor consequences if they are treated quickly. However, the polarized way in which sex ed is taught in U.S. classrooms (when it's taught at all) means that these important public health points are often eclipsed.

Dr. Nancy Kendall summarizes the problems with taking a shame- or fear-based approach to STIs in her ethnographic study of American sex ed, *The Sex Education Debates*:

The framing of STIs as horrifying diseases resonates deeply for many people around the world. For centuries, STIs have been fearful killers, and even today the effects of some STIs are long lasting and life changing. However, adopting a fear-based approach means that teachers and curricula cannot emphasize three important points: first, that the vast majority of people will have an STI during their lifetime; second, that most of the STIs contributing to high teen STI rates are not only fully treatable, they have no significant health consequences *if treated in a timely manner*; and third, that stigmatizing STIs and those who have them makes it harder for people to quickly and easily receive preventative care or treatment for STIs. (133, italics in original)

THIS IS HUGE. WE COULD BE TEACHING ABOUT STIs IN A WAY that helps the 1/4 of teens affected by STIs to more easily seek treatment that prevents them from, say, later experiencing infertility. Or contributing to the spread of completely preventable and treatable infections (not to mention the ones that are lifelong or likely to cause damage). Or experiencing social stigma. Or simply having genital pain or discomfort. No gain is too small to overlook, in my opinion.

I'm having trouble tracking down the original source, but according to a poll reported on in CNN, 68% of teenagers said they weren't using sexual protection because they were worried their parents would find out. So it's not just a formal sex education issue that can be tackled institutionally; it's also a part of family culture and dynamics that we need to change.

As Dr. Kendall writes, "from a public health perspective,

fear-based approaches that do not emphasize prevention *and* treatment and that do not address the negative consequences of stigmatizing people with STIs are likely to be less effective and to have unintended negative consequences" (133).

Not only are fear-based approaches unhelpful from a public health standpoint as discussed above, they also don't bloody work! So why are we doing this to our kids? The sociology and public health research all clearly points to reducing stigma as a major strategy in terms of bettering public health around STI treatment. In my mind, this illustrates just how much of a moral issue sex (and by extension STIs) is, and how we must continue to make an evidence-based case for the importance of sex education.

References:

Kendall, Nancy. *The Sex Education Debates*. University of Chicago Press, 2013.

Link, Bruce G, and Jo C. Phelan. "Stigma and Its Public Health Implications." *Lancet*, vol. 367, no. 9509, 2006, pp. 528–9.

Wallace, Kelly. "Survey Says Teens Skip Birth Control Because They Fear Parental Judgment." *CNN*, 7 May 2015, https://www.cnn.com/2015/05/07/living/feat-teens-birth-control-fears-parents. Accessed 4 September 2023.

TEACHING HEALTHY RELATIONSHIPS EMPOWERS EVERYONE

THE CASE FOR SEX ED PART 7

TEACHING Healthy Relationships Empowers Everyone (The Case for Sex Ed Part 7)

If you sit down and think about it, teaching the basics of equitable relationships as part of a sex education curriculum can improve the lives of teens and everyone.

When we talk about relationships there's a tendency to assume that we mean sexual and/or romantic relationships. Cue freaking out, which, as I discussed a few chapters ago, is because apparently talking to teens about anything sexual apparently is the same as telling them to go do it. But everyone is in relationships, all the time, most of them platonic. We all relate to our family members, teachers, friends, mentors, coworkers, acquaintances, hobby-sharers, and more. And if there's one thing I've learned as a sex educator, it's that solid communication, relationship, and ethical principles tend to apply across multiple categories. If you should be honest and empathetic with your friends, that'll probably work in your relationships too. So in teaching about relationship skills and communication, we teach life skills that apply more broadly.

In sex educator Al Vernacchio's book, *For Goodness Sex: Changing the Way We Talk to Teens About Sexuality, Values, and Health*, he addresses teen relationships as a major area needing more education and attention.

Vernacchio guides his students through the process of figuring out how their values impact their relationship needs and wants over time, stating

It's also important for kids to know that some deal makers and deal breakers can change as we grow. Others will remain set in stone no matter what our age. Thinking about our individual deal makers and deal breakers in relationships is an evolving process. We continually need to call them to mind, evaluate them, and make adjustments when necessary. (80)

This is excellent advice, and I wish I'd had more of this guidance growing up.

Another of Vernacchio's points is that there are multiple ways in which teens are subjected to inaccurate and harmful messages about power and symmetry in relationships, from the media as well as the dynamics they observe around them. According to Vernacchio, the social pressures to be in a romantic or sexual relationship—whether or not it's healthy—are immense, and without education that explicitly addresses how healthy and unhealthy relationships each work, teens might end up in toxic or even predatory relationships.

The components of healthy relationships that Vernacchio

teaches include equitable levels of power, maintaining your individuality within the relationship, being able to express yourself fully without fear of repercussion, and being reliable and present. I think there are obvious benefits to teaching about these healthy relationship traits, though in-depth discussion of what they mean and how they might play out could lead to talking about examples that might include sex, coercion, and other taboo topics.

Furthermore, as reported at NPR, there are findings indicating that when sex ed programs address power in relationships, they're more effective at preventing teen pregnancy and STI transmission. This makes sense, as the types of sexual activity that results in pregnancy and/or STI transmission don't happen in a vacuum: they often happen in the context of romantic and/or sexual relationships where there might be a power disparity or inequality that could be addressed.

There's also evidence that our relationships impact our health. Studies show that spousal conflicts impact one's immune system and ability to recover from disease and injury (Rutherford), while other researchers have found that people with unsupportive, critical partners were more likely to suffer depression (Schute).

While we're all constantly surrounded by and participating in various relationships, it's not necessarily an intuitive process to figure out what makes them healthy. With all the mental, emotional, and physical health risks and benefits that accompany being in relationships, we owe it to everyone in society to ensure that we have a grasp of how relationships work, and how we can improve and benefit from them.

References:

Rutherford, Maryhope Howland. "In Sickness and in Health: Pick Your Battles!" *Luvze*, 15 August 2011, https://www.luvze.com/in-sickness-and-in-health-pick-your-battles-w-videos/. Accessed 4 September 2023.

Schute, Nancy. "Mate Doesn't Have Your Back? That Boosts Depression Risk." *NPR*, 1 May 2013, https://www.npr.org/sections/health-shots/2013/05/01/180290358/mate-doesnt-have-your-back-that-boosts-depression-risk. Accessed 4 September 2023.

Singh, Maanvi. "Sex Ed Works Better When It Addresses Power in Relationships." *NPR*, 17 May 2015, https://www.npr.org/sections/health-shots/2015/05/17/407063066/sex-ed-works-better-when-it-addresses-power-in-relationships. Accessed 4 September 2023.

Vernacchio, Al, with Brooke Lea Foster. *For Goodness Sex: Changing the Way We Talks to Teens about Sexuality, Values, and Health*. Harper Wave, 2014.

LEARNING ABOUT NONCONCORDANT AROUSAL ERADICATES VICTIM BLAMING

THE CASE FOR SEX ED PART 8

OKAY, let's say you *have* acquired some basic knowledge about sex (no thanks to the efforts of those trying to keep young people in the dark). You've probably learned that hard penis and wet vagina = signs of being turned on.*

In her book *Come As You Are: The Surprising New Science That Will Transform Your Sex Life*, Emily Nagoski, Ph.D., describes this as the "standard narrative" about sex and arousal. She writes, "As far as most porn, romance novels, and even sex education texts are concerned, genital response and sexual arousal are one and the same" (192).

The fact that youth (and adults) are getting messages that both idealize and normalize arousal concordance (which is the assumption that genital expression guarantees your own experience of pleasure) means that it's vital to address this issue in sex education materials, for both adults and youth. Because, as Nagoski points out in her book, believing that arousal concordance is universal can have pretty awful consequences for folks who don't experience it.

Feel free to refresh on the basics in my chapter on this in the "How Sex Actually Works" section, but basically, there are some huge problems with how our culture makes arousal concordance the norm: it conflates genital response with being turned on, and it assumes that genital response means you're enjoying it.

This can lead to tons of problems for people, wherein experiences that are not inherently problematic (getting a boner when you don't feel aroused; or being in the midst of sexytimes that you're enjoying, but your body's not responding "the right way" by showing signs of arousal) are pathologized and made to seem wrong. Nagoski presents a handful of examples in her book, and the ones about women's experiences really resonated with me, because I've experienced arousal nonconcordance and felt ashamed of it. It's pretty common for women, apparently, but apart from Nagoski and a handful of other sex educators, no one's getting out the word that there's nothing wrong with you, you're not broken, if you experience this. Chalk this up to another way in which our culture doesn't do a good job of accommodating for how female sexuality is a bit different from male sexuality; overall they're quite similar, but more women experience nonconcordance than men, yet we get shamed for it because cultural understandings are usually predicated on male models.

Additionally, arousal nonconcordance can intersect with and amplify the messages of rape culture, leading to victim-blaming if the person being assaulted has any kind of bodily response. More people are taking the view that when a woman is raped, lubrication can be the body's way of protecting itself from damage, but if we throw in Nagoski's work on nonconcordance, we can also state that the body is simply recognizing that there's something happening that's sexually relevant, and reacting accordingly. It's a value-neutral statement, because we're working to uncouple pleasure (the subjective part of the experience) from arousal (the physiological part of the experience).

Similarly, as Nagoski points out in her book, if a man experiences genital arousal upon seeing a sexual act that he finds repulsive, it's not evidence that he actually likes or enjoys it. But—thanks again, rape culture!—He might perceive it that way. Nagoski's anecdote of a male friend who walked in on a guy raping an unconscious woman at a college party, and just left, demonstrates this. The man was too horrified and ashamed at his own experience of arousal, when clearly he was against rape, that he removed himself from the situation instead of intervening. What might've happened instead if he'd known about arousal nonconcordance?

(Also, thanks to rape culture, there's a tendency to view male-on-female rape as the only kind of rape that happens, while actually men can be raped, and women can be the ones raping and assaulting. Just thought I'd mention that. There's some evidence that male victims of sexual abuse also experience genital arousal during it, so getting out the message of nonconcordance benefits people in these positions, too.)

As a cultural scholar, I know that making information about nonconcordance more widely available might be impeded by cultural lag, or that thing that happens when some parts of a culture change quicker than others. The resulting lag is often noticeable in folklore and expressive culture, since the narratives and beliefs that have become "traditional" stick around as long as they resonate with people, even if people might not fully agree with them (people are complex; who knew?!).

What can we do? Talk about it. Destigmatize the idea that if your genitals and your mind aren't on the same page, there's something wrong with you. Break the association between physical arousal and subjective pleasure. Use your words when you're with a partner, making sure they know what you perceive as arousing, and that they should go with what you say in addition to—or perhaps instead of— how your body responds. Read Nagoski's book, if you're so inclined (I know I loved it; some sections totally blew my mind). Above all, keep advocating for the right of everyone to accurate, shame-free sex ed!

*AMONG THE OTHER PROBLEMS WITH THE HARD PENIS/WET vagina model of arousal concordance, intersex and trans individuals are made invisible. All the more reason to think expansively about arousal!

References:

Nagoski, Emily. *Come As You Are: The Surprising New Science That Will Transform Your Sex Life*. Simon & Schuster Paperbacks, 2015.

KNOWING OUR BODIES MEANS BETTER PUBLIC POLICIES

THE CASE FOR SEX ED PART 9

IN THIS CHAPTER, I'd like to talk about the widespread ignorance and disgust around bodies—especially women's bodies—that could easily be remedied by universal evidence-based sex education. This ignorance has concrete and dire consequences because of how it becomes encoded in politics and public policy, and thus I think we owe it to everyone to do better on this front.

First, there's the issue of gendered access to restrooms. In the 2015 Democratic Presidential Debates, Hillary Clinton's bathroom break became a topic of comment. As Soraya Chemaly points out in a *Huffington Post* article from 2015, Donald Trump's comment on the situation was, "I know where she went, it's disgusting, I don't want to talk about it... No, it's too disgusting. Don't say it, it's disgusting, let's not talk." For someone running for an elected office to claim that bodily functions are too disgusting to talk about is astounding. Toilets and sanitation systems are public health concerns, thus politicians *must* talk about them.

To take a global example, the World Bank estimates that half of schools in lower-income countries lack the bathroom facilities to let menstruating girls have the privacy and sanitation to attend school while on their periods ("Menstrual Health"). And this can align with a series of farther-reaching health and economic consequences that keep young women unable to access as much education, to take on economic opportunities, and so on. Health issues that might seem to only impact half the population can thus impact the entire society, when patterns of inaccessibility restrict the options of a whole swath of people.

Transgender identities are also often singled out for discriminatory bathroom policies, which again is a result of a fundamental misunderstanding of how gender works (which I asserted sex ed needs to address a few chapters ago), and how sexual assault is patterned. It is fairly obvious to me that restroom use is a significant part of the human rights needs of all people, but especially people who are transitioning, and ideally we'll have policies that allow people to use the bathroom of the gender they identify with (as opposed to laws that Indiana and other states have tried to pass to fine people who use the "wrong" bathroom, sigh).

Furthermore, we as a society benefit when women's specific health needs are understood, and policies to address these needs are implemented. Research shows that when women's clinics are closed, and there aren't nearby alternatives, the annual rates of women getting screened for breast cancer and cervical cancer drop ("Closure"). This disproportionately impacts lower-income women, too. Since early detection improves survival rates for these diseases, why aren't we doing more to promote screenings? If, as I contend, it's partly an educational issue, then we can and should do better.

Also, thanks to former-Twitter for this weird bit of discourse, but apparently transphobes are claiming that we need strict policing of single-sex bathrooms because of...how often menstruating cis women need to rinse out their bloody underwear in public restroom sinks?

My good people, I know that bigots will sink however low to try to make their points, but also, let's not forget: period blood is blood, hence technically a biohazard. No one's saying periods are dirty or gross, just like, let's keep things in perspective (and also not let transphobes get away with these sorts of ludicrous talking points).

Finally, every time I see a huge debate about abortion, I wonder how many people actually know that 90% of abortions take place in the first trimester (Diamant and Mohamed, writing for the Pew Research Center). Prior to the second trimester, the fetus is far from viable, only about 2 inches long at the 11- or 12-week mark (Mayo Clinic).

Due to the anti-choice movement's marketing campaigns that focus on graphic imagery of supposedly aborted babies, I fear that a lot of Americans don't have any idea of what actual fetal development looks like. In fact, Snopes.com (which we folklorists generally support!) has even had to debunk an urban legend about it! (Mikkelson) Knowing about how fetal development actually progresses might not dissuade serious anti-choice people from their stances, but it might help informed voters and policy-makers ensure that fear-based campaigns don't get as far as they do. Abortion is health care, and it needs to be treated as such: as an individual matter for a patient and her doctor to decide.

Pregnancy remains one of the most dangerous things a woman can experience bodily. You can search for pregnancy complications on the CDC website and learn about all the fun (read: dangerous) things that can happen to pregnant people: anemia, gestational diabetes, heart conditions, hypertension, hyperemesis gravidarum (you know, the one where you can't keep food down due to persistent nausea), and more. This is one of the major pieces of evidence that counters the "just have the baby" argument that many anti-choice people make. As Natasha Chart writes at *Rewire,*

> To say "Just have the baby" is to say "Just risk a prolonged illness, surgery, and the loss of your income when you have a lot of new expenses." It's to tell someone casually that they should sign up for the possibility of experiencing more physical pain and agony than they thought a person could live through, and maybe having a great deal of it continue for days, weeks, months, possibly even years.

Demystifying how pregnancy works—and the impacts it can have on women's lives and their family's experiences—is an important part of educating the public about bodily matters that require some legislation to help out on a societal level. We need better maternity care, better maternity *and* paternity leave, and better child care. The maternal mortality rate has doubled in the U.S. in the last few decades, with Dina Maron writing in *Scientific American* suggesting that this is both a result of improved reporting and of poor access to prenatal and postnatal care. All of this impacts an entire society, not just the bodies bearing children.

Whether the topic is women's health (the need for bathroom access in general and while menstruating; pregnancy as a risky state; health screening needs) or sanitation and bath-room access for the general public or for transgender people specifically, the absence of comprehensive health and sex education leads to deficient comprehension of policies that have a real impact on many people's lives. I believe that we must do better, and that unbiased, fact-based sex education is one of the things that can remedy this lack.

References:

Chart, Natasha. "Just Have the Baby? A New Mom Reveals Why There Is No 'Just,' and Not Necessarily Any Justice Either." *Rewire News Group*, 27 June 2013, https://rewirenews group.com/2013/06/27/just-have-the-baby-a-new-mom-reveals-why-there-is-no-just-and-not-necessarily-any-justice-either/. Accessed 5 September 2023.

Chemaly, Soraya. "Biology Doesn't Write Laws: Hillary Clinton's Bathroom Break Wasn't As Trivial As Some Might Like to Think." *Huffington Post*, 25 December 2015, https://www.huff post.com/entry/biology-doesnt-write-laws_b_8874638. Accessed 4 September 2023.

"Closure of Women's Health Clinics Due to Government Cuts Affects Preventative Care." *News Medical*, 8 October 2015, https://www.news-medical.net/news/20151008/Closure-of-womens-health-clinics-due-to-government-cuts-affects-preven tive-care.aspx. Accessed 9 September 2023.

Diamant, Jeff, and Besheer Mohamed. "What the Data Says about Abortion in the U.S." *Pew Research Center*, 11 January

2023, https://www.pewresearch.org/short-reads/2023/01/11/what-the-data-says-about-abortion-in-the-u-s-2/. Accessed 9 September 2023.

Maron, Dina. "Has Maternal Mortality Really Doubled in the U.S.?" *Scientific American*, 8 June 2015, https://www.scientificamerican.com/article/has-maternal-mortality-really-doubled-in-the-u-s/. Accessed 4 September 2023.

"Menstrual Health and Hygiene." *The World Bank*, 12 May 2022, https://www.worldbank.org/en/topic/water/brief/menstrual-health-and-hygiene. Accessed 9 September 2023.

Mikkelson, David. "Is This a Photograph of a 12-Week Fetus?" *Snopes*, 26 August 2022, https://www.snopes.com/fact-check/12-week-photo/. Accessed 9 September 2023.

"Pregnancy by Week." *Mayo Clinic*, 3 June 2022, https://www.mayoclinic.org/healthy-lifestyle/pregnancy-week-by-week/in-depth/prenatal-care/art-20045302?pg=2. Accessed 9 September 2023.

BECAUSE KIDS LACKING SEX ED BECOME ADULTS LACKING SEX ED

THE CASE FOR SEX ED PART 10

THIS SEEMS like a rather obvious point, since it didn't occur to me to write it until later in this series. Ah well.

But perhaps it's because it's such an obvious point that it's also a subtle one: we are all shaped by our past experiences, sure. No one would disagree with that assertion. At the same time, there are gaps and absences that are large enough to become noticeable. We are shaped by what we lack, and nowhere is this more true than in America.

With apologies for this pessimistic opening, we see all kinds of lacks shaping people's lives in America: lack of health care leads to adverse health outcomes for many, which is a "duh" point much like this chapter's title...except it doesn't have to be this way. We lack worker protections and we lack maternal mortality interventions (especially for women of color, who are dying at higher rates), and we lack all sorts of things that could be gamechangers for our quality of life.

Lacking adequate sexual health information early in life can alter the course of one's life. And I don't say this in a sex-negative, shamey way, as is often done when talking about the moral panic du jour, when it's teen pregnancies or STI transmission. And these are serious issues, of course, just not always in the way the mainstream media makes them out to be, like, they signal the end of civilization as we know it.

As Kristin Luker points out (and she's not the only one to do so), American teens are pretty sexually active. This isn't an anomaly in and of itself; teens all over the world are pretty sexually active. But what this means for American teens is drastically different:

Teen birth, abortion, and venereal disease rates are among the highest in the industrialized world. More worrisome, about 20 percent of all AIDS cases in the United States are diagnosed among people in their twenties, and because of the long lag time between infection and symptoms, it is presumed that many of these people acquired the disease as teens. (Luker 23).

This is not great on its own merit—though again, I need to emphasize that it's not some massive moral failing, and we can pin a lot of the blame on the shift in the 1980s to absti-nence-only sex ed as well as a centuries-old cultural atmosphere of persistent sex negativity—it has another massive implication.

See, people don't automatically grow out of their attitudes or ignorance. And when a culture consistently sends mixed messages about sex (sex is dirty! but sex sells!) when there's also a vacuum of accurate info about sex, then the lack of sex ed so many people experience as children and teens just accompanies them into adulthood: "Like teenagers, adult Americans get pregnant more often when they don't intend to, pass on more sexually transmitted diseases, and have higher abortion rates than almost any other adults in the industrial-ized world" (Luker 23).

As with so many other issues, we're number one, I guess?

The lack I'm seeing here, which begins in youth and continues into adulthood, is problematic not just because it's a lack of knowledge. The lacking knowledge part does make the whole problem a bit more confounding, because we educators are generally good at what we do and we've been throwing ourselves at the issue of sex education for decades now, but as I've chronicled in the history portion of this book, a good teacher can only do so much if they're already fighting an uphill battle against state censorship (like the Comstock Laws), hostile parental organizations, and so on.

Additionally, in the age of the internet, attaining knowl-edge about sex isn't really a problem anymore. Instead, it becomes a problem of not just how to obtain information, but how to sift through it and how to utilize it once you get it. I love the internet as much as the next millennial, but dang if information literacy isn't an increasingly necessary component to functionally being able to use the internet!

Teaching about sex in a society that simultaneously reviles and is captivated by sex ends up being very tricky. We need to ask ourselves, as educators and citizens, what our goals actually are here. These end up being more "why" questions than "how" questions. And if our "why" of teaching school sex ed, regardless of whether it's abstinence-only or comprehensive, is to address fear, then we have a problem.

Whether it's fear of teen pregnancies or fear of STI trans-mission or fear of queer people or fear of the declining birth rates or rising divorce rates, teaching from a place of fear is often going to be deficient. And I don't mean that we should never do so; like, if I want to take self-defense classes out of a fear of being attacked, that's valid.

But human sexuality encompasses more than fear. Really, every aspect of humanity entails a whole spectrum of emotions and experiences that don't—and shouldn't—just boil down to fear.

When you have not only an absence of accurate sex information but also a framework of fear, you end up giving young people (who then become older people) years and years of enculturation that places sex in a position of mystique while simultaneously instilling feelings of shame and abnormality.

I don't think putting a ring on someone's finger will magically evaporate a lifetime of sex-negative messages, and however many years of abstinence-only education in the classroom. I don't believe a switch magically flips on someone's wedding night, letting them enjoy guilt-free sex—somehow? Once they figure out the particulars?—as though it's possible to shuck off years of avoiding thinking about sex for fear of going to hell or being called a slut or whatever.

By depriving young people of accurate sex ed, we place them in a position where they are likely to carry those lacks— lack of knowledge, lack of guidance on where to obtain good knowledge, lack of a coherent attitude or value system around sex—into adulthood. And even if the young folks are "good" and abstain from the kinds of sexual behaviors they're supposed to, they're still going to carry the shame of knowing it was forbidden when they do start indulging. Sometimes that makes taboo stuff fun, and sometimes it leads to self-loathing. Bit of a risky coin flip there, eh?

Also, when I made the reframe of sex ed from answering "how" questions to "why" questions above, I made a values claim. I'm going into that a bit more here, in part because it didn't really fit anywhere else in the book, and in part because I think we need to be talking about this subtle side of sex ed more.

Luckily for us all, lifelong sex educator and advocate Al Vernacchio has given us this framework in his book *For Goodness Sex: Changing the Way We Talks to Teens about Sexuality, Values, and Health*. He discusses values as "the deepest-set rules that guide one's decisions" (22). They reflect our core beliefs, not just directing our behavior in the what/how sense but also giving an underlying why.

Especially important for our discussion of sexuality is that values must be "chosen freely from alternatives," "prized and publicly affirmed when appropriate," and "acted upon consistently and repeatedly" (25). A lot of mainstream values around sex are, er, kinda the opposite of that: forced on people through social conditioning rather than freely chosen, seen as a private and shameful matter hence not up for public discussion, and seen as pick-and-choose depending on the situation (think of any X in the streets, Y in the sheets meme, or how people will pledge monogamy when getting married and then have affairs).

Our values are both personal and cultural, sure, and they can have an array of orientations towards sexuality: we can view sexuality negatively because our religion tells us to *or* because we had a traumatic experience with it. Alternately, we can view sexuality as a good thing because our religion tells us to (as Vernacchio does) *or* we can be atheists who think sexuality is a good thing because it allows for human connection.

Vernacchio provides some useful guidelines for doing discovery on your own values, and I'll just share a snippet of that here. If we're looking for values, we're looking for consistent patterns in our beliefs and behaviors, so we can uncover the primary beliefs guiding those things. In case this all seems super abstract, here are some pairs of values you can look at, as people often find themselves drawn to one end of the continuum they represent:

individuality vs. community
hierarchy vs. equality
secularity vs. spirituality
introversion vs. extroversion
cruelty vs. compassion
authenticity vs. conformity
isolation vs. attachment
innovation vs. tradition
self-interest vs. other interest (28)

To see how these apply to sex and sexuality, we could just take the last one, self-interest vs. other interest, and list how even when simply having partnered sex, your placement on this value spectrum could mean that you spend more or less time on your orgasm vs. your partner's, that you own more sex toys or lubricants to appeal to yourself or your partner, how you think about sex positions, and so on.

And to apply these categories of value systems to the way we teach sex ed, it's pretty obvious that those values skew more towards hierarchy, spirituality, conformity, and tradition (and, I'd argue, cruelty in how we stigmatize and/or exclude LGBTQ+ teens, teens who have experienced sexual assault and/or pregnancy, disabled teens, and so on). It doesn't paint a pretty picture.

If these value systems inflect early learning about sex in schools, as well as the mish-mash of sexual information we get from folklore, pop culture, our families, and so on, then it's no surprise that there are gaps in people's sexual knowledge, which only increase with age.

To reiterate the point with which I started, sexual health outcomes for teens in the U.S. aren't that great, but neither are sexual health outcomes for adults, which indicates a larger cultural problem with how we treat sex in general. Learning to talk about how our values connect to sex might be one starting point, to help everyone grow into adults who are confident and equipped not just with knowledge but with the values to make sense of all the information out there.

Plus side, I guess this continuing resistance to actually giving young folks medically accurate and inclusive sex education (as well as the tools to determine your values and act accordingly) means that my adult sex ed colleagues and I will always have jobs. Though it'd be cool if we got to spend less time dismantling false and harmful beliefs and just focusing on pleasure.

References:

Luker, Kristin. *When Sex Goes to School: Warring Views on Sex-- And Sex Education--Since the Sixties.* 1st ed., W.W. Norton, 2006.

Vernacchio, Al, with Brooke Lea Foster. *For Goodness Sex: Changing the Way We Talks to Teens about Sexuality, Values, and Health.* Harper Wave, 2014.

IN A JUST SOCIETY, WE LEARN TO RECOGNIZE OPPRESSIVE TACTICS

THE CASE FOR SEX ED PART 11

I TEACH a lot of college courses with social justice content in them (in fact, I have applied to get a lot of my courses the SJD —Social Justice and Diversity—designation at my university). So these topics are on my mind a lot...and I see every reason to pair up a social justice focus with sex education, both the study of it and the practice of it.

In other words, if we aren't applying a social justice lens to sex education, and using sex education to further social justice goals in the world, what the hell are we even doing?!

I guess this is yet another area where I come across as suuuuper liberal/progressive, but like, maybe we shouldn't impose our sexual norms and beliefs on others without their consent. Gasp, shocker, right?! Sex should not be a cudgel to hurt people with, or a tool of oppression. It's wrong to force other people to conform to a narrow view of gender and sexuality and pretend that other genders and sexualities don't exist. Basically, I have every reason to believe it's all good as long as everyone's consenting, as long as we're always checking in with our own and others' boundaries.

But see, this goes both ways: if we can apply social justice principles to sex and sex education, we can look at social justice through the perspective of sex and sex education.

And as we've seen in the history of sex ed portion of this book, past policies around sex education and sex in general have been, er, less than enlightened. In the chapter on the Comstock Laws, I talked about how Comstock and his vice police went after women for providing info about contraception and abortion, to the point where at least two of his victims committed suicide rather than go to jail. In the chapter on World War I, I talked about how the U.S. government doled out safer sex information and exams to white soldiers, but let African-American soldiers carry on without that same protection. The list of biased sex ed practices goes on and on. Meanwhile, on the home front, women suspected of being sex workers and/or diseased were rounded up under the American Plan and forcibly examined, treated, and detained, all without a warrant.

Or, to take another example, maybe some of the "No cops at Pride" discourse could be better understood in light of how the police used to not only round up sex workers under the American Plan but also used to round up queer people in their own queer spaces to out them and/or arrest them. Authority figures have not always been friendly towards those of us who are considered sexual outliers, and it's important to know that history.

Also? Lots of history is already sexual in nature. You can't talk about King Henry VIII without talking about his multiple marriage attempts, for instance. The desire to have certain kinds of relationship and reproductive access has informed so much history, I don't see why we can't just admit that instead of pretending that sex and history are totally separate topics that never interact (and spare me the arguments that learning about sex will scar kids; they're pretty perceptive and resilient, and there are plenty of ways to keep it age-appropriate as needed).

Learning about this stuff should be a regular part of history curriculums from at least high school onward, in my opinion...not just because sexuality history is a legitimate part of history, but also because it helps teach us how to spot nasty patterns: moral panics, scapegoating, and more.

And if we want to be a functioning society, we need a better-informed citizenry that can spot a conspiracy theory a mile away; that can identify when a population is being unfairly blamed and detained; and that can see through propaganda when it's being presented as objective fact.

Teaching about the history of sex education provides the perfect examples of all these topics and more. And I think we owe it to citizens of all ages to fill them in on the historical and political reasons why important information about their bodies has been withheld from them. So let's put on our critical thinking hats and do better!

CONCLUSION: HAVING LEARNED
ABOUT SEX ED, NOW WHAT?

I HAVE SO MANY THOUGHTS! There are so many conversations yet to have! But I'll try to distill them here for you.

While writing this book in the summer of 2023, I attended a dance workshop weekend with Amy Sigil and Brittany Laleh Banaei (Amy in particular is a big name in my corner of the dance world; she is a creative powerhouse!). Brittany gave an awesome lecture on the cultural conversations happening in our little corner of Middle Eastern and related fusion dances, and one of the things she said stuck with me: Dance is a human right.

As a lifelong dancer, dance is a huge part of my life (and somehow I've managed to barely talk about it in this book, lol). And you know what? I think dance *is* a human right: we all have bodies, so we should all have opportunities to move them! Expressive movement is joyful, therapeutic, so many things.

Brittany also said that dance is a liberatory practice, as in, it has the potential to free our minds and bodies, unite us with communities of likeminded folks, and help us empathize with others who might be different from us, so we can all help liberate one another.

Sex education is also a liberatory practice and a basic human right. We all have bodies, and in addition to their potential to be dancing bodies, they have the potential to be sexually active (or inactive, as we so choose) bodies. We are, as I wrote earlier in this book, all sexual beings. Sex ed can help us access information to explore our sexuality, in whatever consensual modes we might wish.

Isn't that amazing? Isn't that something we should want for one another?

Like, I don't personally care what you get up to sexually as long as it's consensual. But I want something delightful for you, something embodied and joyous, something as transformative as you want it to be.

And universal, comprehensive, medically-accurate, inclusive sex education is one tool to help us all get there.

Another tool? Just better education in general. The more we develop critical thinking skills, the less we'll be fooled by moral panics and conspiracy theories that perform ideological sleight of hand: placing the blame on marginalized folks while the real people in power chuckle all the way to the political podium or bank. The more we study history, the less we're doomed to repeat it. And so on.

We should also want progress. Ideally, the kind we can measure.

The good news is, there has been progress in the U.S., at least some. As Lauren Bialystok and Lisa Andersen wrote in their recent book on sex education's history and philosophy, "teen birth rates have fallen in the United States from 59.9 births per 1,000 girls aged 15-19 to just 18.8 in 2017" (171).

Other evidence is not looking so great; STIs are on the rise again, with the CDC estimating, for instance, that reported syphilis cases increased 32% from 2020 to 2021 ("U.S. STI Epidemic").

Among other trends I've noted in this book, American sex ed is profoundly negative: it assumes the worst of sexual activity, especially when it's done by teenagers outside marriage (or teens in general, or unmarried people in general, or queer people, and so on). And so much of these hypothetical worst-case scenarios could be ameliorated by more conversations about informed consent, more access to health care, more focus on systemic injustices like racism and misogyny and transphobia and more.

And you know what? I'm not convinced that sexuality is the force for evil that so many make it out to be. This isn't just because I'm a godless atheist, but also because we have peer-reviewed studies showing that being sexually active can provoke introspection and feelings of self-worth.

As Nicole Fava and Laina Bay-Cheng summarize these studies,

... empirical research with young women has demonstrated sexual exploration to be associated with greater sexual subjectivity, sexual assertiveness, willingness to voice opinions to a partner, and the rejection of sexual double standards... In addition, more sexual experience was found to relate to positive sexual self-concept and approach motives for sex, which in turn predicted greater satisfaction with one's most recent experience of sexual intercourse. (384)

Isn't that amazing? Why isn't that part of our conversations?

Sex education should be, and can aspire to be, a number of awesome things. Here's a partial list:

- Responsive to the needs of youth, rather than the fears of adults;
- Treating children and teens as fully deserving of basic human rights, including the right to accurate information about their bodies, no matter who their parents are or what their parents believe;
- Attuned to larger cultural conversations about consent and pleasure, affirming that we all deserve these things;
- Honest about the risks of sexual activity...as well as which disenfranchised groups often bear the brunt of them (Bialystok and Andersen remind us that girls, queer teens, and disabled teens are more likely than their mainstream counterparts to be sexually assaulted and have worse health outcomes as a result; 166)

I agree with authors Bialystok and Andersen that we "have the knowledge and the means to choose sex education programs that are more likely to accomplish shared goals and elevate the well-being of the most disadvantaged. What we need is political will" (167). This will look different in different regions of the U.S. (and world), for sure. But get educated, get involved, and don't let a vocal minority (in this case, those who cling to abstinence-only sex ed as the only viable sex ed) dictate what we all get.

Getting involved can look different depending on where

you live, what your skill set is, and what your bandwidth for activism is. And I haven't had a typical sex ed career trajectory either, which has definitely caused me to grapple with some impostor syndrome...but in reality, people come to sex ed from a variety of walks of life. Some are nurses, some are sex therapists, some are school sex ed teachers, and still others are dildo-slingers. Whether sex ed happens in a sex toy shop or a classroom, it's all valid, and it's all needed.

Some places to get started might be at a local Planned Parenthood, at a church (often Unitarian Universalist) that offers the comprehensive Our Whole Lives curriculum, at your local school board in order to advocate for accurate and inclusive sex ed, or starting a sexuality discussion group for adults in your community.

Again, this book feels impossible to wrap up since it's been such a journey, but here goes. Speaking on behalf of Americans, we're pretty fucked up around sex. And honestly, I don't think any culture or society gets it 100% right; we all have our own traditions and beliefs, a.k.a. our sexual baggage. But we can learn to think and act in new ways. And we can do better in the future.

Please join me in advocating for a brighter future for sex education, one where we explicitly analyze the folkloric and cultural messages surrounding us while simultaneously addressing institutional and educational policies around sex. I want a future where sex education gives accurate and culturally-relevant information, such that adult sex ed is not meant to fill gaps but rather enhance what we already know. I want more education about the prevalence of relationship abuse so we can identify it and stop it sooner. And less stigma around STIs so we can all seek treatment sooner and have detailed conversations with our partners about our safety practices and boundaries.

Let's ditch fear and embrace the reality of how diverse humans are in our genders and sexualities. Let's use folklore and history to better understand who benefits when we're afraid. Let's question social norms around sex and make more of an effort to protect the vulnerable (with their consent of course; no need to play out the cliché savior trope!) and have a blast doing so.

Now that I've told my part of this story, this history, this interwoven tale of folklore and gender and sexuality and feminism and more, I can't wait to see what we do next.

References:

Bialystok, Lauren, and Lisa M. F. Andersen. *Touchy Subject: The History and Philosophy of Sex Education.* University of Chicago Press, 2023.

Fava, Nicole M., and Laina Y. Bay-Cheng. "Trauma-Informed Sexuality Education: Recognising the Rights and Resilience of Youth." *Sex Education*, vol. 13, no. 4, 2013, pp. 383–94.

"U.S. STI Epidemic Showed No Signs of Slowing in 2021—Cases Continued to Escalate." *Centers for Disease Control and Prevention*, 11 April 2023, https://www.cdc.gov/media/releases/2023/s0411-sti.html. Accessed 9 September 2023.

RESOURCES

BOOKS

General books on sex:

Corinna, Heather. *S.E.X.: The All-You-Need-To-Know Progressive Sexuality Guide to Get You through High School and College.* Da Capo Press, 2007.
This is the book I wish we handed to every teenager. It has sections covering every form of contraception and a buffet of gender and sexual orientation info, to sexual healthcare for every gender, and, one of my faves, lots of info about healthy vs. unhealthy relationships. Even if you're an adult, there's something for you here!

Herbenick, Debby. *The Coregasm Workout: The Revolutionary Method for Better Sex through Exercise.* Seal Press, 2015.
Even if you're not interested in experiencing exercise-induced arousal or orgasms (popularly labeled "coregasm"), this book is full of amazing information.

Hite, Shere. *The Hite Report: A Nationwide Study of Female Sexuality*. Seven Stories Press, 2004.

This is a classic survey on women's sexuality, initially released in 1976, that reports on and analyzes women's experiences with solo sex, partnered sex, orgasm, and more.

Moon, Allison, and Kate Diamond. *Girl Sex 101*. Lunatic Ink, 2014.

Illustrated narrative journey through women-centered sexual encounters, with lots of practical information about consent, pleasure, and more. LGBTQ+ inclusive.

Nagoski, Emily. *Come As You Are: The Surprising New Science That Will Transform Your Sex Life*. Simon & Schuster Paperbacks, 2015.

Science + feminism, what's not to love? Seriously, if you only read one sex book this year, read this book.

Winston, Sheri. *Women's Anatomy of Arousal: Secret Maps to Buried Pleasure*. Mango Garden, 2010.

Winston brings decades of experience to the table in order to explain what's actually going on with areas of women's bodies that are largely misunderstood, when they're taken into account at all. I'll caution skeptically-minded readers that she occasionally goes in a bit of a "woo-woo" direction, but most of her assertions are empirically valid.

Books on sex and folklore:

Bennett, Gillian. *Bodies: Sex, Violence, Disease, and Death in Contemporary Legend*. 1st ed., University Press of Mississippi, 2005.

Ugh, this book is just so good, I don't know why I didn't talk about it in the body of my book. If you want bosom serpents, poison maidens, and body snatchers (texts about them, which are then analyzed) then this book is your jam.

Dundes, Alan. *The Meaning of Folklore: The Analytical Essays of Alan Dundes*, edited by Simon J. Bronner, Utah State University Press, 2007.
Not every essay is on sex, but a lot of them are. If you're looking for a comprehensive bunch of essays that touch on tons of aspects of folklore—everything from basics of the field to specific genres like cockfighting and the blood libel legend—this is a great introduction to the scholarship of Alan Dundes, my mentor and one of the most influential folklorists of the 20ᵗʰ century.

Goldstein, Diane E. *Once Upon a Virus: Aids Legends and Vernacular Risk Perception.* Utah State University Press, 2004.
Fantastic book on urban legends that circulate on HIV/AIDS, demonstrating tons of connections between folklore and risk perception.

Goodwin, Joseph P. *More Man Than You'll Ever Be: Gay Folklore and Acculturation in Middle America.* Indiana University Press, 1989.
This is one of the first ever published studies of gay men's folklore, and it is accordingly awesome. Goodwin collected and analyzed tons of jokes, personal narratives, and other aspects of folk culture, including those focusing on coming out and on AIDS.

Kitta, Andrea. *The Kiss of Death: Contagion, Contamination, and Folklore.* Utah State University Press, 2019.

This book isn't solely about sex, but it contains chapters on HPV and fears around promiscuity as well as on literal kisses of death, which are documented in both the Motif and Tale Type Indexes plus in pop culture.

Weems, Mickey. *The Fierce Tribe: Masculine Identity and Performance in the Circuit.* Utah State University Press, 2008.

This important book documents gay men's folklore and culture through ethnographic participant-observation that Weems did at a series of parties and performances.

Whatley, Mariamne H, and Elissa R Henken. *Did You Hear About the Girl Who...?: Contemporary Legends, Folklore, and Human Sexuality.* NYU Press, 2001.

If I weren't listing authors alphabetically by last name, you can bet this book would be first in my sex + folklore listing! It's that good! It presents a snapshot of what young Americans believe about sex, and how these beliefs impact the efficacy (or lack thereof) of institutional sex ed. By reading this book, you'll better understand why teen pregnancy and STI trans-mission rates continue to be high(ish), and you'll walk away with a sense of how your own cultural context has influenced your views on sex.

Woods, Emma. *Bite Me: The Myth of Vagina Dentata.* Independently published, 2022.

The vagina dentata (literally, toothed vagina) is found in folklore all over the world. This book documents and analyzes the motif very astutely.

Books on the history of sex:

D'Emilio, John, and Estelle B. Freedman. *Intimate Matters: A History of Sexuality in America*. Third ed., University of Chicago Press, 2012.

This is THE book to read if you want to understand why American attitudes about sex are the way they are. From colonial times through the present, the authors sift through all the historical evidence they can get their hands on to present a coherent, nuanced picture of how sex has been legislated, thought of, and acted out in America (also, make sure to get the 3rd edition as it's the most recent, with expanded chapters on modern times).

Grant, Melissa Gira. *Playing the Whore: The Work of Sex Work*. Verso Books, 2014.

This is a bit more contemporary, but it ties into the history of how sex work has been policed and criminalized in many countries, including the U.S.

Klein, Marty. *America's War on Sex: The Attack on Law, Lust and Liberty*. Praeger, 2006.

If, like me, you're pissed off about the arbitrary laws governing sexuality in the U.S.—the crap that is federally-funded abstinence-only sex ed, for example—this book explains why these sex-negative systems are so entrenched and remain in place.

Knowles, Jon. *How Sex Got Screwed Up: The Ghosts That Haunt Our Sexual Pleasure. Book Two, from Victoria to Our Own Time*. Vernon Press, 2019.

This is a chonker of a book, but it's comprehensive and

contains tons of facts about sex-negative attitudes and practices in the West.

Laqueur, Thomas Walter. *Making Sex: Body and Gender from the
Greeks to Freud*. Harvard University Press, 1992.

This is technically more about gender than sexuality, but
these are so intertwined in the West that it makes sense to
learn about the one-sex vs. two-sex model from antiquity to
the Victorian era since a lot of these ideas are still with us and
shape how we perceive men's and women's bodies and
identities.

Melody, Michael Edward, and Linda Mary Peterson. *Teaching
America About Sex: Marriage Guides and Sex Manuals from the
Late Victorians to Dr. Ruth*. New York University Press, 1999.

Basically what it says in the title: a historical look at sex
guides from the late 1800s up through almost-now, including
those *Joy of Sex* books.

Nielsen, Kim E. *A Disability History of the United States*. Beacon
Press, 2012.

Interested in eugenics? This is a great (read: depressing)
starting point.

Ross, Loretta, and Rickie Solinger. *Reproductive Justice: An
Introduction*. University of California Press, 2017.

This is a crucial read if you want to understand how biased
and bigoted the U.S. policies around sex have been (especially
directed against people of color).

Stern, Scott W. *The Trials of Nina Mccall: Sex, Surveillance, and the Decades-Long Government Plan to Imprison "Promiscuous" Women.* Beacon Press, 2018.

This is specific to the time period around World War I and shortly after, but it's essential if you want to understand the American Plan (how the U.S. government unlawfully detained and imprisoned and assaulted women suspected of being sex workers and/or or having STIs).

Books on sex education (how it can/should be practiced, its history, etc.):

Herbenick, Debby, with Susan C. Stone. *Yes, Your Kid: What Parents Need to Know about Today's Teens and Sex.* Benbella Books, 2023.

I haven't even read this yet (it's coming out just as my book is set to release) and I can already tell you it will be an amazing and refreshingly honest resource.

Irvine, Janice M. *Talk About Sex: The Battles Over Sex Education in the United States.* University of California Press, 2004.

This book covers roughly the 1960s to the 1990s to analyze how the conversations around school sex in the U.S. became so steered by sex-negative conservative and religious viewpoints.

Jensen, Robin E. *Dirty Words: The Rhetoric of Public Sex Education, 1870–1924.* University of Illinois Press, 2010.

Super useful historical overview of the Gilded Age and Progressive Era timelines and players that shaped early U.S. sex ed.

Kendall, Nancy. *The Sex Education Debates*. University of Chicago Press, 2013.

Kendall did fieldwork in five U.S. states in order to understand how each school system implements federal, state, and local regulations about sex education. The results are fascinating, and Kendall's ethnographic approach gives us a glimpse into how sex ed policies play out on the ground.

Lord, Alexandra M. *Condom Nation: The U. S. Government's Sex Education Campaign from World War I to the Internet*. Johns Hopkins University Press, 2009.

Useful overview of how much the U.S. government has had a heavy hand in steering sex ed in this country.

Luker, Kristin. *When Sex Goes to School: Warring Views on Sex--And Sex Education--Since the Sixties*. 1st ed., W.W. Norton, 2006.

This is another overview of sex ed in the U.S. throughout the 20th century, but it also utilizes a lot of the author's interview data from different communities and different positions on sex ed, which is noteworthy.

Moran, Jeffrey P. *Teaching Sex: The Shaping of Adolescence in the 20th Century*. Harvard University Press, 2000.

This is a history of U.S. sex ed from the early 1900s to roughly the 1990s. It's good for helping one understand the major players, policies, ideologies, and so on.

Rayne, Karen, et al., editors. *How I Got into Sex ... Ed*. Center for Sex Education, 2014.

Filled with short essays by those working in all areas of sex education, this is a delightful book that illustrates just how varied our paths are.

Sohn, Amy. *The Man Who Hated Women: Sex, Censorship, and Civil Liberties in the Gilded Age*. First ed., Farrar, Straus and Giroux, 2021.

If, like me, you learned a little bit about the Comstock Laws and went, "oh wow that sounds like a major shitshow," then this book gives all the details on this purity crusader and the powerful women he fought to take down.

Vernacchio, Al, with Brooke Lea Foster. *For Goodness Sex: Changing the Way We Talk to Teens about Sexuality, Values, and Health*. Harper Wave, 2014.

This book is fantastic because it challenges us to rethink how we view teenage sexuality, providing multiple examples from Vernacchio's long career as a high school sex educator of how to talk to teens about sex (which also includes relationships, gender identity, body image, and technology). Even if you don't have kids, this book will leave you with insightful conversation-starters and concepts for how to manage what often feels like an awkward topic even among adults. I wish every high school teacher and administrator had to read this book!

Books on trauma:

Gordon, James S. *The Transformation: Discovering Wholeness and Healing After Trauma*. First ed., HarperOne, an Imprint of HarperCollinsPublishers, 2019.

A useful trauma book that goes into both the neuroscience and some things everyday people can do in their lives to address their trauma.

Haines, Staci, and Felice Newman. *Healing Sex: A Mind-Body Approach to Healing Sexual Trauma.* Updated 2nd ed., Cleis Press, 2007.

A book specifically intended for survivors of sexual trauma who still want to enjoy sex (or learn to enjoy sex again). Aimed at women but I think people of any gender would benefit from the in-depth discussion of triggers, dissociation, consent and boundaries, and more.

Lipsky, Laura van Dernoot, et al. *Trauma Stewardship: An Everyday Guide to Caring for Self While Caring for Others.* First ed., Berrett-Koehler, 2009.

This is less about the immediate effects of trauma and more about vicarious or bystander trauma, the trauma we incur while adjacent to it. If, like me, you are a teacher (or in any field where you work closely with humans), this is an incredibly useful book, since it's so easy to get dragged down by the struggles of those we are trying to help/teach/heal/etc.

Maté, Gabor. *When the Body Says No: Understanding the Stress-Disease Connection.* J. Wiley, 2003.

This book is more about chronic stress than trauma specifically, but it includes a lot of information that is helpful when addressing trauma, too.

Nagoski, Emily, and Amelia Nagoski. *Burnout: The Secret to Unlocking the Stress Cycle.* First ed., Ballantine Books, 2019.

So useful for talking about trauma in the broader context of chronic stress and burnout (which the body tends to interpret in similar ways anyway).

van der Kolk, Bessel A. *The Body Keeps the Score: Brain, Mind, and Body in the Healing of Trauma.* Penguin Books, 2015.

This is *the* trauma book, according to me and a lot of peers. Lots of useful concepts and takeaways.

Books on feminism, gender, and related topics:

Bornstein, Kate. *My New Gender Workbook: A Step-By-Step Guide to Achieving World Peace through Gender Anarchy and Sex Positivity.* 2nd ed., Routledge, 2013.

Bornstein has done a lot of notable work on gender, and I think this is a really fun and accessible book.

Manne, Kate. *Entitled: How Male Privilege Hurts Women.* First edition, Crown, 2020.

Easily one of my favorite books of the last decade. Manne unpacks the myriad of everyday ways that patriarchy and misogyny take their toll.

Muscio, Inga. *Cunt: A Declaration of Independence.* Seal Press, 1998.

Super accessible book on feminism, starting with the very pertinent question of why "cunt" has always been such a bad word. I'm citing the 1998 version here because it's the one I read as a teenager that deeply impacted me, though there have been updated and revised versions since.

Taylor, Sonya Renee. *The Body Is Not an Apology: The Power of Radical Self-Love.* First ed., Berrett–Koehler Publishers, 2018.

I'm somewhat arbitrarily putting this book under the feminism/gender section, because it touches on a variety of other topics too, like racism and ableism and transphobia and fatphobia and all the power structures that keep us from genuinely inhabiting and loving our bodies. It's a fantastic read; highly recommended!

Books centering LGBTQ+ folks:

Blank, Hanne. *Straight: The Surprisingly Short History of Heterosexuality*. Beacon Press, 2012.

As Blank meticulously documents, the word "heterosexual" didn't exist until the 1860s. But it quickly became the norm and things just got even weirder from there.

Fielding, Lucie. *Trans Sex: Clinical Approaches to Trans Sexualities and Erotic Embodiments*. Routledge, 2021.

Fielding is a friend and colleague who does amazing work. This book is aimed at therapists working with trans and non-binary clients but could be helpful for educators and those in adjacent fields, too.

Serano, Julia. *Whipping Girl: A Transsexual Woman on Sexism and the Scapegoating of Femininity*. Seal Press, 2009.

Serano is both a trans woman and a biologist, so, putting it mildly, she knows her stuff. Excellent intro to trans issues written by an insider, with plenty of fodder to refute the transphobic nonsense we're seeing all the time in the news and media.

Books on relationships (monogamous or not):

Beckett, Cooper S. *My Life on the Swingset: Adventures in Swinging & Polyamory*. Hump and Circumstance, 2015.

Known for hosting a long-running podcast on ethical non-monogamy, Beckett also blogs, and this book is a collection of blog posts and short essays that documents his growth from recently monogamous newbie to full-on sex geek.

Bergstrand, Curtis R, and Jennifer Blevins Sinski. *Swinging in America: Love, Sex, and Marriage in the 21st Century.* Praeger / ABC-CLIO, 2010.

Yes, it's a fascinating sociological study of swingers, but the authors spend a lot of time defining and discussing monogamy in addition to non-monogamy, so there are tons of great insights in here for people of any relationship status.

Easton, Dossie, and Janet W Hardy. *The Ethical Slut: A Practical Guide to Polyamory, Open Relationships & Other Adventures.* 2nd edition, updated & expanded / ed., Celestial Arts, 2009.

Quite classic, this book is often the one anyone considering exploring open relationships gets handed first, and for good reason.

Gottman, John Mordechai, and Nan Silver. *The Seven Principles for Making Marriage Work.* 1st ed., Crown, 1999.

I'd be remiss if I didn't have at least one Gottman book in here; he's famous for having a lab setting where he can watch couples interact and predict with stunning accuracy whether or not they'll remain together. His advice is thus evidence-based and pretty solid on the whole.

Labriola, Kathy. *Polyamorous Elders: Aging in Open Relationships.* Rowman & Littlefield, 2023.

This is (to my knowledge) the only book on ethical non-monogamy specifically as practiced among aging populations. It contains numerous personal narratives along with thematic analysis of the kinds of issues middle-aged-and-older polyamorous people experience.

Marin, Vanessa, and Xander Marin. *Sex Talks: The Five Conversations That Will Transform Your Love Life*. Simon & Schuster, 2023.

Really excellent book on relationship and sex communication, focused on unpacking shame and taboo topics so partners can actually, like, talk to each other about sex.

Mirk, Sarah. *Sex from Scratch: Making Your Own Relationship Rules*. Microcosm Publishing, 2014.

This book isn't really pro-monogamy or pro-nonmonogamy; instead, it features Mirk's experiences and tips alongside those of guest authors to showcase a variety of relationship types and choices. Good for taking a DIY approach to figuring out which types of relationships work for you.

Patterson, Kevin. *Love's Not Colorblind: Race and Representation in Polyamorous and Other Alternative Communities*. Thorntree Press, 2018.

An incisive and necessary (but still totally approachable) look at how racism impacts those in alternative relationship styles and communities.

Perel, Esther. *Mating in Captivity: Unlocking Erotic Intelligence*. HarperCollins, 2014.

Perel has worked as a sex therapist with couples in dozens of countries, and thus she brings a cross-cultural awareness to this book about the whys and hows of sex, desire, and attraction in long-term relationships.

Powell, Liz. *Building Open Relationships: Your Hands on Guide to Swinging, Polyamory, and Beyond!* Dr. Liz Powell, 2018.

As with many books that are technically about non-monogamous relationships, this one has excellent advice and resources for people in monogamous relationships too, such as worksheets to learn how to identify and discuss difficult emotions and sections on learning how to name the kinds of people or engagements you desire.

Sheff, Elisabeth. *The Polyamorists Next Door: Inside Multiple-Partner Relationships and Families.* Rowman & Littlefield Publishers, 2014.

This is the only longitudinal (as in, spanning multiple years) study of polyamorous families, and as such, it's a must-read in my opinion. Sensitively written and insightful.

Taormino, Tristan. *Opening Up: A Guide to Creating and Sustaining Open Relationships.* 1St ed., Cleis Press, 2008.

As with *The Ethical Slut* (mentioned above), this is a classic book on navigating ethically non-monogamous relationships.

PODCASTS, SHOWS, & TALKS

The Bawdy Storytelling podcast is a delight and Dixie de la Tour, the head wrangler, is a national treasure (she also does local tours for her in-person shows!).

Emily Nagoski has at least two TED talks that I know of; the first one, titled "The Keys to a Happier, Healthier Sex Life," should be required viewing for everyone, in my opinion!

Life on the Swingset is a fun podcast that features interviews and banter with a number of open-relationship-adjacent and sexuality-related speakers.

The Principles of Pleasure is a documentary-style show on Netflix that goes into both the scientific and social aspects of sex, focusing on, you guessed it, pleasure, with a focus on marginalized folks.

Sex Education is a TV show that's fictional but I had to include it here because of the name (I watched the first episode but didn't get any further; from what I understand it promotes decent info while being entertaining).

Sex Nerd Sandra is one of the classic podcasts about sex that ran for over 200 episodes. Definitely worth a listen!

The Sexplanations podcast, also on YouTube, features Dr. Lindsey Doe sharing medically accurate and inclusive info about all aspects of human sexuality.

A Touch of Flavor podcast is specifically about non-monogamous relationships (building 'em, keeping 'em healthy, etc.), but as always, a lot of healthy relationship advice applies to different relationship styles.

What Excites Us is a podcast by sex educator Gwyn Isaacs with a ton of special guests and discussions on both niche and mainstream topics.

Vaginas, Vulvas, & Vibrators is a podcast focusing on women's health and sexual wellness. Very focused on empowerment, which is lovely.

SEX EDUCATORS AND GROUPS TO FOLLOW

AASECT is the American Association for Sexuality Educators, Counselors, and Therapists. It's the main organization that trains and certifies sex educators, counselors, and therapists, though in many cases anyone can attend their conferences and workshops.

Crista Anne is a sex educator and blogger who became well known for her Orgasm Quest social media series, about her journey towards sexual pleasure while on antidepressants.

ASHA, the American Sexual Health Association (formerly the American Social Hygiene Association), is a non-profit that provides education and advocacy around sexual health in the U.S., including but not limited to info around STIs (in keeping with the first iteration of this organization as a group that focused on venereal diseases in the early 20th century).

Robin Wilson-Beatty is a disability and sexuality educator who offers services such as workshops and consulting to help with accessibility, cultural competency / inclusion, and more.

The Center for Sex Education puts on an annual conference and publishes lots of educational materials, aimed at sex educators in all sorts of settings and educational levels.

Dirty Lola is a dildo slinger, educator, and entertainer on a wider variety of topics. She's featured on *The Principles of Pleasure*.

Debby Herbenick is one of the researchers on sexual and reproductive health doing scientific studies of how people experience their bodies and sex lives. A professor at Indiana University, she conducts a large-scale survey of American sexual health and behavior and has published numerous books and articles.

The Kinsey Institute. Duh. It's research-oriented and you can't necessarily walk on in without an appointment (if you happen to be in Bloomington, Indiana), but the collections (films, archival, etc.) are notable in scope.

The Leather Archives & Museum is located in Chicago and is a super cool (I've visited) place that documents and shows exhibits on the history of leather, kink, and BDSM culture(s).

Aida Manduley is a social worker and sex educator whose work focuses on social justice, intersectionality, Latinx community organizing, and more.

Joellen Notte is a sex educator who focuses on the intersections of depression and sex and explores this topic in her book *The Monster under the Bed: Sex, Depression, and the Conversations We Aren't Having* (which is here instead of my books section of the resources list since I haven't read it yet).

Our Whole Lives is an inclusive, medically accurate sex education program developed by the Unitarian Universalist Association that contains whole curricula, sorted by age group, to be used in a variety of sex education settings. It's appropriate for use in both faith communities and secular spaces.

Planned Parenthood is, how shall I put this: however you might feel about abortion, this organization steps up to provide health care (sometimes reproductive, sometimes not) to lots of people who couldn't otherwise afford it ('Murica!).

Reid Mihalko is a sex educator who provides sex education for adult audiences on bunches of topics, ranging from relation-ship skills to how to have "the talk" before hooking up with someone (search online for his "safer sex elevator speech"). He also provides workshops for fellow sexuality professionals to up their business game.

Jennifer Rehor is an AASECT-certified sex therapist who works with LGBTQ+, kinky, and non-monogamous clients. I haven't read her book *Women and Kink: Relationships, Reasons, and Stories* yet but it's on my list.

Michelle Renee is an intimacy coach and surrogate partner, and I mention her here in part because I haven't had time to talk about sexual surrogacy in this book at all and it's an interesting facet of the sexuality world that a lot of people don't know about. Look up her web presence to learn more.

SIECUS is the Sexual Information and Education Council of the United States, and they provide a variety of resources and fact sheets to document and advocate for social issues around sex education and sexual health more broadly.

SisterSong is an organization based in the U.S. Southern states with national ties, focusing on the reproductive health of women of color and other historically excluded and marginalized groups.

Smitten Kitten is a feminist sex shop in Minneapolis that has a slick online presence with educational resources and shopping guides on its website. There are of course other feminist sex shops worth mentioning (Good Vibrations; The Pleasure Chest), but Smitten Kitten gets a special shout-out for its resources, including one of the best lube breakdowns I've ever seen.

TASHRA is The Alternative Sexualities Health Research Alliance, an organization that researches, works with, and advocates for people in non-mainstream sexual communities (e.g. kink, BDSM). A huge focus of theirs is on fighting stigma and discrimination.

The Woodhull Freedom Foundation is a non-profit organization that focuses on the intersection of human rights with sexuality and related topics. They put on a great annual conference, too, called Woodhull's Sexual Freedom Summit, and if you don't get the Woodhull reference, go back and reread the history section of this book!

INDEX

ACKNOWLEDGMENTS

First, I must thank my cover designer, Cover Villain, for absolutely nailing the concept for this book's cover. Next, thanks go to Susan Redington Bobby (www.professorofwords.com), who edited and indexed this beast. Finally, I am grateful to my early readers who took the time to send feedback and encouragement: Jennifer Stevenson and Metis Black among others.

I was humbled to receive support from Bill Taverner and Lucie Fielding during this project. My colleague at Butler University, Charlene Fletcher, helped me locate some historical resources. The interlibrary loan folks at Butler also helped me source some stuff that probably sounded very strange at the time, so my thanks go to them. My students have suffered through a lot of this material, sometimes one lecture at a time, sometimes a whole course at a time, not to mention all the tangents I went on when stuff that came up in class reminded me of something I was working on for this book. Sorry / not sorry.

My friends scattered across various writer's groups online have helped me with a variety of tasks, from nailing my book's description to staying sane during the writing process.

I wrote large portions of this book while visiting my parents, while buying a house (stressful, do not recommend), and while exploring cafes near my new house. My favorite writing spot ended up being GoldLeaf; check them out if you're in Indianapolis.

Much love to the friends and loved ones who put up with me and/or fed me during this turbulent writing process. You know who you are.

ABOUT THE AUTHOR

Dr. Jeana Jorgensen studied folklore at the University of California, Berkeley under Alan Dundes and went on to earn a PhD in folklore from Indiana University. She has authored nearly 30 academic articles and book chapters in addition to blog posts, poems, stories, and rants. She spends entirely too much time on Twitter (@foxyfolklorist), dances, and plays with her sourdough starter.

To learn more about her upcoming books and sign up for her newsletter, you can go to: www.folklore101.com